St. Martin's Paperbacks Titles
by Jim Morris

War Story

Fighting Men

THE DEVIL'S SECRET NAME

JIM MORRIS

St. Martin's Paperbacks

To Kathryn

RENAULT: What are you doing in Casablanca?
RICK: I came for the waters.
RENAULT: There are no waters in Casablanca.
We're in the middle of a desert.
RICK: I was misinformed.

—*Casablanca*

THE DEVIL'S SECRET NAME

Copyright © 1990 by Jim Morris.

Cover photo © Corbis.

ISBN: 0-312-99341-2
EAN: 80312-99341-2

Printed in the United States of America

Dell paperback edition / May 1990
St. Martin's Paperbacks edition / January 2005

St. Martin's Paperbacks are published by St. Martin's Press, 175 Fifth Avenue, New York, NY 10010.

10 9 8 7 6 5 4 3 2 1

ACKNOWLEDGMENTS

There are many people to thank for their help on this book: my wife Kathy, who wrote the first draft of the story of her experiences in Cambodia, Tom Reisinger, who graciously told me his story of that experience, and, of course, the prince of darkness himself, RKB, "god-king of the killer elite."

Great thanks are also due to Dennis and Patrice Bartow of Daring Books, Maggie Lichota of Dell, whose contribution cannot be overestimated, and the entire Dell editorial staff, whose support, encouragement, and tolerance were so helpful, and Paul H. Williams, for his fine hand with the English language.

Others who helped are too numerous to mention, except for the Committee for State Security of the Union of Soviet Socialist Republics, without whose active meddling in the affairs of the world, there would have been no story.

FOREWORD

Jim Morris's remarkable career in Special Forces and journalism put him on the front lines of Vietnam and almost all the brutal wars of the '70s and '80s. He has fought, written vividly while under fire, and gone to substantial lengths to help repay America's debts to some of those, such as the Montagnards, who fought alongside us but were then forgotten or abandoned. Few Americans are better equipped by their personal histories and skills to help us all understand the background of what we now face in the 21st century.

This is not the conventional view. Many, perhaps most, would say that the Cold War is over and that we now face a completely different kind of enemy—international terrorism—for which the wars of Jim Morris's experience have little relevance. I would strongly disagree. Morris puts it succinctly:

> *A statement one hears often: 'We don't want another Vietnam.' From a strategic standpoint it's not 'another' Vietnam. It's the same one. We've just got in the habit of naming wars after the patient rather than the disease.*

Exactly right, then and now.

In the present circumstances we can learn from some of the mistakes we made during the Cold War and its brutal manifestations in many corners of the world. As I wrote in 1992, the end of the Cold War put us in a position as if we had slain a dragon, against whom we had been struggling for nearly half a century, and then found ourselves in a jungle full of a lot of poisonous snakes. The snakes—proliferation of weapons of mass destruction, rogue state aggression, terrorist groups, international organized crime, etc.—though smaller than the dragon, could kill as well, and were generally harder to keep track of.

But although the manifestation of the enemy has changed, as Morris pointed out in the post-Vietnam context, its essential nature has not. Generally speaking the "new" enemies of today wear the scales of totalitarianism just as much as the old. Whereas in the '80s we tended to make the mistake Morris points out—"naming wars after the patient rather than the disease"—our current mistake is to name wars after tactics, e.g., our "Global War on Terrorism." World War II in the Pacific was not just a war against kamikazes: it was a war against the totalitarian movement that was Japanese Imperialism. If we focus only on the tactic of terrorism, we run the risk of ignoring the other elements of our current enemies' assault, such as the lessons of hatred taught in the Islamist madrassahs of Pakistan, and the Saudi Wahhabis' massive worldwide propaganda effort (some $70 billion spent on it over the last quarter-century or so) on behalf anti-Semitism, suppression of women, and jihad against all infidels. The central feature of the enemy is not his location or his tactics.

The heart of today's enemy, like that of the Nazis and the Communists, is again totalitarianism. Speaking of the post-Vietnam communist attacks, Morris notes that:

> ...while the roots of these insurgencies come from within, the rain, the sunshine, and the fertilizer come from the Soviet Union. Their ultimate objective is to wipe democracy, personal freedom, and human dignity from the planet.

So, too, the totalitarian objectives of our current enemies. They have replaced the dream of world communism with a dream of a world caliphate under their control, but their Islamism—a totalitarian movement masquerading as religious belief—has about as much to do with the great religion of Islam as Torquemada and those who joined him in the autos-da-fé of the Spanish Inquisition had to do with the teachings of the Sermon on the Mount.

Can we win this current war? If we see its nature clearly. I would call it "The Long War of the 21st Century" because I believe it will last for decades. Like the Cold War, a central feature will be the clash of ideologies. There will be fighting, and more of it on the home front than in the Cold War, thus stressing the importance of making our societies much more resilient against terrorist attack.

But there is certainly reason for hope if we look at what we have accomplished. The world has moved since August 1945 from having 20 democracies to having 121—89 of them operating generally under the rule of law, another 32 with serious problems of corruption but still with regular and generally fair elections. (These are Freedom House figures, from its annual publication, *Freedom in the World*.) This did not happen by accident. The result is that some 63 percent of the world's governments, and about the same share of its people, live in democracies. And some of these democracies are in, to many Americans, rather surprising places—e.g., Mongolia and Mali. Modern democracies virtually never fight one another, nor do they generally harbor terrorist groups. Most of the successes of reversing proliferation in recent years—e.g., Brazil, Argentina, and South Africa turning away from their nuclear weapons programs—have come about not through arms control agreements but because the nations turned democratic.

Although these extraordinary changes have occurred in a world in which we and our allies were protected by our armed forces and much (though certainly not all) Soviet aggression was deterred thereby, many of the successes were brought about by other forces. For instance, in Poland, the Pope and the AFL-CIO were probably the most important supporters of solidarity and Poland's transition to democracy.

Ultimately, in my view, we will not win this war until we (the U.S., Britain, Australia, and various other allies at different times) do for the Middle East what we did for Europe. It took three world wars, two hot and one cold, and some 200 million deaths over three-quarters of a century to turn Europe into what it is today: with only a few exceptions, a continent of democracies, a continent at peace. The Arab Middle East is a hard case—one of the hardest, but it is not an impossible one. The majority of the world's 1.2 billion Muslims live in democracies—in Indonesia, Bangladesh, India, Turkey, Mali, etc. Jim Morris has given us some important insights from the late Cold War that can help us understand how to think about the challenges of the Long War of this century. The spirit of patriotism and resolution that he and his American colleagues, his Montagnards, and many others showed is the spirit that will lead us to prevail this time as well.

R. James Woolsey
Director of Central Intelligence
1993–95

1
FLAME OF THE FOREST

In the spring of 1973 I heard that my old interpreter from Vietnam, Kpa Doh, had become a major in the Cambodian army, and was at Ft. Benning, Georgia, taking the Infantry Officer's Advanced Course. I went to see him. He told me it was his intention to return to Vietnam after the war, to wage revolution against the Vietnamese on behalf of his people, the Montagnards of the Central Highlands.

"How you think I should do this?" he asked.

Kpa Doh had been chief interpreter for my camp on the first and best of three tours with Special Forces, the Green Berets, in Vietnam. Civilian life had not been especially kind to me, or I to it, and ever since leaving Vietnam I had dreamed of going back.

"That's kind of a tough question on short notice, Kpa

Doh," I said. "Let me do an area study and some planning. I'll come over this summer and tell you what I think."

What I wanted to do was evaluate his plan in light of Mao Zedong's teachings on the War of National Liberation, to see whether he had a chance.

I had two college degrees, but the most intellectually demanding study I ever undertook was the Special Forces Officer's Course at Ft. Bragg, and what we learned was Mao. He had devised a model for revolution that was brilliant, practical and comprehensive. You could lay his theory over the American Revolution of 1776, for instance, and it fit perfectly. It's a template for any revolution, communist or not.

At Ft. Bragg we had been shown *Viva Zapata!* as a training film. Again, so we could watch Mao's principles worked out in detail. They were all there.

The basic tenets of Mao's model for revolutionary warfare are easy to remember because they are organized in three sets of threes.

There are three *sine qua non*s of revolutionary warfare. In all of recorded history no revolution, barring the occasional *coup d'etat*, has succeeded without them, and I know of none that failed in which all three were present.

The first is support of a significant percentage of the population. A majority is not necessary. Fifteen percent will do it. Of the majority, it is only necessary that they be indifferent. It is also necessary that the guerrillas have secure areas from which to operate. A handy border to duck over, which government troops are forbidden to cross, is best, but an impenetrable swamp or mountain vastness will do in a pinch. The third necessary ingredient is help from a foreign government, which can provide arms, ammunition, medical supplies, money. Perhaps the most invaluable thing the outside source provides is legitimacy. Without it the guerrillas have the feeling that they are only bandits in an evil place.

The revolutionaries themselves also fall into three distinct groups. First are the guerrillas, then the underground of spies and saboteurs in towns and cities, and then the auxiliaries, the aforementioned fifteen percent who provide active support.

Revolutions then proceed in three stages. The first is political organization. Second comes guerrilla warfare, small-stage raids and ambushes up to battalion-size. Only in the third stage, when the guerrillas graduate into a regular, conventional army, do they attempt to take and hold territory. By then government troops are usually in rout, and territory falls easily into guerrilla hands.

According to Mao, Kpa Doh didn't have a chance.

I left in May to check out the situation in Vietnam first, then go on to Phnom Penh.

It was limbo time in Vietnam. The American combat units had gone home; all that was left was a kind of caretaker advisory effort. There was also an international commission to control the "truce," and next to no fighting. This was the time of the "decent interval," Kissinger's term for that face-saving period after the U.S. withdrawal, before the inevitable fall.

My aircraft arrived at Ton Son Nhut at one in the morning, an hour after curfew. When the bus let me off at the Continental Palace Hotel, it was closed and barred. There was a bell for the night porter, but I didn't know that and couldn't see it in the dark. Saigon was not a good place to be roaming around after curfew.

Fortunately, the Continental had an open terrace. I mounted the two steps from the sidewalk, took off my hat and sat down on one of their wicker chairs, and put my feet up on a small table.

Five years, and I was back in the country that had mutilated my body and reduced by half the number of living people I call "friend."

In the park across the street, a propaganda banner whipped by the wind popped loose on one end and flapped frantically. Occasionally a crumpled newspaper skittered across the square. The scene was lit by the kind of ghastly yellow streetlight which makes everything look like a colorized Dracula movie.

Every ghost I knew marched through me that night, from the *yang*, the spirits of the mountains, to the company of my dead friends. It wasn't frightening—sort of cozy, in a grim way. It was always Halloween in Vietnam.

At five a.m. a ferocious siren sounded for a full minute. Soon after that the petulant sputter of a single Honda 90 rattled hollowly between the silent buildings. Two ladies bobbed by in black pajamas and conical hats, carrying long balance poles, with baskets suspended by ropes on either end.

A jeep containing four "white mice," Vietnamese national policemen in white uniforms, careened around a corner and ran over a cat.

A tallish porter from the Continental, about a hundred years old, in a dirty white uniform three sizes too large, came out with a three-foot-long broom, and a dust pan on a three-foot-wire handle. He gave me not so much as a glance with his expressionless eyes. He began to sweep the terrace with a desultory shuffle.

A small boy came up and offered to sell me a three-day-old *Stars and Stripes* for thirty cents. A nine-year-old girl with one arm held a basket containing garlands of white blossoms to my nose and insisted, "You buy frower!"

The traffic in the street continued to build: Hondas, cyclos, jeeps, more Hondas, blue-and-yellow thirty-year-old Renault taxis, International Control Commission-Saigon jeeps, ARVN military vehicles, all roaring by at thirty miles an hour, with no discernible muffling, all emitting a vile, noxious, blue smoke which fogged the air by six o'clock.

Represented on paper, comic-book fashion, the resulting RO-A-A-A-A-R-R-R-R!!!, *screeeeeech*, HONK! and SLAM! of red-and-black cartoon letters would overlay each other in a blur that would fill the entire page.

The crowd in front of me had grown, too. There was a

guy on crutches, with one leg missing, wanting to sell lacquerware, a healthy fellow with used books who had been there the first time I stayed at the Continental ten years before, a lady selling incense made by kids at the Buddhist orphanage, several beggars, mostly with missing limbs and/or napalm scars. In the early Sixties the beggars had been just as numerous, but suffered from leprosy, yaws, and malnutrition.

I could no longer see the street. These people were six inches from my face, tugging and gesticulating wildly, crying for relief. Since there was no possibility of alleviating one one-thousandth of the human misery displayed before me, I rose, towering over the crowd, and shouldered my rucksack.

"HEY! WHERE YOU GO?" shouted a cyclo boy. Several taxi drivers and a guy on a Honda 90 also yelled, "HEY! WHERE YOU GO?" From all corners of the square, young honeys in hip huggers, sheer blouses without bras, but with hungry, hostile smiles, began walking briskly in my direction. I surged through the mob of clutching, crying people. "Ride!" *"Eat!"* "FUCK!" *"BUY!!"* *"YOU WANT CHANGE MONEY???"*

Get me out of here!

Pleiku: flat, red dust everywhere, churning under two-and-a-half ton truck wheels, big, bluegrey skies stretching off to the mountains in the distance.

Along the roads into town were Montagnards, men in black, red-bordered loincloths wrapped around their waists, pulled up tight between their buttocks, with a flap in front. The women wore shimmery, black, tubular skirts; some had been put in blouses by missionaries, but they didn't take them very seriously, and if a button popped and a breast showed nobody seemed to care, or even notice.

From a leisurely French mountain town, with one family of Vietnamese, fifteen years before, Pleiku had grown into a quagmire and a pesthole. Plywood, packing crate shacks lined every road, filled with Vietnamese people who had come from God-knows-where, for God-knows-what reason. Some had been forcibly resettled by the government, and there was also a large community of pimps, whores, bartenders, and other parasites who had come to live off the U.S. Army, and were now reduced to slim pickings from the ARVN and the ICCS.

I went looking for Sprague's house.

"The Ahmy! I hate the fuckin' Ahmy!" Sprague spat out the words at me, staring in distaste at my G.I. rucksack and cammie jacket. He grinned the hard, twisty smile of a retired, Special Forces master sergeant with no quit in him.

In truth, he didn't look very military for a retired master sergeant. His silver-grey hair slopped down over his collar and curled out over his ears. He came from the part of Boston where they have not yet discovered the letter *r*, and twenty years of southern army posts had yet to put it into his diction.

His living room in the USAID compound was filled with Montagnard memorabilia: crossbows, arrows, carvings, woven cloth, mostly in red and black, because those were the only dyes Montagnards knew how to make.

On his wall was a brass plaque that read, *"Special Forces has done so much for so long with so little that now we are expected to do everything with nothing forever."*

Indeed, about the only things Sprague found in my favor when I first arrived were that I, too, had worn a green beret and we shared a taste for rock 'n' roll.

He had a huge reel-to-reel tape deck, playing the Blue Ridge Rangers, all of whom were John Fogerty, formerly of Creedence Clearwater Revival, overdubbed on every instrument. On top of the tape deck was a color photo of three young people, two boys and a girl, the boys bearded and long-haired, the girl with dark, straight hair, parted in the middle in the style of the day. They were Ed's three older kids, in college in the States. His wife and the younger kids lived in Taipei, where he could see them sometimes.

My first impression of Sprague was that he was a crotchety old fart, and I couldn't figure what he was doing here, since most of his contemporaries had returned home to drink beer and reminisce.

But the answer was simple enough; he had a bad case of what the French call *Le Jeune Mal*. He was a Far East addict, with a serious Montagnard fixation.

Ed was excited because his son, Mark, a former one-hitch Special Forces medic, but not a Vietnam veteran, was arriving the next day, after which we would go to Cheo Reo, and then to an outlying Jarai Montagnard village for the weekend.

Because the road simply stopped at the river, the Vietnamese seldom went to that village. Sprague stopped his Bronco and we all got out: Sprague; me; Mark, Sprague's Jesus-haired son; H'yak, Sprague's lovely, brown-eyed Montagnard maid; and Ksor Bem, an eighteen-year-old who was a cousin in Sprague's adopted Montagnard family. Bem was a thin, lively little dude in a newsboy cap, tank top, purple flare jeans, and two-tone purple saddle-shoes.

It took us a few minutes to unload our stuff, take off our shoes and boots, and roll up our pants legs. The river was wide and flat, and we had brought a lot of stuff: food for the family, bedrolls, and so on. The water was warm and bright, deep enough to get our pants wet, rolled up or not.

On the other side we walked on a winding path of hot sand that burned our feet, making me skip and look for grassy patches. As we came up the path the Yards came out to look at us. They had seen Sprague many times before, of course, and H'yak and Bem, but Mark Sprague and I were new and unusual. Before the U.S. Army pulled out they had become used to G.I.s but neither Mark nor I had seen a barber or a razor in a long time.

It was a very clean village, no trash piles or other debris, just row after row of large longhouses, up on stilts thick as telephone poles. The houses were about thirty feet across in front and maybe a hundred feet long, six feet off the ground on their poles. Entire extended families lived in the houses; cousins, aunts, uncles, everybody. A few men wore loin-cloths, but most had on western pants or cut-offs. We moved through the village, past cows, chickens, and sad, draggy, prehistoric-looking grey pigs that snuffled in the mud under the longhouses.

"Hiam droi jian muon!" people greeted us as we passed.

"Hiam muon!" we replied, with a quick nod of the head.

We scampered up the notched log that served as stairs on the longhouse. As we entered, the first thing to hit my eye was a poster of the rock group, Canned Heat. Times had changed.

There was a large crowd of people waiting for us. Sprague made as many introductions as he could as we trooped inside.

The walls were soft rattan, but the rattan floors of former years had been replaced by planks, and most of the long-houses were roofed with USAID tin. Easier to build, of course, but in no way an improvement in looks or comfort.

Sprague wasted no time breaking out his portable cas-sette player. "Got a new Jawge Hahison heah!" he said. At the sound of that magic name forty people clustered around to hear, "All Things Must Pass."

Soon Sprague turned down the music and some men ap-proached with a big jug of rice wine, reeds and glasses.

Sprague took me aside and explained that Mark was to be initiated into the family with the rice wine ceremony. "It don't mean nothing when they don't do you," he said to me. "They're accepting Mark because he's my son."

I nodded. I knew the custom well. I'd already been given four bracelets, but they hadn't been sent home with my stuff after my last wound. I had lost them all.

The old Spirit Man came in and took off Mark's right hiking boot, placing his foot on a Montagnard ax blade, which looked something like a metal boomerang. He put some cotton between his toes, siphoned rice wine through the reed and liberally doused Mark's foot with it.

Throughout the ritual the Spirit Man kept up his chant, calling on the *yang* of the mountains, and the *yang* of the forests, to bless Mark.

They put the bracelet on Mark's arm.

After the ceremony Nyot, the drummer from Ayunapa, an all-Montagnard rock 'n' roll band that Sprague sponsored, got out his acoustic guitar and sang Jarai Cheo Reo folk songs. Their weird, eccentric rhythm, played on gongs instead of a guitar, had haunted my dreams for nine years. Even now I cannot summon that sound consciously; it is too alien. But in the dark hours just before dawn, the jungle, the heat, and that rhythm chase themselves through my dreams.

"This is a new one," Sprague said of a song just completed. "It's the story of a Montagnard soldier and his girl. She sings, 'The helicopters came and took my man away. He's been gone for such a long time. Oh, helicopters, please bring my man back to me.'"

The next morning we got up, eager for a swim and a bath. The river was only a short distance away, but half the kids in the village, and all Sprague's friends and family came along. The boys capered and chattered, making faces at us all the way; the little girls were demure, eyes shining.

I kept my cut-offs on and waded into the river, soap in hand. Pretty soon we were all in the water, laughing, lathering ourselves until we were covered with foam, and then diving underwater, letting the current carry us a little distance downstream.

A boy, about nine, came up and splashed water on me. I grinned and surged through the water after him, running, laughing. . . .

Memories and a heavy sadness rolled over me. Nine years before, same river, same jungle, ten miles north. My patrol came across three Bahnar Montagnard boys, in their teens, clearing a field by the river. We surrounded them on three sides, river on the fourth side, wide as a football field. Who would try to escape across it?

The boys would. They did. We only wanted to question them. I surged after them, over the bank and into the river, weighed down by my rifle, ammo, canteen, surging through the water that splashed before me in sunbright shimmers, same as now. Yelling at my Jarai troops not to shoot, and yelling at the boys to stop. But my two Americans fired warning shots over their heads. The Jarai didn't understand the difference between warning shots and aimed fire. They had been fighting the Bahnar with crossbows for nine hundred years. They opened up, full-auto, shooting to kill.

Maybe the fact that I was there saved two of them. The Jarai had to fire high to avoid hitting me. One of the boys was hit, bright red blood cascaded down his back. We put a bandage on his wound and tried to raise a chopper on the radio. But we couldn't, so we stood there and watched him die.

And that's in my dreams with the gongs in the mornings.

I caught the kid, threw him up on my shoulder, and strode back through the water to the deepest part, spun around enough times to make him dizzy, and threw him into the water. He came up and splashed me again, now joined by three of his buddies.

I gave up, sank to the bottom, and floated out of range.

After the swim we returned to the longhouse. Sprague put on Creedence and, as if by magic, the jugs appeared again.

The history of mankind has been, among other things, a search for the highest expression of the human spirit. Several hundred years ago, the Yards discovered how to distill alcohol and quit worrying about it.

Bem and some of the other young men laughed and

pointed at me. "King Kong!" Bem said. "They call you King Kong, like from movie, 'cause you so big. 'Specially when you carry little boy."

I laughed. Sprague changed the tape and Nyot hung a nine-inch loop of quarter-inch brass welding rod on my right wrist, a Montagnard bracelet. It felt great.

A little later, bladder full, I lurched up. Absolutely smashed, I wandered down the notched log, stepped around a couple of pigs, passed two bare-chested ladies with baskets slung over their backs, crooked pipes in their mouths, and found a convenient bush to step behind.

Coming back I stopped. Rock 'n' roll music poured out of the longhouse, and I was drunk and happy, but I wanted to be alone for a few minutes. A big tree stood in front of the longhouse, a big, gnarled Flame of the Forest, with lurid blossoms in the upper reaches. It was beautiful, and it had a low fork that I could get my foot into.

It was an easy climb. I stopped when I was even with the door of the longhouse, looked in for a moment, then went on up twenty more feet. Bem came out and said, "Hey, King Kong! You climb tree?"

"Yeah!"

"You no 'fraid?"

I laughed out loud. "Are you crazy? I used to be a fucking paratrooper." I charged on up, bare toes hunting for stubs and limbs, higher and higher in the Flame of the Forest.

2
THE
PEACH-COLORED
LOTUS

In Phnom Penh that summer the press corps gathered every evening at a little outdoor cafe in front of the Ministry of Information. We sat under another spreading Flame of the Forest tree, its huge branches gnarled and beautiful, dropping fire-colored blossoms over the thirty-odd journalists.

The war in Vietnam was quiescent, but in Cambodia it was hot. The Khmer Rouge were slowly tightening their stranglehold on Phnom Penh, and the Cambodian army fought back in its languid way, sure that the Americans would bail them out in the end.

The ministry posted a single, double-spaced typewritten page daily, a summary of the day's military activities, in French. Every day someone would get up and amble over to see whether it contained anything newsworthy. It never did.

At the table were Malcolm Browne, the distinguished Far East correspondent of the New York *Times*, and Dieter Ludwig, a cameraman for German television who wore a Rolling Stones T-shirt and blond hair to his waist. The others represented all politics, fashions and lifestyles between. I had secured credentials from *Rolling Stone* as a cover, and they were legitimate, but I had my other reasons for being there. I was meeting Kpa Doh when he returned from the field.

Al Rockoff, a gnomelike free-lance photographer, crinkly hair tied back in a ponytail, sat cross-legged, rolling the tobacco out of a Juan Bastos cigarette, refilling it with something more to his liking from a film can.

I introduced myself to Malcolm Browne and told him I had enjoyed his book, *The New Face of War;* that I had been in Special Forces and shared many of his conclusions.

We were interrupted by an overwhelmingly healthy young man seated across the table, who broke in to announce that he, too, had been in Special Forces. He looked like Superman, except for blue jeans, a sly smile, and a predatory glint in his eye. He has since become immensely respectable and does not wish his name used in this book, so I will call him by the nickname he subsequently acquired, Captain America.

We shook hands and felt each other out in conversation. He had been an ROTC lieutenant, and had only been out of the army for six weeks. "Right after graduation, I went to Kathmandu. That way, when I went on active duty the government had to pay my travel from Nepal to Fort Bragg and back."

While either going to or coming from Kathmandu, Captain America had hitchhiked, at the height of the war and in civilian clothes, all over Vietnam. G.I.s had greeted him with shouts of, "What the fuck are you doing here?"

It is not often one meets a madman of these proportions.

I invited him to join Rockoff, the photographer, Haney Howell, the CBS correspondent, and me, for dinner.

Later that evening I stepped outside of Haney's apartment at the Hotel Royale to bum a light from the security guard in the parking lot. He stood beside a peach-colored Lotus owned by a Cambodian film director. It seemed an odd sort of status symbol in a country where you couldn't drive more than fifteen kilometers in any direction without a military escort.

The ground rumbled under my feet. Bomb run somewhere out in the countryside. It felt and sounded exactly like the New York City subway system from street level, bombs falling out of the night sky, twenty-five miles away.

Next morning Rockoff asked Captain America and me if we'd like to go out to the Battle of Ang Snoul. I agreed; Captain America was eager.

For the Cambodian Army the war consisted of trying to keep the roads open to the cities they did control; Phnom Penh, Kompol Som, Battambang.

We walked to the market and got a ride on the back of a three-wheel Lambretta minibus.

The sounds of battle were audible a long way out. Our driver wouldn't go any further than a mile from Ang Snoul, so we got out and walked along the blacktop highway, listening to the rat-a-tat WHOOM!!! soundtrack get louder. We walked into the town which had been rocketed by the Khmer Rouge and looted by the Cambodians; there were no civilians.

Television doesn't convey that noise, nor do motion pictures. These were tremendous shock waves, from 106mm recoilless rifles and mortars that leave your ears ringing, shake the ground under your feet and hit your stomach with palpable tremors of air.

I hadn't heard those sounds for five years, not since the NVA mortared a field hospital while I was on the operating table. We came upon Haney and his crew—Joe Yue, who was putting on his camera brace, and Sophan, who fiddled with the knobs on the sound equipment.

Christine Spengler, the French photographer, fresh and pretty in a red-and-white checked top and Levi bellbottoms, photographed some Cambodian G.I.s playing cards in front of a gutted store. They looked up and grinned gold-studded smiles for the camera.

Al announced he was going forward to get some shots of the fighting. Once past the town, the layout of the battle became clear. The Khmer Rouge had the road from about a mile out of Ang Snoul, and apparently controlled the woodline on the other side of the paddies that lay just outside the town. The Cambodes were drawn up in a long line, pretty much out in the open, about a hundred and fifty yards from the woodline. A frontal assault had broken down and they were all down behind some paddy dikes, not moving.

Way off to our right, cannonlike 106mm recoilless rifles mounted on armored personnel carriers, slammed away at the woodline.

"I'm going out to those 106s," Captain America announced, strolling across the paddies toward the battle.

"I'm going forward for some shots of the infantry," Al said. I stuck with Al; he was the guy who knew the territory.

Both of them had fought in paddies before; I had not. I had fought in jungle-covered mountains, the brush sometimes so thick you couldn't see somebody three feet away. This was a whole different game, flat, with no cover. If you walked, you did it in full view of an enemy a hundred and fifty yards away.

Al walked boldly down the road, although the firing now came from our right *rear*. He strode across paddy dikes out toward the troops, who lay flat on their bellies behind the dikes, which only gave about a foot of cover. They looked at us as though we were insane, a position with which I was in total agreement.

"Hey, man!" I called to Al.

He turned around and said, "Just keep on the dikes and you won't get your feet wet."

"I wasn't thinking about that. Those fuckers can see us."

He explained that firing broke out sporadically at different parts of the line and you could walk around when they weren't firing in your sector. When they did fire at you, the thing to do was to get down.

"What about snipers?"

He shrugged. Apparently his regard for Cambodian marksmanship was low.

We settled in by a big tree in the middle of the field and Al started taking pictures of the Cambodians.

Psnap! Psnap! Two bullets passed about six inches from my head.

"Hit it!" I yelled. I was flat on my face behind a paddy dike, with no recollection of having moved at all.

After a while the firing drifted off again. Captain America strolled over. He'd borrowed an M-79 grenade launcher from one of the Cambodes. He and Al got into a contest to see who could come closest to a little house that had somehow remained standing to our left front. It took them six grenades to totally destroy it.

Brigadier General Les Kossem's villa sprawled behind a low wall, just off Monivong, one of the main streets of Phnom Penh. As Kpa Doh and I entered, the guards lounging in the courtyard, wearing a variety of knives, grenades, and automatic weapons, mostly AK-47s, came to attention and saluted. In the courtyard there was also a jeep-mounted recoilless rifle, a couple of .30 caliber machine guns, a 60 millimeter mortar, and a number of the general's sleek, happy children playing.

General Les Kossem advanced through the door, slender, tall for an Asian, maybe 5'11", looking about twenty-seven except for the deep lines around his eyes and mouth. He wore a blue baseball cap, sky blue jumpsuit, and a forty-five in a shoulder holster. His smile was boyish, friendly and eager.

His people, the Cham, were coastal fishermen from central Vietnam. They are Moslem, and his father had come to Cambodia as a political refugee. ·

I had first read about Les Kossem in 1968, in a top secret CIA report on FULRO—*Fronte Unife de Lutte des Races Opprimees:* Unified Fighting Front of the Oppressed Races. FULRO had been conceived as a revolutionary organization of ethnic Vietnamese nationals both in Vietnam and in exile. They were Cambodians, Cham, and Montagnards; peoples who had been subjugated by the Vietnamese.

The general's house was a meeting place for cabinet ministers, university professors, and high-ranking army officers, all from families originally from South Vietnam. They sat around on the verandah in their white shirts and ties, sweating freely, fanning themselves and plotting revolution against the Vietnamese.

While there, we drank copiously of a bottled orange drink called Howdy Cola, poured into huge, iced glasses. They talked slowly and reasonably, citing historical precedent, unreeling this pipe dream which had no consonance whatever with political or military reality.

FULRO, and more specifically Kpa Doh's Montagnards, lacked two of Mao's essentials for a successful revolution; they had no serious backers among the superpowers, and no support among the Vietnamese people. Being ethnically dissimilar to the Vietnamese, they could not blend into the general population. Also, the Vietnamese outnumbered them fifteen to one. They had no chance within the present equation.

I told Kpa Doh if he tried to go back and lead a revolt he would fail, and he would get a lot of people killed.

He shrugged. "I must still try."

Okay, what were the Vietnamese's weak points? The main one was that, whatever Vietnamese were in power, they would be heavily dependent on U.S. aid for survival. Aid was controlled by Congress, and Congress was influenced by public opinion. Maybe the outside support could be obtained.

In small ways I'd been able to affect that before; good PR had kept the Pentagon from disbanding the Green Berets, and I'd been part of that, and I'd done PR for the defense fund on the Green Beret Murder Case. Nixon had freed the seven defendants because of adverse public opinion.

The story of their release had come over the wire while I was being interviewed about the case by Mike Wallace for *60 Minutes.* We had gotten a lot of publicity in that situation, and it had done the trick. Maybe we could use the press to pressure the South Vietnamese into granting Montagnard autonomy.

Toward that end I convinced Haney to do a story on one of the Montagnard battalions which had come over the border with Kpa Doh. This battalion had been the Strike Force at a Special Forces camp called Buon Sar Pa. During the Montagnard revolt of October 1964, they had machine-gunned their Vietnamese commanders and dumped the bodies down a three-hole shitter. That had made it awkward for them to stay in Vietnam when the revolt failed, and there was work available for trained soldiers in Cambodia.

The plan was for me and Captain America to stay in the field with them for a couple of weeks after the TV crew went home, to function as free-lance advisors. Then I'd go home and write it up for *Rolling Stone.*

The day before we were scheduled to go out to the battalion, Kpa Doh and I were walking along a residential street in Phnom Penh. "You know, Kpa Doh," I said, "I never have been convinced that Cowboy was dead. During Tet I manned a mortar with a sergeant who said he got away on a bicycle." I was referring to another of our Montagnard interpreters, Philippe Drouin, a.k.a. "The Cowboy." Phil had been my best Montagnard friend, and my patrol buddy.

He was the only Asian I'd go with on patrol without taking another American along.

By the time I returned for my third tour, Cowboy had become a colonel in FULRO, but his arrogance and high-handedness had created problems for him within the organization. Finally, he killed a Vietnamese Special Forces sergeant in a barroom fight and the Darlac Province chief was after him. He didn't have enough friends in the organization to save him, and, according to the CIA, had been killed by other FULRO factions seeking an accommodation with the Vietnamese.

"Oh, he is dead, for sure," said Kpa Doh. "Man who kill him live two block from here. You want to go see?"

I shook my head. I had no desire to meet my best friend's executioner. I wondered what Kpa Doh's position in that fracas had been. Then I shook it off. It was an intramural squabble, no business of mine.

"Okay, let's go!" the Cambodian colonel snapped crisply. I strode out through his front office, and stopped on the second floor balcony, overlooking the security detail.

The security detail was definitely professional. The men were neither overexcited nor oblivious to the fact that we were heading out through country where ambush was not only possible, but likely. They stood, smoking calmly, weapons draped casually across their bodies. They wore crisply tailored fatigues and old green berets mashed down over their brown, flat noses.

Most of them wore U.S. parachute wings from their days in the Mike Force in Vietnam, and Thai wings over their right pockets, earned when they trained with the Thais after joining the Cambodian Army.

Kpa Doh's wife, Miss Mlo, came out of the house on the other side of the headquarters building. She scooped up her littlest son and took him inside the house, where the oldest couldn't beat on him for a while.

I smiled. She was one of the prettiest women I have ever

known; slender, graceful, with huge eyes, and long, glossy, black hair. She didn't look old enough to be the mother of three wispy roughnecks—or the son who had died while Kpa Doh was in the States. He had told me about it the night he invited me to Cambodia. "When I get letter . . . I cry," he had said.

I remembered the night the first one had been born, almost ten years before. Kpa Doh was on patrol, and Miss Mlo panicked. She wanted him home. He was twenty klicks into VC territory, and I had to tell her to forget it. I was still maybe not her favorite person.

I stood in the steamy heat on the balcony for a long time while the soldiers below became more and more impatient. Apparently what the colonel meant when he said, "Okay, let's go!" was, okay, let's begin to get ready to think about it. The cockiest of the soldiers took off his armored vest and began to run through a series of karate forms, punching the air, kicking a jeep tire.

"I tell you, Morris, I never see army like this before," Kpa Doh said as he came up beside me. "Supply officer no want give gas for operation. Now we have hard time to go because he want to sell gas. He want to give money to girl downtown. My men know the girl he have." His voice grated harshly, the result of a round he'd taken through the vocal chords in 1965 or '66.

Before he got caught up in the war, he had sung professionally, propaganda songs on the radio for the Diem regime. He had detested Diem, but it was a gig, and nobody took the songs seriously. That was where he met his wife; they sang duets.

He pointed out a fat Cambodian in fatigue pants and an undershirt, poking avariciously around the vehicles, a cigarette dangling from his lips.

In Cambodia, everybody was on the take. Every worthless officer debutante in the Cambodian Army tooled around Phnom Penh on government gas in a jazzed-up jeep with glossy, olive drab paint and white sidewalls. Except

Kpa Doh; he drove a beat-up old civilian jeep, passed on to him by an American friend in the USAID program. Kpa Doh bought his own gas, usually heavily laced with water, in one liter bottles from street vendors.

"Why don't you just shoot the son of a bitch?" I inquired.

He gave me a reproachful look. "He is my colonel's cousin."

"Okay, kidnap the girl and sell her back to him for the gas."

He looked interested.

"If I were you, Kpa Doh," I said, "I'd be picking myself an escape route. This little country isn't going to make it."

I only said it once. I wish I'd said it a hundred times.

The colonel must have persuaded his cousin, because we finally got started, three army trucks and the TV crew's grey Peugeot, toward the river.

The Tonle Sap River was wide, brown and flat; the shore cluttered with sputtering Hondas, throbbing military vehicles and pushcart vendors selling square coconut popsicles on bamboo sticks to the throngs waiting for the ferry.

Drifting across the river on the ferry, we passed what was left of a beautiful steel and concrete bridge. The North Vietnamese had blown it, dropping three spans out of the middle. Twisted steel shot off the end of the bridge into space. It had been built with U.S. money and the North Vietnamese were willing to sacrifice 86 out of a 120-man unit to destroy it.

It had been a long time since I'd been out with an M-16. We were okay as long as there were civilians going up and down the road; generally, civilians do not wander through the killzone of an ambush. But the civilians soon petered out and we were out there by ourselves with nothing on either side but rice paddies. Low jungle started one or two hundred meters back from the road. Occasionally, we passed a farmer working a water buffalo; sometimes houses, up on stilts, built open to catch the breeze.

"Isn't this beautiful country, Morris?" Kpa Doh asked.

"Yeah, beautiful for ambushes." I muttered, chewing nervously on a toothpick. I jacked a round into the chamber, selector on safe, my finger on the switch.

About five minutes after I armed my rifle, the others did, too. They knew the country, so I hadn't missed it by much.

We crossed a little river and entered into a fair-sized village. We pulled into a schoolyard, ringed by wire and trenches. The battalion's mission was the defense of an administrative district, and they had inherited the school as their headquarters from the previous battalion.

Brigade headquarters had been informed a TV crew was coming, and every staff officer for a hundred miles, including the crooked supply officer, came out to pose for American television.

They crowded in front of the camera, guns holstered low, glancing at the camera from the corners of their eyes.

Haney led me aside and said, "Sorry, ace, but we've been shooting without film for half an hour. We can't get anything with these shitheads in the way."

"Yeah," I muttered. "I can see that."

He slapped me on the shoulder. "But I know Kpa Doh now, and if this outfit ever gets in some heavy action, I'll hurry down and shoot that. We can use the action as a carrier for the Montagnard story."

You take what you can get. I thanked him.

Before they left, Joe Yue asked me and Captain America if we wanted to go back to town. There were rumors that the battalion was to be assaulted that night.

We both laughed and shook our heads. This was the best dug-in defensive position we'd seen in Cambodia, and there weren't enough Khmer Rouge in the province to overrun it.

Haney and his crew jumped in their air-conditioned Peugeot and headed back to Phnom Penh with our escort, and our rifles: mine and Captain America's. We were to draw others from the battalion.

As soon as the TV crew left, we went inside headquarters and borrowed a couple of rifles and some ammunition.

That was when the holes in their defenses started to appear. They could only give us four magazines apiece. In a serious firefight that would last maybe ten minutes. Then we'd be lying in the dirt, in the dark, trying to load magazines by the intermittent light of drifting flares, frantic to get the weapon back in operation before the next rush.

They were short of magazines because the supply officer who hadn't wanted to provide gas to come out here had sold them. The only possible buyer was the enemy.

I was beginning to understand how this war worked. The Khmer Rouge didn't get supplies down the Ho Chi Minh trail. It was much easier and cheaper for the Chinese to send them money to buy stuff from the Cambodians. The U.S. supplied both sides and the Khmer Rouge let the Cambodes hold the cities while they consolidated their hold on the countryside.

When we made the rounds of the defensive perimeter with Y Bun Sur Paul, the battalion commander, that night, Captain America pointed out a number of minor flaws . . . poor fields of fire, things like that. He had never worked as an advisor, and he baldly explained the deficiencies to Y Bun, which is not the best way to advise. You almost have to apologize for suggesting you might know something your counterpart doesn't. Then you carefully explain that although you have learned far more from him than you could possibly teach, there is this one little item he might find helpful.

Y Bun pointed out some cows, grazing inside the outer perimeter wire.

"If we get hit tonight, we'll have steak for breakfast," I said.

"The Cambodes I was with in Vietnam used to eat VC liver," said Captain America.

"You ever try it?" I asked.

"Sure."

"Cooked or raw?"

"Cooked, of course," he snapped.

After a supper of rice, an indecipherable goulash, and Howdy Cola without ice, Captain America and I sat on the verandah of the headquarters, enjoying the sunset and the evening breeze.

As he started the daily entry in his spiral notebook, he asked me if I'd seen anything abnormal in Phnom Penh.

"In all honesty, Captain, the most abnormal thing I saw in Phnom Penh was you."

"Well, fuck you!"

"No, really. I never met a cannibal before."

He looked at me, amazed. "You mean to say if everybody around you was eating VC liver, you wouldn't do it?"

I shuddered. "Absolutely not."

He shook his head.

Y Bun and Kpa Doh came up to tell us, as tactfully as possible, that we would have to return to Phnom Penh the next day. Y Bun said that if we got waxed, and there was a diplomatic flap over it, he would be in serious trouble. He also said the local people hated Americans so much, because of the bombing, that our presence was threatening the rapport he was trying to build with the people of the district.

The Cambodian battalion which had preceded them had lost no opportunity to alienate the population. He figured that eighty-five percent of the locals were with the Khmer Rouge. During the short time he'd been here he'd been winning them back by being nice and having his soldiers be polite and helpful.

All this was part of the Civil Affairs/Psychological Operations program I'd laid out for him when I first visited the battalion a month before. I was pleased that he'd listened, and that my advice was working.

But I should have realized that after ten years of war they didn't need a junior Jesus to tell them how to run raids and ambushes in their own jungle. We had already done that job.

I felt like Kid Shileen, the old drunken gunfighter in the movie *Cat Ballou.*

Captain America thought I was nuts. To him this was an excursion, an outing, not a serious mission. We were on an *adventure,* in *Cambodia,* for chrissakes, and what did I want anyway?

Our only hope for a little action would be if the Khmer Rouge hit the camp that night. Captain America went to sleep out on the perimeter.

I lay down in the headquarters with my boots on and my rifle beside me.

Couldn't sleep, though. After a while I got up and went outside to listen to the troopers and their wives talking in their coughing language, laughing in the cool evening air, scented with tropical blossoms and woodsmoke. Their kids were asleep by then. The soldiers kept their families dug in behind the perimeter.

I had missed those sounds and smells.

Around four-thirty in the morning, Captain America saw something poking around the perimeter and squeezed off a burst. Scared the hell out of the whole camp, but nobody fired back.

The next afternoon we went back to Phnom Penh. I got ready to leave the next day. Maybe I could get these people some good publicity back home. If I could get the rest of America to see them like I saw them, we could get backing for their revolution, or at least pressure the Vietnamese for fair treatment.

Before he said good-bye, Kpa Doh asked me if I would forward a letter to John Wayne. In 1966, while doing research for *The Green Berets,* Wayne had lived for two weeks with the Pleiku Mike Force, which Kpa Doh had commanded. He wore the Montagnard bracelet Kpa Doh gave him until he died.

Kpa Doh was angling for an assignment to the Command and Staff College at Ft. Leavenworth. If he got it he would need a dress uniform, and he couldn't afford one. His letter asked John Wayne for two hundred dollars to buy a dress uniform.

Captain America urged me to stay, said we could go out with Cambodian units and do some fighting. I said no. In my opinion, the Cambodians were going to lose, and deserved to lose. I'd been shot four times in Vietnam. I might risk it again for the Montagnards, but if they didn't need me, I sure wouldn't do it for fun.

John Wayne's secretary wrote me later that he had sent Kpa Doh the two hundred dollars, but Kpa Doh never got to go to Ft. Leavenworth. Rockoff said that his unit was one of the last to break up when the Khmer Rouge took the country. He changed to civvies and took his family to the French Embassy. They were among the roughly two hundred Cambodians ejected from the embassy in the final days, led away, presumably for execution, by the Khmer Rouge.

My plan to publicize the Montagnards failed. I couldn't even sell my story to *Rolling Stone*. When their editor read it he realized that, in essence, they had financed a mercenary for the Lon Nol government. Hardly in keeping with their editorial policy, and not something they wished to publicize.

By 1973 the American public was so tired of Vietnam they didn't want to hear anything more about it.

3
FAYETTEVILLE, ARKANSAS

June 1981, the last day of my last semester. I had finished teaching three classes of bonehead English, and completed the coursework for an MFA in Creative Writing. In the preceding week I had taken three finals, and given three, and I was done. I dropped my tabulated, signed gradebook on the stack of identical books on Dr. Van Scyoc's unoccupied desk, and checked my box for the last time. I felt that sudden let-down which comes from a release of tension when you're still wired.

Leaving the building, I walked down the hill from the English department. The campus thronged with young, attractive, and, at that moment, very worried students. The air was clear and clean, and the trees green.

I was in love, and living with the woman I loved, in a nice house on a tree-shaded street in a pretty town. Other than the fact that I had no money and no prospects of money, it was just about the best time in my life. But it would soon be over, and I had nothing lined up to replace it. I had applied for teaching jobs, but had no acceptances yet.

I walked into our empty house—Kathy was taking her finals too—threw my books on the sofa, and went to the kitchen for a beer, Coors. Not then sold in Arkansas, it was a status item, especially imported by pickup truck from Oklahoma. It was only noon, but I was dead beat from lack of sleep and release from nervous tension caused by taking all the courses I'd put off for three years in one semester, while simultaneously teaching three sections.

The next day I planned to take off with a backpack for four days alone in the Ozarks. Then I'd have a full summer to read for comps.

But first I was going to finish this beer and take a nap.

I kicked my sneakers off and propped my feet up on the coffee table. I put my lips to the can, and the phone rang. I let it ring three times while I took a long swallow. Then, languidly, I reached out and snatched up the receiver. "Hello!"

"Morris? This is Jim Graves at *Soldier of Fortune*. Can you go to Beirut for us?"

I sat up, electrified, my feet slapping the floor. "Sure. No problem. When?"

His voice cracked over the line. "Thursday. Fly to Boulder tomorrow. We'll brief you and give you some things for the Phalangists. Here, I'm going to put Venter on the line."

"Hello, Jim. Hello!" A middle-class British accent on the line, strong baritone voice. I didn't know Venter, but I'd read some of his stuff, solid new journalism about the wars in Rhodesia and South Africa. His photos were excellent, and he'd had to stick his neck out a long way to get them. "I'm just back from Beirut for *Eagle*," he said, referring to *SOF*'s principal competition within the genre. "It's a great story. The Phalangists—nobody knows anything about them, and they're really very good. Got in a hell of a punch-up . . . rockets and machine guns on the rooftops. My guide went for more ammo and fell seven stories down an elevator shaft. Jesus! He was a great kid. Engineering student. I can't stay to brief you, but I'll write you a long letter. Cheerio, mate!"

I sat for a long moment, stunned. My life hadn't taken such a sudden unexpected turn since 1962, when I'd gone to the Pentagon to see about getting out of the army and come away assigned to a three-year tour in the 1st Special Forces Group on Okinawa. Just as I had on that occasion, I started to laugh, a rolling, belly-flexing guffaw that didn't stop for three minutes.

My relationship with Bob Brown, the founder, publisher, and editor-in-chief of *Soldier of Fortune*, went back to '76, just before the magazine started. I had read in the paper that some guy out in Boulder, Colorado, was starting a trade journal for mercenaries.

That struck me as about the squirreliest idea I'd ever heard, but I had an entire cardboard box full of unsold stuff I'd written about the war, and about my later trip to Vietnam and Cambodia. In 1976, unless your work was subtitled *mea culpa*, all you had to say to a publisher was "Vietnam" and a steel curtain descended in front of you.

So I called Brown, who, as it turned out, had commanded a Special Forces "A" Detachment in Vietnam, just as I had.

"Great!" he bellowed over the phone when I told him about my writing. "I'm going to an Army Reserve summer camp in Illinois next week. I'll drive down and look at your stuff." Sure, why not? It was only five hundred miles out of his way.

Brown drove up in an old dun-colored two door, covered with road dust and crammed with luggage and uniforms. He pulled into the parking lot in front of my apartment and exploded out of the car, barefoot, wearing cut-offs and an old J.C. Penney sport shirt. He grabbed my hand, a broad-shouldered guy with thinning sandy hair, long torso, and short, pale, hairy legs; talking a blue streak, cackling insanely during the pauses, snarling outrageous war stories from Vietnam, from Rhodesia, from some strange coup attempt in Haiti. Colonel Brown.

At dinner, the lady I was with was nonplussed when Brown ate his salad with his hands.

The bond between Special Forces people is a little hard to explain to someone who has never experienced it, but it's closer than friendship and closer than most family. Brown and I had so many overlapping experiences that as soon as we met, I felt I had known him all my life. If it weren't for that, and the fact that my work habits as a writer were not yet professional, I would not have done what I did, which was to give him my cardboard box full of Vietnam stories.

He didn't have to ask; I was desperate to be read. I had no carbons.

He took the box to Boulder and lost it. It disappeared into the maw, the Fibber McGee's closet, of his so-called filing system—apparently forever.

Over the next three years I made four trips to Boulder and turned the *SOF* office upside down each time. No stories. Mary Lou Jones, Brown's associate editor, searched between times as well. No stories.

By that time I was in print again and no longer desperate for publication. And I was a little put off by the rabid tone of Brown's magazine, the mad-dog ferocity of the ads. Brown knew what would sell; his style was your basic snake-eater animal act, on display in bars at low dives worldwide. Personally I prefer a more low-key approach. I try not to talk about heroics for fear someone will ask me to do some. I decided to chalk the loss of my stories up to experience and forget it. But I still loved the guy, and went to see him every time I was in Boulder.

Three years after I gave Brown my box of stories, and long after my G.I. Bill had run out, I entered the graduate program in creative writing at the University of Arkansas. Being a teaching assistant was a way to make a few bucks while I wrote, and, who knows, I might learn something. As it turned out, I learned a great deal; the program was hard, but very good.

Like most graduate students, I didn't have much money, so I was delighted, if puzzled, a year or so later, to receive a postcard from a guy at *SOF* I had never heard of, saying my story had been accepted, and they would be sending me a check for $250.00. I called to find out what story. I hadn't sent them anything since Brown lost my cardboard box.

His new managing editor, Bob Poos, had gone through their entire inventory and found my stuff.

Before I finished at Arkansas, they bought two-thirds of my cardboard box. It has never been a mistake to trust Brown, but sometimes it looked like one for a long time.

Poos, a former Marine drill instructor, former AP reporter in Vietnam, molded Brown's combination wild-west show and G.I. Joe comic book into a professional, slick-looking magazine. In addition to what was in the cardboard box, I did a couple of long pieces about genuine heroes I'd known in Vietnam, but I'd never thought about going overseas for them. Couldn't have even if I'd wanted to; I was teaching and taking courses.

But I had a window of opportunity here, and this was my first chance to do something really exciting in eight years. The thought of passing it up never crossed my mind.

I had the summer free except for my reading, and I could take my Cliffs Notes along and study in Beirut.

At this writing it is eight years later, and I still have seven books to read for my comps.

Two days later, walking back from the *SOF* offices to Brown's house, I found an eagle feather in my path. If you believe in omens, you couldn't ask for better.

4
OUR MAN IN BEIRUT

I sort of expected my Lebanese contact on Cyprus to be like Sydney Greenstreet or Peter Lorre, wearing a panama hat. What I got was a collegiate-looking kid in a new Corvette, who grabbed my hand, shook it, and said in perfectly accented American English, "Hi, my name's Masoud."

Masoud gunned the 'Vette through the narrow, twisting streets of Limassol. People, small cars, and motorcyclists flew from our path and flowed back around the 'Vette. We pulled up in front of a pleasant restaurant with a verandah overlooking the city.

We ate seafood on the verandah. Over a plate of shrimp, a salad, and a bottle of excellent white wine, Masoud told his story. He had been a junior, majoring in electrical engineering at Oklahoma State when the war with the Syrians got hot in '78.

He returned to Lebanon to find himself in charge of a squad of what the papers call the Christian Phalangist Militia. He told me about it in grammatically correct, but eccentric, English. The eccentricity was that even though he had six months of combat experience, he didn't know any military terminology, at least not in my language.

"One night one of my boys woke me up; I looked out through a chink in the wall and saw about six thousand enemy. So I called the boys with the mortars and had them fire right on us. We were in very strong houses, and they were in the open, so that drove them away."

We swapped war stories for a while until he finally said, "You know, the things they do to our people, after a while they drive you crazy. So once, when we captured a Syrian, I tied him to the back of my jeep and drove him all over town, on cobblestones, down alleys. When I got through there was no more left of him than this." He held up a plate of shrimp shells and sauce.

"It gives me the creeps to think about it now," he said. "It scares me to think I could ever have been like that. When I go home I ask the boys not even to tell me their stories. They are fanatics."

That night I got the shakes. I thought back on my briefing from Jim Graves, the new managing editor at *SOF.* "Look, Jim," I had demanded, "every combat situation is different. Before I go in, I like to know what I can do and not do, where I can go and not go. And most important, who are the good guys and who are the bad guys?"

Graves looked up from his desk and shot me an evil grin. "Well, Jimbo," he said, "that's what we're sending you over there to find out!"

Maybe I shouldn't write about fear; maybe I should play it stoic and close to the chest, but I think it needs to be talked about. Everybody goes through it. This fear is as much a necessary part of preparation for combat as is cleaning your weapon.

I wasn't mad at anybody in Lebanon. So the deal I made with myself was that I would take it a step at a time, and reserve the right to back off anywhere along the line. I would not, for instance, go into combat against a well-armed, well-trained, determined enemy, with a bunch of clowns.

That was the intellectual part. Physically, I got alternating chills in the gut and a lethargy that made me want to stay in my nice warm bed. What was needed now was for my body to accustom itself to the fact that the decision had been made. Once that happened, the transformation began, a transformation as complete as man into werewolf. I am convinced that it is a sustained, low-level release of adrenaline that keeps you alert and ready for combat.

All the tension I had accumulated since 1973 in Cambodia disappeared. A lower-back pain that had plagued me for three years vanished instantly.

It was an old, sweet feeling, one I had missed, and the closer I got to combat the sweeter it would be. That's the *Devil's secret name*, that feeling that suckers you into *the game*.

The next day Masoud arranged for my passage to Jounieh, a Christian-controlled port twenty miles north of Beirut. Boat travel was necessary because I had no visa, and because the airport was in West Beirut, under the control of the enemy.

Once we were underway I ordered a beer at the bar. One of the other passengers, a chubby Lebanese in one of those shiny, brightly colored shirts, the kind favored by Vegas dealers and low-level mafiosi, approached me in true Peter Lorre style, and identified himself as an agent of . . . Christ! I didn't even know what these people called themselves.

I had been told they were trying to shake the "Phalangist" tag. The word comes from *phalanx*, a Greek word meaning a military formation. The Christian Phalangist parties were political organizations formed for the purpose of organizing a militia to defend their homes, shops, and towns, when the central government was too weak and indecisive to do so. Unfortunately, the name "falange" is also associated with Franco's fascist party in Spain, not a good tag from a public-relations standpoint.

At any rate, I was sitting at the bar, sipping a Heineken and chatting with the ship's heavily-muscled West Indian steward, when this sharp-nosed bureaucrat, scowling, sweating heavily, his belly jiggling against a shirt designed for a man with no waist at all, approached with my passport in his hand. "You have no visa!" he announced.

I nodded. "True. There is a man in Jounieh who is supposed to pick me up."

"His name!"

I gave him the name.

Just saying the name had an effect similar to that of racking back the bolt of an automatic weapon. The whole tone of the conversation changed. "Well, if you know Joe, then you won't have any trouble."

I grinned. I wanted to see if I could make him sweat again. "Oh, I don't know him. My Cyprus contact is supposed to have called him that I was coming."

The beads of sweat popped right back out on his brow. "I will radio ahead and see if it is okay. You may have to go back to Cyprus."

I shrugged. "I get paid the same, either way."

Not true. Brown would have my guts for garters if I went this far and didn't get a story. But I wasn't too worried; a high-handed air and a few names work wonders in these ceiling-fan countries. That's how I thought of Lebanon then: Vietnam with sand.

The only ocean-going vessels I had been on before were submarines. So that night I borrowed a blanket and slept on a foam pad on the flying bridge, under the stars. At night, on the sea, the stars are almost as bright as they are on the desert. I finally fell asleep with my glasses still on.

The next morning we were scheduled to arrive in Jounieh at 8:30, so I bounded down the ladder at first light, eager for coffee and breakfast.

The revolutionary bureaucrat came up to me at the bar, which also served as a lunch counter. "They didn't know you were coming and they can't find Joe." Not good news, but I still wasn't worried. A couple of phone calls should fix it. I gave him some numbers from my notebook.

When we had eaten breakfast I went to the bow to watch slick blue water run under the boat, and a grey line of mountains appear on the horizon. The first Lebanese boat I saw in the water was an ancient fishing sailboat which looked like the Flying Dutchman, reinforcing all my prejudices. But the second was a low, sleek outboard, pulling a skier.

Oh, Lord, I thought. *They told me this was going to be different, but this is different from the different I had in mind.*

The ten or eleven Lebanese men on the bow began singing a folksong, a rhythmic Middle Eastern chant, and one began beating his right fist into his left palm, muttering along with the music: "Syrians—kill fuckin' Syrians."

Shortly after that, a motor launch with two open rows of hard-backed wooden benches came out to our ship. Standing up in the boat was another overweight official in a slick shirt. He carried a handy-talkie in one hand and wore a snub-nosed revolver on his right hip. As soon as the launch pulled alongside, two highly bronzed young men in obscene Mediterranean bathing suits came aboard and began transferring our baggage.

But the thing that held my attention was the shore in front of us, crowded with swimmers; its little amusement park going full blast—complete with two gaily colored Ferris wheels, a merry-go-round, and some bumper cars.

The guy with the pistol on his hip and the bureaucrat

from the boat engaged in animated conversation over my passport. A moment later my sweaty friend from the boat came back to where I sat and whispered in my ear, "As soon as we dock, take your bag and go across the street. Stand by the BMW."

The guys in the nasty swimsuits lobbed a couple of lines onto the dock as we coasted in. I grabbed my black B-4 bag which, with its 20 pounds of Second Chance armored vest, three sniper manuals, and sixteen copies of *SOF*, immediately threw my lower back out of alignment. I lurched onto the Lebanese shore.

It's easy to forget, but there is a legal government there. Its representative stood on the dock in rumpled khakis, with some sort of off-the-wall black epaulets on his shirt. My two accomplices, both of whom seemed much more in charge than the official representative, chatted with him while I heaved past as inconspicuously as a tall man with a red beard carrying a hundred-pound suitcase can.

I got across the street okay and stood admiring the palms and the handsome people on the beach. But I didn't see a BMW anywhere.

Just as the official from the ship approached me, an old blue Plymouth sedan, with two red lights exactly like the ones on American cop cars, drove up. "Get in that car," said my sweaty friend. I was not eager to do it.

Two young guys got out. They wore green fatigues and black berets, and carried folding-stock AKs slung over their shoulders. These lads were not part of any mariachi band. They handled their weapons with the familiarity with which most people handle their wallets. One of them opened the trunk for my suitcase and camera bag.

The other shot me a quizzical look. He didn't know whether he was picking up a prisoner or a VIP. I didn't either, but I nodded imperiously toward the door handle. He popped it open and I entered like an ambassador.

We drove through a nice seaport and resort town, with signs advertising seafood, scuba gear, and discos, in

French, English, and Arabic; the big movies were *L'Histoire d'O* and *The Wild Geese*. After a drive of about three miles, the car turned into a walled compound with a small guard-house at the entrance. Inside were civilian villas, sur-rounded by spiny tropical vegetation and flowers. The guard at the gate, a listless lad of seventeen or so, appeared to have his attention focused on something else, probably his radio, from which Top 40 music poured. If necessary, he'd be a snap to disarm and get past. But then what?

We went inside the first building. I had been informed that this was a militia without rank, but, rank or no rank, one sweep of the eyes sorted out the chief clerk, sergeant major, and adjutant, and tabbed this as an MP outfit, since the adjutant, a small, bespectacled, finicky-looking man, had handcuffs on his belt.

I was pleased they were on his belt instead of my wrists. These people didn't know me, and had reason to be ner-vous. If they decided they didn't like me, or my magazine, I was in a world of hurt. Even if by some feat of *James Bond-ismo* I bashed and battered my way out of this compound, I'd be conspicuous, ignorant, and illegal.

I sat for a long time behind a desk across from the adju-tant, nervous and sleepy from my night on the bridge of the ship. Then the guard who had driven me here approached and loomed over me, concentrating, looking for words in English, "Woood yooo lihk zome coffee?"

After I'd drunk my coffee, I was ushered into another office to meet Joe. He welcomed me and we had a pleasant chat. He had gone to college in the States and for a time had been a police reporter in Miami. He called the Lebanese Forces G-5 to tell them I was coming. In the American staff system, G-5 handles propaganda, and the public relations is a separate function under G-1, Administration. But the Leb-anese saw no reason for such an arbitrary distinction; G-5 handled all information functions.

* * *

No guard this time, only the same driver who had driven me from the harbor, smiling and friendly. Before we reached our destination, my driver wrote his name and phone number in my notebook so we could go out and hell around a bit before I left Lebanon.

Back in Jounieh, I had begun to wonder whether the war in Lebanon was a joke or a comic-opera game. As we came into East Beirut all such misconceptions were dispelled. The closer we got to the center of town the greater the destruction: apartment houses with great shell-hole gouges, and collapsed buildings. But the streets were filled with European and American cars, some of them also pockmarked with shrapnel holes, and the sidewalks were thronged with people dressed no differently from those in Little Rock, Arkansas.

What really amazed me was that everywhere I looked there were construction cranes and new high-rise buildings going up. Some buildings under construction were already pockmarked with shell holes, and others bore patched holes, but they just went right on slapping them up. I thought, these people must be either the ballsiest in the world, or the smartest, or the craziest, or all of the above. Although I was to learn a great deal about Lebanon and the Lebanese in the coming weeks, nothing contradicted this initial impression.

My driver turned off a main boulevard and shot up a long hill, into an area of narrow two-lane streets fronted by high-rise apartments with balconies. The construction looked like something you'd see in Miami, Florida, but the doorways were barricaded with 55-gallon drums filled with dirt and topped with sandbags, and the street was full of young men wearing fatigues and carrying slung weapons, mostly AKs, but a few M-16s.

Very few of these people wore caps with their fatigues, but a semi-military haircut was in style, short, but no crewcuts, no sidewalls. I saw no rank or unit insignia of any kind. These troops looked pretty sharp, but casual about it; no spitshines. Their uniforms fit well, and that lost, hangdog look often found in Third World military units was totally absent.

We stopped in front of an apartment building. My driver led me around the barricade and up the steps to a second floor apartment. A plant hung just inside the door. Across the room was a conversational grouping of plush furniture, seating a three-man French TV crew, in animated conversation with a tall, skinny, bearded Lebanese wearing a crewcut. He wore a genuine Vietnam-issue Special Forces tiger suit and a .45 in a spring-clip shoulder holster. He had on the last pair of WWII wrap-around combat boots I ever saw or expect to see.

All of these guys looked up when I came in, then went back to their conversation. I set my bag down and looked around.

In the dining room, several young men in fatigues sat at a large table, poring over newspapers, magazines and photos. Working with them was a truly stunning girl, model-thin, with long strawberry blonde hair. She wore tight, faded jeans, sneakers, and a white top. She appeared tired, strained.

The guy in the tiger suit got up. He and my driver exchanged a few words in Arabic. He turned to me with an expression of weary exasperation. We shook hands. "My name is Samir," he said.

My driver said good-bye, reminded me to come see him in Jounieh, and left. Samir gestured toward the couch and we sat down across from the TV crew. By way of a conversation opener, I asked him where he had gotten his tiger suit.

"A friend in your Special Forces got me six pairs," he said. "This is the last."

A kid whom I took to be an American student walked in the door I had just entered. He walked with a slouching saunter and wore Adidas sneakers and beat-up grey cords.

He had the scraggly beard and long hair I associated with college students. But over his Izod shirt he wore an old French army cammie bush jacket.

Hey, kid, I thought, *that thing can get you killed here.*

He went into the dining room, leaned on the table where the young people in fatigues worked and began jiving in French with the exquisite young woman. She looked up and they smiled at each other.

From what sounded like two blocks over, I heard a burst of AK fire, followed by another farther away and then a muffled *crump . . . crump.*

I looked up, startled. "We are two hundred meters from the front," Samir said. His accent was English public school, overlaid with the musical, rolling Lebanese lilt. Wearily he lifted his wrist, pulled a green and black tennis sweatband away from the face of his watch, and said, "Would you like to go to lunch?"

If he wasn't worried about being two hundred meters from the front, then I saw no reason why I should be. "Sure."

We got up and sauntered out of the apartment. "Do you like Lebanese food?"

I nodded. It seemed an appropriate thing to do; I had never eaten any.

Outside, a kid in jeans expertly steered a skateboard down the slope of the street and around the rubble. Around the corner another bunch of kids played soccer.

Our restaurant consisted of two rickety tables set outdoors behind a sandbagged wall. The kebab was done on an open grill made from a 55-gallon drum, halved lengthwise. But what a lunch: the best tabouleh, homus, kebab, fresh fruit, and arak, a clear liquor that turns milky white when mixed with water. It tastes like licorice, but watch it!

"This country is sure different from what I expected."

He smiled. "You expected a desert."

I nodded.

While we ate I watched Sam closely, trying to take his

measure. I liked what I saw. He was wary at first, but when he saw I had no preconceived notions, he warmed up quickly. I never saw a man slide into and out of a thousand-yard stare as quickly as Sam did. He had the spaced-out mystical-militant quality of an El Greco monk trapped by the Inquisition. The feeling I had about Sam was that somehow he had been burned clean.

Lebanon's form of combat had its compensations, like this lunch, and the high incidence of truly lovely women; but when it got hot, it was very, very hot, and none of the parties was a signatory of the Geneva convention. Sam had lived through seven years of this stuff. I could only guess at his weariness.

Once when I saw him slide into that long-gone stare I asked him what he would have done if this war hadn't interrupted his life. He replied, "Oh, I'd have found one someplace."

I asked him about the atrocities Masoud had described on Cyprus.

"Yes," he replied. "The Palestinians excel at that sort of thing. But our boys decided if those were the rules, we would play, too. They backed away pretty fast."

Raised in Cairo, Sam had spent a year and a half in an Egyptian Commando unit as an 18- and 19-year-old kid. He was under no illusions about the general quality of Egyptian forces, but claimed his unit had been exceptional. The quality of their desert training, specifically, had been excellent.

He told one story about this Egyptian training. "There was a group of us sitting cross-legged around our instructor on the grenade range. He pulled the pin on a Russian grenade and threw it in my lap. 'Get rid of it,' he said. I knew it was either a dud, or had a long fuse, so I threw it back at him and said, 'Get rid of it yourself.' It had a long fuse, but it wasn't a dud. He left me alone after that."

He was quite frank about the fact that he had gone into G-5 work because his nerves were shot. "It's quite amusing, really," he said. "I get shot at twice as much as before, because I'm always taking journalists to where the action is. Before, I stayed in my unit, and only fought sporadically."

As we talked, we found that we had read an amazing number of the same books. I asked if he had read *The Centurions* and *The Praetorians*, by Jean Larteguy, two Special Forces' favorites. He had not only read them, he had read all of Larteguy, and met him when he came to Lebanon.

At the end of lunch my situation was very different from what it had been at the beginning. For the first time since 1968, when I left the 5th Special Forces Group in Vietnam, I felt completely at home with my environment, at ease and happy. These were my kind of folks.

Walking back across the street to the press bureau, we passed the American college kid we had seen earlier, unloading the French TV crew from a white VW bug, into which they and their equipment had been jammed. The kid had an AK slung over his shoulder. *Hmmmmmm*, I thought, *things are not always what they appear*.

When we got back upstairs and flopped down on the couch, Sam said, "Well, what can we do for you?"

"I've got a bulletproof vest and a sniper manual from Venter to deliver to a guy named Rocky in a place called Sodeco, and another couple of manuals for a guy named Tony in Hadath. Let's get rid of the bloody vest first. Then we'll play it by ear."

He went to check with Lebanese Forces command to see if it was okay if I went to Sodeco, wherever that was. I had visions of a tiny village near Beirut that we would have to tiptoe over the mountains at night to get to. I still had a firmly fixed idea of Vietnam in the desert, with these guys playing a role sort of like the Hoa Hao, a militant Buddhist sect in the Delta. I unzipped my bag and dragged out the vest.

The college boy with the AK and the French TV crew came clattering up the stairs.

Sam came back and said, "Okay, you're supposed to spend the night in Sodeco; Rick will take you."

"Who's Rick?"

He indicated the college boy.

"Who's that gorgeous French creature?"

"That's Christine. She's Rick's friend. May I see the vest?"

I handed it to him. Rick left the Frenchmen, who sat down with their beers, and came to examine the vest. He was distant and none too cordial. He looked tired. He and Sam spoke to each other in bursts of rapid-fire French, too fast and complicated for me to follow. But after they spoke, Rick was open and friendly.

The vest had two tiers of alloy plates in front and back that slid into OD-nylon pockets. Second Chance makes heavier ones, with more armor, to cover the crotch, but that was a lot more weight than I'd wanted to carry. In any case, the heavier vests would not have covered the area under the arms. They had been made primarily for police work, just as the Army and Marine flak vests were made for indirect-fire weapons. Sam and Rick wanted something that would cover you both ways.

"You ready?" Rick inquired.

I looked around the apartment, considering that once again I had gotten myself into a situation where I was racing off to get shot at with people I didn't know. "Just like that, huh?"

"Unless you've got something else to do here."

I made a transatlantic call to *SOF*, to tell Graves I was there, was okay, and was going out.

"What's it like?" he asked.

"So far it's been a Humphrey Bogart movie."

"Well, don't get yourself killed just to get a story."

"I won't." I hung up the phone. "Okay," I muttered. "Let's go." I picked up my camera bag.

"Don't take that!" Rick commanded.

"That's just my camera bag."

"I know, but our people cross over into West Beirut all

the time; some of us work over there. We have relatives over there. We can't afford to have our faces shown. We can't let our positions be revealed either."

Great, I thought. No photos. Brown's going to love that. Rick was telling me rule number one for this war, and once more I was thinking when I should have been listening, an omission I was to regret later. Just as rule number one for Vietnam had been never set a pattern, rule number one for Lebanon was never let them know who you, personally, are. Because, if you do, they will definitely send someone to do a number on you.

But all I could think about was the bloody photos—in the end, they gave me more photos than I could ever use.

We went back downstairs and got in Rick's beat-up old VW bug. He eased it past the quiet block of apartments, and the pinball arcade, and accelerated at the end of the block. But the instant we hit a major traffic artery, two blocks down, he floored it and we roared through empty, shattered streets. We blasted through a red light, entering a major intersection at about 85 kph. "Stop at that light and you'll draw mortar fire almost every time," he muttered, and gave me a piratical grin, taking quick glances down the six intersection streets to see whether he might be run over by an oncoming tank.

He twisted down three or four more streets, slewed sideways into the entrance of a parking garage, and parked correctly between two white lines.

"Is that a stock VW engine in there?" I asked, when I caught my breath.

Rick grinned wryly as he opened the car door. "Not exactly," he said. "Okay, this is it."

No midnight infiltration over the mountains. Sodeco was a neighborhood in Beirut, like Flatbush is a neighborhood in Brooklyn.

A handsome, well-built young man with curly brown hair and an engaging smile walked toward us. He wore a pair of fatigue pants and an OD T-shirt. He looked to be about 20 or 21, and carried himself with an unselfconscious air of command.

"This is Rocky, the Sodeco commander," Rick said. We shook hands and I passed him the manuals and his bullet-proof vest. Rocky and Rick grinned greetings. They were obviously friends.

"See you in the morning," Rick said. He jumped in the bug and screeched backward up the ramp, through a blue haze of exhaust; he went so fast that if I'd blinked, I'd have missed it. A squeal came from upstairs as he speed-shifted into low and roared off down the street.

Rocky took me on a walking tour of his section of town. A couple of his boys went along with us. One of them had a pistol on his hip, but nobody carried a rifle. The buildings in the neighborhood were all concrete, closed in, and shot straight up for many stories. Holes, pockmarks and rubble were everywhere. We walked easily until we approached a little open area in front of a church. "Stay on the right here," Rocky said. "On the left side of the street a sniper can hit you."

I remembered downtown Nha Trang during Tet, where a foot either way made the difference.

Rocky wanted to show me the church. It was shot all to hell. But I was interested in why they weren't armed, and were unconcerned, if this was such a hot area.

"Venter told me you had a hell of a fight when he was here," I said.

"Yeah," Rocky replied. "Up on the roofs. His guide got on the elevator on the twelfth floor. Unfortunately the elevator was in the basement. It shook Al up pretty badly . . ."

On the roofs there were no ground assaults, but nowhere to hide except behind a few sandbags.

We went on back downstairs to the parking garage. "You want a beer?" Rocky asked. This was a front-line position and I had to settle for a Lowenbrau, but it was ice-cold.

There were also a couple of nice-looking girls downstairs, one in heels and a purple pair of those ugly, baggy pants which were in fashion then. She held her cigarette at an affected angle, and had a toy poodle on a leash. The other girl wore jeans and a T-shirt. The one with the poodle looked French; the other was dark enough to be Lebanese.

From the way they were jiving the young men, I began to understand that here, a first-rate resistance fighter got all the best girls. I smiled. I had finally come to a place where people had their priorities right.

Just at that point, Rick came screaming back down the ramp in his bug and screeched to a stop beside me. "I came to pick you up. Headquarters wants you back at G-5." He hadn't shut off his engine and the garage was filling up with noxious fumes. I didn't like this. I was all jazzed up for a firefight and . . . ah, well, no point in arguing. Rick wasn't a decision maker.

"Maybe next time," I said to Rocky, and got in the VW.

We backed up the ramp and screamed once more through the blasted streets. "Why did they pull me out?" I asked.

"I don't know," he said. "I'll try to find out when we get back."

"Are you Lebanese?" I asked. "When I first saw you I thought you were an American college student."

He laughed. "I'm almost 30. I was born here, but my father is American. I went to college in the States. I have a B.A. and an M.A. in political science from Berkeley."

"Berkeley?" I grinned.

"Yeah, I used to have hair halfway down my back and a ring in my ear, to blend in, you know. But I always spent my summers training and fighting here. There was only one guy I was really tight with at Berkeley, and he was a Marine colonel back for an advanced degree."

We pulled in at the G-5 apartment house, skipped around the sandbags and went upstairs.

Sam looked up from the couch where he sat chatting with a Swedish TV crew. "Hello," he said. "How was the trip?"

"Not very satisfactory," I grumbled. "Look, if I'm going to get a story for a combat magazine, I have to see some combat. I'm no good to anybody dead, but the more action I see and get away to write about, the better story for all of us."

"We'll see what we can do," Sam said wearily.

A moment later Rick came back. "That was it," he said. "They expect a heavy attack on Sodeco, and they don't want you caught in it."

When working entirely at the sufferance of somebody else's army it is best not to throw a tantrum. "I'm not the reporter from *Women's Wear Daily*," I snapped. "Next time gimme an AK and let me stay."

They both grinned. "We buy our own," Rick said. "I doubt anybody is going to want to give you his and do without."

Rick and Sam went out on the balcony. I followed them. We sat down in wicker chairs and propped our feet up on the rail. Christine came out and joined us. She leaned easily against the balcony and threw her long hair back to let the breeze air her neck.

"You don't get paid, you buy your own guns, your own ammo, your own uniforms, and there's no rank in your army?"

"That's right," Sam said.

"I don't see how you can fight a war that way."

Rick grinned. "We can do it because our fighters are very good."

"What happens if you want to leave?"

Rick shrugged. "I've been working straight through for a month, being with the reporters during the day, and doing some other little things at night. Next week I'm going to take a couple of days off and go to the beach."

I shook my head. "How do you know who's in charge?"

"Well," said Sam, "we don't have rank, but we have job titles. When the war is hot, everybody takes orders. When it's not, we talk it over. When it dies down for a while, we go back to our regular jobs."

"Rick," I asked, "why don't you wear a uniform?"

He grinned his old grin. "Our G-5 asks me the same question all the time," he said. "I don't like them. Besides, you see those boots?" He nodded toward Sam's combat boots. "Those are boondockers." He wiggled his sneakers at me. "These are better for city fighting. I have a friend who fights in flip-flops. He's not any good in boots." He shrugged.

What was his headquarters to do? They couldn't bust him; he had no rank. They couldn't fine him; he didn't get paid. They couldn't fire him; he was too valuable.

After a while Rick said, "Look, we've got to leave. You're welcome to crash here tonight. Anything you like in the fridge is yours."

I sat on the balcony for a long time watching the sun go down and the streets clear.

Some of the guys from the G-5 section sat inside, sipping beer or coffee, watching a *Charlie's Angels* segment on a 24-inch color TV with subtitles in French and Arabic. Completely oblivious to the automatic weapons fire in the street outside, they stared fascinated as those three adorable kumquats battled imaginary bad guys with .32 caliber automatics.

I heard no indirect fire, but lots of AK and M-16 bursts from a few blocks west, toward Sodeco.

5

THREE SISTERS FROM HADATH

Sodeco wasn't hit that first night, so it hadn't really mattered where I slept. But I still had two sniper's manuals to deliver, so the following day Rick drove me to Hadath, a suburb of Beirut. There is no real break between the two; Hadath is an old town that the city has grown beyond.

As usual Rick drove at top speed, and took a route that went all the way around Robin Hood's barn. Sometimes he sneaked slowly down narrow streets, driving carefully to avoid hitting anyone, then turned a corner, already accelerating, bursting across a street with a clear line of sight to Palestinian-controlled territory before a sniper could squeeze off a round.

"The Palestinians tried a probe on Hadath the day before you arrived. There's a small Lebanese army platoon in position there, between the Palestinians and our guys, but they were outnumbered and had to withdraw. Then our boys counterattacked and drove the Palestinians off."

We coasted down a long hill, between narrow, close-set buildings, burst through one turn, rounded another, and pulled up across the street from an imposing building, which looked like a police station, but with the usual arrangement of sandbags outside.

"Nothing to worry about," Rick said. "But it's best to cross this street rather quickly."

"Sniper?"

He nodded.

The space in which the sniper had a clear shot was only about six feet wide, in the middle of the street. We hopped across it and went into the building, the Hadath headquarters of the Kataebe Party, now given over to the Lebanese Forces.

A couple of lads in fatigue pants, T-shirts, and flip-flops and a dark and animated girl with big eyes and blue jeans sat in wooden chairs in the shade of the building, talking, smoking cigarettes, and drinking Turkish coffee. They were four feet from the sniper zone, totally unconcerned.

Rick asked a question, and when they replied, turned to me and said, "Tony's in a meeting. He was due back an hour ago." I had been informed that the commander in Hadath was "Sheïk Tony," but other than the name, I knew next to nothing about him.

Rick had to get back to the bureau, so he turned me over to a hard-looking kid in a black T-shirt. His name was Rais, as near as I could make it out, and he offered to take me on a tour of the front.

The front was all streets, alleys, and buildings. These buildings were old, constructed of solid masonry. Turning them into fortifications hadn't been much of a trick, but getting to and from them was a tortuous job. To avoid being shot at, we crouched low, leaped ditches and dodged down alleys. We arrived at a small chink in the masonry wall of an almost totally destroyed building, through which I could see the Syrians' sandbagged emplacements in a half-completed building across a 200-meter wasteland of rubble.

We went through a half dozen of these outposts, until he was satisfied that I had the idea.

Rais was in Lebanese Forces, but he had spent a year in the Lebanese Army and was on friendly terms with the platoon between them and the Palestinians, so he took me to their Command Post. A dozen or so Lebanese soldiers stood around outside a house, drinking coffee. They seemed like nice boys, but handled themselves more like high school kids than soldiers.

The difference between them and their Lebanese Forces' counterparts was amazing. The army kids were younger and less sure of themselves than the militia. There were Christians and Moslems in the platoon, and although they seemed to get along well, it was obvious they did so by not talking about certain things.

The uniforms of both groups were almost identical, except that the army guys wore helmets or helmet liners. They carried their rifles like someone had handed them these things fifteen minutes before, and they were looking for a place to put them. By contrast, the Lebanese Forces militia usually went bareheaded, carried their weapons with the familiarity bred of good training and long, continuous use, and, to a man, wore gold crucifixes on chains around their necks, usually with another medallion, a small, gold map of Lebanon.

As one of the soldiers brought me a cup of Turkish coffee, their platoon leader drove up in his jeep. Rais introduced us, and I took my coffee and followed him down into his CP, which was in a shelled-out basement apartment.

He gestured me into the seat of honor, an easy chair, half-torn apart by shrapnel. I balanced my coffee on my knee.

The lieutenant sat down facing me on a couch that was as ripped apart as my chair, and a G.I. brought him his own cup. The furniture was arranged so as to face a black-and-white portable TV, sitting on top of two ammo crates. The sound was turned way down, and the picture was awful, but through the snow I could make out Henry Winkler as Fonzi, as Ron Howard stood by with a stupid grin on his face.

"Pretty nice," I said. "Is there one for the enlisted men?" I was just kidding. The line was the caption to one of Bill Mauldin's WWII Willie and Joe cartoons. The lieutenant assured me, however, that the lounge was for the entire platoon.

The lieutenant was sharp enough. His closest U.S. equivalent would be a Sigma Chi who had gone through ROTC. He was about 28 years old, in excellent physical condition, and he seemed intelligent and knowledgeable. However, he had a six-block front to cover with nineteen men, which was not a possible mission. Bunched up, as they were, they could be flanked. Spread out they could be easily penetrated.

In theory, both his platoon and the Syrians were here to keep peace between the Palestinians and Lebanese Forces. But, in fact, the Syrians were sending shells and rockets into Christian areas on a daily basis, and were perfectly happy to let the Palestinians try a probe whenever they felt like it.

With nineteen men, spread that thin, all the lieutenant and his men could do was zing a couple of bursts at the attacking Palestinians and then get the hell out of their way. But the firing alerted the Christians, so they always drove the Palestinians back. There were more than 500 armed and trained members of Lebanese Forces in the town—more than enough to chew up anyone the Palestinians could squeeze through the alleys and across the rubble.

The lieutenant was Christian, as were most of his men, but there was very little love lost between the Moslem members of his platoon and the Palestinians. He was more than happy to be the early warning system for the defenders of Hadath.

But that wasn't what the lieutenant wanted to talk about. He wanted to talk about the Infantry Officers' Advanced

Course at Fort Benning. He wanted to get there the next year. I assured him that he would do well, as I had no doubt he would. He would also probably profit from an association with officers from several different countries. But I doubted that the advanced course itself had much to teach that was applicable to his present situation.

It was way past time for Tony to return, so Rais and I went back to the Kataebe headquarters.

We went the usual circuitous route; a cautious walk down a trench, a quick sprint down an alley, camera case thudding against my groin.

I decided the next time I went to Lebanon, or any other war, for that matter, I was going to take a BAR belt for my camera stuff. If possible, I'd also take a few extra bucks and buy an AK on the way in and sell it on the way out.

Correspondents say you can shoot pictures before and after a firefight, but not during, so I might as well go ahead and get me some boom-boom time.

When we arrived at the Kataebe headquarters, a different set of kids was taking a break in the shade. But just as we arrived, a new Audi screeched to a halt across the street. It snuggled against the curb, so that its near side was a good eighteen inches away from the sniper zone. Three doors sprang open, and three young men got out and stepped briskly across the street. Two were in uniform, but the big guy who had been in the right front seat wore a blue warm-up suit, and had a .45 tucked under his left armpit. "Hi! I'm Tony," he said, and stuck out his hand for a shake.

I had been told the commander in Hadath was "Sheik Tony," but I had no frame of reference for a sheik in a warm-up suit who looked like Buddy Holly, except for about twenty extra pounds of solid muscle. He grinned disarmingly and blinked through thick, black-framed glasses, then led us into the headquarters with a long-legged, confident stride.

We went down a long corridor and a dark hallway, into a fair-sized room lit by a naked light bulb. Mounted on a wall, on a standard sheet of four-by-eight plywood, was his situation map, which showed every house and alley in Hadath, with Syrian, Palestinian, Lebanese Army, and Lebanese Forces positions marked in different colored crayons; weapons positions, sniper positions, and observation posts were marked with different colored pins.

It was not a military map; it seemed the sort of map the city water department would have. Had I not toured those positions it would not have made much sense. Tony pointed out what, at first, looked like a major street. When it was identified I realized it was a tiny alley down which Rais and I had scuttled like crabs, sometimes walking, sometimes ducking, sometimes sprinting.

"This is my apartment," Tony said bitterly. Small wonder he was bitter. It was marked as a Palestinian sniper position.

Tony introduced me to the two men with him. The short, compact one, Max, was his artillery commander. The stocky, good-natured guy was chief of his mortar section. His name, he said, was Bob. They invited me to tour their artillery positions, and to join them for dinner afterward.

Outside we quick-stepped across the street. Bob put the Audi in gear, gunned around the corner before the sniper could take aim, and then started driving normally—that is, like a maniac.

Tony wanted to drop by his dispensary before we went to the artillery positions. In addition to being commander, he was a fifth-year medical student, and he took a personal interest in treatment. "I still have two years to go on my medical studies," Tony said. "I should have finished by now, but the war . . ." He shrugged.

The dispensary was run by two attractive young nurses in civilian clothes. One wore jeans, a T-shirt, and platform shoes, her hair hanging down to the middle of her back; the other was in a fashionable summer frock. Despite looking like a pair of disco queens, they were all business.

There were eight or ten wounded or ill people waiting in

the anteroom. The treatment room was well-equipped with examination tables and instruments, but there was little medicine on the shelves, and all the expendable items seemed to have been expended. "What are you short of?" I inquired.

"Everything," Tony said. "All that you see here is outdated."

After another short race through the streets, we pulled into a parking garage. Among the cars there was also a motor pool for a commando platoon down there. Two or three young guys in fatigue pants and black commando T-shirts bent over an engine under the open hood of a Land Rover pickup, with a 106mm recoilless rifle mounted in back. There were two or three jeep-mounted 106s, and a jeep-mounted .50 caliber machine gun drawn up in the same line. The vehicles were all clean, and freshly painted olive green, but their bodies were dented all to hell.

The three guys under the hood and the two or three others hanging around were all laughing and jiving. As usual, the guys with the most difficult, most dangerous duty had the highest morale.

Max, Bob, and Tony led me down a long, narrow tunnel, which had been chopped out of the raw concrete; electric wire and naked bulbs hung from the ceiling. We emerged from it into another room, freshly made from thick concrete. That wet concrete smell still hung in the air. Maps, charts, and plotting instruments lay on plywood tables, slanted like drawing boards, leaning against the wall to the right.

"Ah! Your FDC."

"What is FDC?" Max inquired.

"Fire direction center."

"Yes, this is my fire direction center."

I talked about his gear for a few more minutes. It soon became clear that neither Max nor Bob knew much about artillery, at least not the way they teach it at Fort Sill. Not that they didn't know what they were doing, or that their stuff wasn't set up efficiently. It just didn't look like what I was used to. And none of their terminology was like anything I had heard before. "Where did you guys get your training?"

"We didn't," Bob said, grinning. "We captured the guns and figured out from there."

"Jesus, how did you do that?"

Max shrugged. "I'm an architect and Bob's an accountant. The math wasn't that hard."

"You worked out your own firing tables?"

Bob nodded. "Yes, we can usually hit a target after two shots. We have to be very careful. We all have friends and relatives on the other side. We don't want to hurt anybody but the Syrians."

I thought about the rubble upstairs. "It doesn't seem as though they're that cautious."

Bob sneered in contempt. "They open the gun and look down the barrel. If they can't see the building in front of them they start firing over here. They keep it up until we hit their positions. We have to be quick and accurate."

"Two rounds?"

"Right! Two rounds."

We went down another long tunnel, and emerged into what amounted to a large, vacant lot, with sandbagged emplacements for their mortars. These were among the best-made mortar positions I have ever seen, neatly and cleanly dug, and sandbagged so carefully that nothing but a direct hit would have much effect on them.

Their pride and joy was a huge, newly captured Soviet 160mm mortar. They were in the process of constructing a pit for it when I saw it. Its tube was longer than that of a 105mm howitzer, and the baseplate was wider across than I am tall.

After that we went to dinner. The original plan was to treat me to some Lebanese food, but the restaurant they wanted to go to was closed, so we wound back down the mountains, raced through streets and stopped at a couple of check points, laughing and talking about the war, politics, girls, everything.

During the course of the conversation, Max said the thing that stuck most in my mind during the entire time I was in Lebanon. I don't remember how it came up, but it fit smoothly into the flow of conversation. It had to do with why his people had risen, almost to a man, to fight with rage and intelligence against clearly impossible odds. "I think we fight," said Max, "for the human dignity."

We had our dinner on the veranda of a pizzeria. Tony reached over and took his .45 back from Bob, who had been holding it for him while he drove. He put it in his lap and carefully looked over the four or five people eating on the verandah. It was wonderfully cool out there, and the lights of the city shone all around us. "What?" I asked, nodding toward the pistol.

"We might get a bomb or a grenade," Tony said. "It's not very likely, but you never know." It all seemed so quiet and normal out here.

As we talked, Max mentioned that he worked in West Beirut. Every morning he got up, put on his suit and tie, picked up his briefcase, and drove into enemy territory, to the office of his architectural firm. Then, at night, he drove back, put on his fatigues, and went down to the FDC.

"I don't tell them I am a fighter," he said. "If anybody talks about the war, I just act as though I am afraid."

"I'm sure the Syrians didn't plan on anything like this uprising," I said to Max. "I wonder what the Syrians think about you guys?"

Max deals with the enemy in his business on a daily basis. To do so, he has to see them as people. But he misunderstood my question and started explaining the Syrians' rationale for being in Lebanon.

Tony would have none of it. The bastards had invaded his country, delayed his career, usurped his apartment, and God knows what else. He totally lost it, screaming in Arabic, raging and waving his arms.

What impressed me most about this incident was the way Max handled it. Despite being a kid in bop glasses and a jogging suit, Tony was his commander, with responsibility equal to that of a lieutenant colonel in the U.S. Army. In every army with which I am familiar, if the main man put on a display like that, all his flunkies would fall immediately into line, tug at their forelocks, and exclaim, "Yassa, massa! You sho' right. Them bassar ain't got no rationale."

Max did nothing of the sort. He patiently sat and waited for Tony to sputter to a halt, then went right back into his explanation.

Actually, Tony was right. The bastards' rationale was totally false. But I was impressed by the fact that Max could fight them effectively and still see them as people.

I slept in Tony's Tactical Operations Center that night. The next day he had to rush off and do something important, and none of the guys I had met the day before seemed to be around. I was actually quite pleased with the chance to be alone to collect my thoughts. I found a chair out in front of the headquarters, propped my feet up on a couple of sandbags and spaced out, watching flowers and palms rustle in the breeze in the back yard of a pockmarked villa across the street. I went over everything that had happened since Cyprus, sorting out what was usable and what was not, how to tell it, and in what order.

Several times young men stopped and exchanged a few words. A kid named Jamil stopped. He was going out to drive around in a van to collect foodstuffs for Lebanese Forces from merchants and households. It seemed to me that he had been carefully selected for this job, since he was about as engaging and non-threatening as it is possible for a man to be; a skinny, doofus kid, with a grin that never left his face. He wore jeans and a checked sport shirt. The only military things about him were his baseball-style fatigue cap and the old, long-barreled .38 in the waistband of his jeans.

All the kids who were trying to improve their English

chatted with me; Jamil was no exception. "Last year I spent six months in San Francisco," he said. "I meet many heppies. You know heppies?"

A while later, a pleasant-looking kid, a boy of about seventeen, came lurching up the steps. His left leg was stiff all the way down, and his left arm was braced from the shoulder out, at a 45 degree angle from his body, and bent at a 45 degree angle from his elbow. When he saw me he gave a big, delighted smile, and said, "Bonjour!"

"Hi!" I replied.

"You speak English?"

I shrugged. *"Je parle Francais un peu, pas tres bien."*

"I woood prefer English," he said. "I am learning."

He was a B-10-rocket gunner who had been wounded in a shoot-out with the Syrians.

"Tony was a B-10 gunner at Tall Zaatar," I said, something I had learned the night before.

The kid's smile widened. "He is my brother. Not my real brother, but he teached me the B-10. Three days I stay at his apartment. He teach me everything about the B-10."

I had never before heard a trooper say of his battalion commander, "He is my brother."

After the B-10 gunner had gone, I sat there for another hour or so, until a remarkably beautiful young lady tapped me on the shoulder. "Are you sad?" she asked.

I suppose a man staring into space with a blank look on his face looks neither happy nor busy, although in truth, I was both.

The girl was just plain beautiful; big dark eyes, olive skin, aquiline nose, glossy dark hair; she was just a kid, maybe eighteen or nineteen, with the careful smile and manner of a "nice girl."

"I'm fine," I replied.

Clearly she didn't believe me. "Come inside for coffee," she said.

We went inside the communications center of the headquarters. One entire wall was filled with ranked row upon row of two-way radios, some military, some commercial. A girl wearing fatigues sat and muttered Arabic into a microphone. A speaker sputtered back at her. Her sad look had nothing to do with a long shift in the communications center. I never found out what caused it, but in Lebanon the possibilities were endless.

There were three more women in the room. One, also in fatigues, lay dead asleep on a small bed against the wall opposite the console, her boots neatly lined up beside the bed, OD socks still on her feet.

The other two were girls about the age of my new friend, wearing civilian clothes; jeans and pants. They and my friend were all pretty, and obviously sisters.

For the next three hours they entertained me to make sure I was not blue and lonely, not moping around in front of the headquarters. They told me jokes; they fed me coffee and a great lunch. Since their English wasn't much better than my French, we spent a lot of time groping for the right words. Sometimes it took all four of us to put together a sentence for one of us, all of us laughing at the fluffs we made.

Although they were sisters, the girls were very different. Farrah, the oldest, was a beauty queen, with a great body and long, wavy hair that framed her face and fell below her shoulders. She wore a carefully chosen, fashionable top, pretty little sandals that offered her feet no support whatsoever and showed off her painted toenails.

When we got to the inevitable part where I whipped out my wallet and showed the pictures around, she studied Kathy's picture long and hard. "Nott badd," she said at last, clinically.

Gina, the girl who had brought me in from outside, had the most beautiful face, but she was obviously not interested in her looks. She planned to be a journalist, and showed me an article she had written, printed by one of the Kataebe magazines. I couldn't get much out of it, since it was in Arabic. I encouraged her though, and offered to send her some texts from the University of Arkansas bookstore when I got home.

I did so with reservations, because I liked her. All the newspaper people I have known in the States are burnt and bitter by 35, from too much coffee, booze, cigarettes, dinner from cardboard cartons, and marriages that don't work because of the above. Still, some people are suited to such work, and Gina didn't look like a potential housewife to me.

The youngest girl, Lida, interested me most. The whole time I was there she was smiling and laughing, but it was the sort of laugh you'd expect from your teen-age point man, terribly one-pointed, and a little crazy. She wore jeans, a none-too-fresh yellow T-shirt, and combat boots.

Later when I mentioned the three sisters to one of the guys, he said, "Oh, Lida. She's a fighter." He did not mean only that she had a lot of moxie. He meant that when the Palestinians came to town, she grabbed her AK and went into the line with the guys. Most women are not good for heavy work, and sometimes their presence creates havoc in the ranks, but there were plenty of them who could not be faulted for guts; Lida was one of those.

Several young men came through the communication center while I was there, and it was interesting to see how they and the girls handled each other. There was a lot of kidding, but it was all pointedly nonsexual. They treated the girls like comrades, who happened to be made of Dresden china.

Later I mentioned this to a lady in a fairly high staff position at Lebanese Forces headquarters. "Yes," she said, "the boys act like brothers . . . and like boys." From this I deduce that there is some hanky, but very little panky, unless the boy is dead serious. Every one of these girls has about forty big brothers to hammer into a bloody pulp anybody who does her wrong.

The girls were careful to make sure of my religious convictions.

"Do you believe in Jesus?"

"Yes."

"Mary?"

"Yeah, sure."

"Do you like Lech Walesa?"

They took me on a walking tour of Hadath. One of the funniest and scariest things I have ever seen was Farrah, running through a sniper zone in those damned sandals.

They showed me the main street of Hadath, gutted and boarded up, their uncle's restaurant, gutted and boarded up, their parent's pharmacy, gutted and boarded up. "They want us to go to the mountains with them, but we want to help the fighters."

They showed me their church, a beautiful, modern structure, as modern as the one in Sodeco, and as badly shot up. They showed me the refugee families living in the church basement.

I wanted a shot of Farrah and one of the guys walking down the street, from the back, no faces. People are not much interested in rubble; they are interested in people. I wanted a human interest shot. Her eyes grew huge, and she flatly refused. I couldn't really blame her. If she were recognized crossing into West Beirut, she would be subject to arrest, interrogation, torture, rape, and murder; not necessarily in that order, and, except for the first and last, not necessarily just once.

When Tony returned that afternoon, he and I went back over to his mortar emplacements, so I could take a few pictures of the way they were dug in. One of his artillerymen came out while I was shooting and went into a panic for fear I would give their position away. Tony assured him all would be well.

It was mid-afternoon by then, and Tony still hadn't had lunch. He drove to a small *patisserie* and we went inside. We each had a strawberry tart and a glass of milk. I remembered Asian LRRP rations with the Mike Force, and the famous ham-and-lima-bean popsicle from frozen Chosen. These tarts had an incredible, light flaky crust, and were surmounted by red, luscious strawberries that burst in your mouth like ecstasy bombs. The milk was so cold it crackled in your throat.

"I still can't get over this."

Tony shrugged. He had never tasted C-rations. "You have to eat," he said.

Tony was the biggest hero in Hadath. He practically had to browbeat the proprietor into taking money for the food.

We went back outside. Three teenagers came walking slowly down the street. They walked slowly to give one of them, the girl, a break. She was pretty, almost as pretty as Farrah, but she walked with a bad limp, and wore an obvious above-the-knee prosthesis. The Syrians had blown her leg off.

I've seen a lot of dead men, and made a few, but none of them affected me like the sight of that pretty girl, who would never dance again, whose body would always hurt, who would never get to run for the Lebanese equivalent of homecoming queen.

Later that afternoon Sam came to take me back to the G-5 bureau. On the way I told him something I had in mind. "It sounds like a good idea to me," he said, "but I didn't expect it from a magazine."

"Well," I said, "you'd kind of have to know the magazine. It started out as a trade journal for mercenaries, but it's grown to be the unofficial magazine of the Combat-Arms Old-Boy Network, worldwide. Obviously you guys should be in it."

He and I sprinted up the stairs. I called Tim Leifield at Paladin Press and ordered $1,500 worth of demo and ranger manuals. Then I called Brown at *SOF*.

I had my spiel rehearsed. What I was going to suggest was going to cost him a fair amount of money. But, well, you have to know Brown.

"Robert, these are the good guys, and I think they have a chance to win." I was about to mention our larger duty to mankind, when he cut in. "Great! How can we help?"

"Well, I wouldn't want you to send a Military Training Team. Heaven forfend the thought. But I have a friend who is much better qualified to make a survey of Lebanese Forces technical innovations than I am. And, who knows, they might pick a few points up from him. He's the best small-unit leader I ever met. His leg's kind of gimped, but his brain works great."

"Who is he?"

"Name's Larry Dring. He's going to learn as much as he teaches. He's no journalist, but he's a great storyteller. We'll debrief him when he gets back, and get another good story out of it."

"Roger that!"

That was all it took. We talked for a minute more, and I hung up the phone.

Something had clicked in me. For a lot of years I had been like half a puzzle, looking for the other piece. I took the phone out of the bedroom, where I had gone for quiet, back out into the outer office, where eight or ten people were working, howling into telephones, poring over newspapers.

6
A NIGHT ON THE TOWN

One of the first things Sam did when I moved into the G-5 headquarters was to show me a special phone. "On this phone," he said, "you can call anywhere in the world and talk as long as you want." It took me a while to get used to this idea, but finally, after I asked him several times, he said again, "Yes, really, any time you want, for as long as you want."

The guys in the G-5 section were in the habit of working very late, and they also did odd combat jobs, defending their neighborhoods, and Rick had hinted that they were running an effective psy-war operation against the Syrians, Palestinians, and Mourabitoun, in West Beirut, and elsewhere. Usually they slept until eight or nine in the morning.

I got in the habit of getting up around seven and fixing myself a cup of coffee. Then I took the phone out on the balcony and called Kathy in Fayetteville. With the time difference, I'd catch her at midnight the night before. The air was still cool, so I'd sit there with my coffee and watch the sky shade in over the buildings, and listen to the first firefights of the morning.

Ordinarily we'd talk until the first of the G-5 guys got up. I'd give her a summary of the preceding day's events and assure her that I was still in one piece. She had signed up for two summer dance classes, and had broken a bone in her foot the week before I left. She needed some classes to graduate, so she was dancing in pain every day. I wanted reassurance that she wasn't killing herself. Finally, she would ring off to get some sleep before her eight o'clock class.

One morning Sam came out on the balcony with his first cup of hot, sweet, Turkish coffee, just as I started on my third. "How is Kathy?" he asked.

"I don't think she ought to be dancing on that foot," I said. "She's a smart girl, but she's got more guts than sense."

"Is she Lebanese?" He was kidding. He knew she was mostly Irish and English, and about an eighth Cherokee.

"No, but she might as well be."

We shot the breeze in a desultory way for a while. When we went back inside he said, "I want to show you something." In an inner office room he shook out the contents of a maroon cotton bag. Inside was a grab-bag collection of passports, driver's licenses, and other IDs from various Arab countries, Leftist countries, Muslim countries, from southern Africa, from Asia, from I.R.A. provos—an international bazaar of anti-Western types. "All of these are from people we have captured in combat," he said. "This is our 'Civil War.' Webster's defines civil war as one between citizens of the same country. Very seldom do we fight Lebanese, Muslims or not. Our war is with the Palestinians, whom we gave refuge, and who have taken over large parts of our country, and with the Syrians, who view Lebanon as a rebel province, and with these people." He shuffled the mound of documents. "I asked one of these people why he was here. He said, 'To fight the Zionists.' Do I look like a Zionist?"

That afternoon Fouad carefully nosed the Land Rover around a herd of goats. They ran bleating to get out of his way. The herdsmen scarcely looked up as we passed. Even in this Christian area of the Sannine mountains, the herdsmen wore the Lebanese hillbilly costume; burnoose, a white shirt and black trousers, tight at the calf, but baggier than any other trousers I have ever seen.

Below us the road twisted downward. Around us, mountains dived steeply, flattened into a wide valley far below, and climbed sharply back up through row on row of gray-rock mountains, sparsely vegetated, beautiful, climbing into snow-capped peaks.

Fouad, a Lebanese Forces nurse, Claude du Plessis, and I had left Beirut early that morning. We had been driving for more than two hours. Fouad, the Lebanese Forces Information Officer, is a man about my size, six-two, weighing 190 to 195 pounds. His powerful shoulders were a trifle stooped from hours over the books; he was a lawyer in civilian life, with both Lebanese and French degrees. The Lebanese nurse sat quietly. She wore fatigues, boots, and a bush hat and held her aid bag in her lap.

Next to her was Claude, photographer for a French news service, who had even less English than I had French. We had shared a room for several days, but I barely knew him, since we couldn't talk to one another. He was taller than I and about twenty pounds lighter. He wore his frizzy brown hair almost shoulder length and smoked Gitanes incessantly. Around the bureau he wore strange-looking French-made cowboy boots, but he had put on combat boots for this job, and wore jeans, a black T-shirt, and an old safari jacket with the sleeves cut off, pockets jammed with film.

After another half-hour's drive, we came to a stop in a little shaded grove of trees, under which a couple of tents and some poncho lean-tos had been set up. Three or four Lebanese Forces fighters sat around, cleaning weapons, smoking, drinking coffee. We got out of the car. Fouad spoke to one of the fighters, who disappeared into the tent. He came out a second or so later, bringing with him the first bum I had seen in Lebanon: a small, bleary-eyed man with a three-day stubble, his face slick with sweat. He wore a dirty white T-shirt, and his left arm was missing from two inches below the elbow.

"This is Michel," Fouad said. "He is commander of this outpost." Michel looked sullenly at me, then extended his hand. We shook. My right hand is brittle and wasted because the arm is missing two nerves and an artery, a wound from an RPD automatic rifle. The hand looks okay, if you don't look too close, but a lot of meat has withered off it. The last time I broke it, it wasn't set properly and the bones meet at a jagged angle.

Michel's right hand, however, was incredibly strong, since he had to do everything with it. He grabbed my hand in a bone-crushing grip.

I tried to keep a straight face and ignore the pain. He noticed that my hand didn't feel right and dropped it.

He spoke briefly to Fouad, in French, and disappeared into the tent. "He apologizes for his appearance," said Fouad. "He was out all night on an operation."

I started to ask for a description of the operation but restrained myself. Michel was obviously a soldier to the core; if he had been out all night and slept all morning, he hadn't told the tale yet, and it would come rolling out of him in due course, probably sooner than later.

Michel popped back out of the tent, wearing his fatigue shirt. He expertly flipped a patrol harness over his shoulders. It was put together from Russian gear, and the ammo pouches were smaller than ours. His M-16 had an extra-long sling, which he draped around his neck, so the weapon hung about where Elvis used to wear his guitar.

We got back in the Land Rover. Michel took the nurse's

place, and the vehicle headed into the mountains. It was all barren rock up there, with not a sign of cover. Fouad drove, keeping the mountain between us and the Syrian positions on the next ridge line over. The Land Rover rumbled and lurched over the rocks. Michel directed him to pull into a concealed position between two fingers of bare rock, and we got out and started humping. I was glad I lived in the Ozarks as we pounded up the steep trail, but even so, I was breathing like a bellows to keep up.

At last we came to a shallow depression in the rock, just big enough to hold a small tent. A squad of troops was living in it. Three or four of them sat around outside. "The men who were with me last night are sleeping inside," Michel said in English. He had a very heavy French accent.

"What was that operation?"

"We mine the Syrian positions."

"What?"

"It is maybe one and one-half kilometers to the Syrian positions, but it takes three hours to walk there. Then we go to the road maybe fifty meters from their positions and plant the bouncing-betty mines in the road."

"How many men did you take with you?"

"Six, but for the last fifty meters to plant the mines, only me and one other."

Michel led us further up the mountain to an observation post at the very peak. "Stay close to the rock here," he said as we went up. "They shoot the rocket every time they see anyone move." I hugged the rock, snuggled right up to it.

At the peak we four squeezed ourselves into a tiny perch behind a rock that gave us three feet of cover. Except for Michel we were all big men, and Claude and I both had big camera bags as well.

"You must take off your glasses," Michel said to me. "They will shoot at the glare."

"These are prescription shades," I insisted. "If I take them off, I can't see at all."

He favored me with a look that is cultivated, but seldom achieved by all the world's drill instructors.

"Got any tape?" I inquired. "I can cut about 90 percent of the glare by taping the outer edges."

Without a word he took his canteen out and made a tiny mud puddle at my feet. I daubed mud on the outer edges of my glasses. Not as good as tape, but it ought to help.

While I was doing this, Claude shot pictures with his long lens. Then I looked over the top of the rock, moving slowly. Over the next ridge line I could see a dirt road S-curving along the ridge, but I couldn't see any tracked vehicles or personnel.

For a moment I wished the Syrians would shell. I wanted some action for my story. Then I felt guilty. These kids got shelled almost every day. I didn't want one of them killed or wounded just so I could write about it.

I snapped a couple of shots, but there really wasn't anything to shoot, and I didn't have a telephoto lens, even if there had been. After that, we crept back down to the tent. Some of the guys who had been out with Michel on his raid the night before were awake.

They sat on top of this barren rock for a week at a time, getting shelled almost every day, and still they were laughing and joking. I really liked those kids.

I had worn fatigues, and they wanted to know whether I was an Israeli. To a man they fervently wished for an Israeli intervention.

One of them, a slender, good-looking young man, came up and said, "Hi!"

"Hello!"

"You ever been to Dallas?"

"Sure," I replied, in amazement. His English was almost as good as Rick's. "How do you know Dallas?"

"I worked there for two years. I was a flight instructor." I grinned. "How'd you like it?"

"Great!" He grinned back. "I like the pushover." He put the accent on the second syllable.

I laughed and shook my head. "So why are you here?"

He shrugged. "My country is at war."

That must have been some decision. A young man can have a good time in Dallas, Texas.

"So why are you here on this rock?"

He shrugged. "We have no airplanes."

Nobody made him do this. He had left one of the good-time centers of the world, and paid his own way back to risk his life, to squat on this barren rock.

I decided to see exactly how far this went. "What'll you do after this is over, stay in Lebanon or go back to Dallas?"

He shrugged. "I'll probably have to go back to Dallas. There aren't enough flying students in Lebanon."

"What's your name?"

"Roger."

That's the only name in the Lebanon chapters I haven't changed, but since, in my short time in Lebanon I met five Rogers, it's not much of a risk. So, to all the girls in Dallas, Roger says, "Hello."

Fouad, Michel, and Claude were ready to go back down the mountain, so I said good-bye to Roger. We walked with a good interval between each of us, pausing at Michel's CP to drop him off and share a cup of coffee with the folks there.

Then we wound down the mountain, and the traffic and the civilian population picked up. Fouad got on the CB radio mounted under the dash, probably telling them that we were coming in. I'm not sure because he spoke in Arabic. But a few English words had come into general use in Lebanon, and I was able to pick them out.

There were some significant differences in American and Lebanese radio procedure: Instead of "Roger," he said, "Okay," and instead of "Out," he said, "Bye-bye."

When I mentioned this to him later, he said, "Well, we must still laugh."

I thought I had seen some driving in Lebanon before, but Fouad was the prince of kamikazes. Once we reached the

Jounieh-Beirut Highway, traveling an entire city block without four near-collisions counted as a breathing space. He used the horn and he had a siren. He also had a complete inventory of hand gestures for any other driver who got in his way. I was only familiar with one of them, but none seemed complimentary.

Travel on the shoulder of the road, where there was one, was routine. Once, when traffic on our side of the road jammed up, he unhesitatingly jumped the center island and ran three blocks in the left-hand lane, traveling at sixty miles an hour and shaking his fist at oncoming drivers if they didn't get out of the way fast enough to suit him.

"Listen," I said, as laconically as I could manage under the circumstances, "if you're looking for work after the war, I can probably get you a job driving in Burt Reynolds' movies."

He smiled, hit the siren and accelerated into a space two feet narrower than the Land Rover.

Because of the Palestinians' tendency to take their war with them wherever they go, Rick advised me to do my article under an assumed name, and not to do the interview Fouad had set up for me with the Lebanese Forces paper.

We were talking about it out on the balcony, over a Coke. "I don't see how it can cause a problem," I said. "They're not going to use my name in the interview. It's just that Fouad thinks a pat on the back from a former Green Beret major would be good for morale."

"I don't like it," Rick said. "I just don't like it."

Sam said nothing, but he looked glum.

The young lady who conducted the interview was very polite, as was her interpreter, a young man. We sat at Fouad's antique dining table in his apartment across the street from the press bureau. It was a beautiful apartment, except for a couple of shrapnel cracks in the smoked glass mirror on the wall by the coffee table and some rents in the sofa from the same source.

The first thing the interviewers asked about was the quality of their troops, which I couldn't praise highly enough.

Then they asked me whether I thought they could win, and if so, how?

I responded that, like them, I was a Christian, and that I believed both in prayer and miracles. And on a more practical level, I knew of no historical case of an army with true spirit losing a defensive war to one that lacked it.

Last, they asked me why I was involved in their cause on a personal level.

"Well," I replied, "I once had a friend, a very close friend. He and I fought together, off and on, for ten years. When the United States pulled out of Cambodia, he was a major in the Cambodian army. I have reliable information that he and his wife and three little boys were executed in the street out in front of the French embassy. I guess I've just seen enough of that stuff."

There was another reason I took this action, which, for a journalist trained to be "objective," seems unprofessional. Before I went to Lebanon, I didn't know anything about the war there. But as a veteran, it had been my habit to read everything that appeared in the papers about combat anywhere. I couldn't make any sense out of what I read about Lebanon.

As it happened, the entire Beirut press corps lived in the Commodore Hotel, located in West Beirut. The hotel was Palestinian owned, and that part of the city was under the control of the Syrians. Almost the entire Mideast was covered from there. While I was in Lebanon, the Israelis bombed the nuclear reactor in Iraq, and things were hopping in Iran, but it was relatively quiet in Beirut itself.

For the entire time I was in Lebanon, I lived in the Lebanese Forces Press Bureau. I did not see another American in that time, much less another American reporter. Sure, they were busy, but for twelve days they didn't cover one side of the war they were in the middle of. On the 2nd of August of that year, the Denver *Post* printed a story by Michael Kennedy of the Los Angeles *Times*. He wrote, "Syrian soldiers peer into each passing car as it passes. Often the Syrians ask for passports and want to know where the passengers are going. 'I told them, we are going to the port,' the driver said. 'You do not tell them you are going to the other (Christian) side.' "

Well, if you couldn't tell them you were going to the other side, what do you suppose would have happened to any reporter who told the true story of what was happening and tried to maintain his residence in the Commodore? People disappeared over there all the time, and at that time seven of them had been journalists. A guy from ABC was killed just after I left. Nobody knew why; he was just dead.

What do you suppose would happen to anybody who wrote that the Syrian so-called "Arab Deterrent Force," was sanctioned by the Arab League to conquer Lebanon in order to hold down Lebanese fighting the Palestinian "state within a state," thereby freeing Palestinians to fight the Israelis?

You couldn't really blame the reporters. Most of them were locked into their assignments for a number of years. Many had established themselves as Middle East "experts." They'd all be out of business if they couldn't go into or even pass through an Arab country without fear of assassination. So nobody covered the Christian side, and nobody covered the story of why they couldn't cover the Christian side. There was no possibility of objective journalism in Lebanon. The only honest thing to do was announce your bias and drive on. That was what I was doing.

We had lunch after the interviewers had gone. In the kitchen, Celeste, Fouad's lady, a wonderfully sweet, zaftig young woman, had supervised their Ceylonese maid's cooking. The results were perfection.

"This is delicious," I said, over the main dish, a light fluffy meat. It was like nothing I'd ever eaten before. "What is it?"

"Lamb's brains," Fouad said, rolling both the *l*'s and the *r*'s.

Amazing. I ate them with relish.

After lunch he asked me whether I'd like to see some training. I was feeling a little heavy, but I was eager to see Lebanese Forces' techniques. Dreading the ride and the sun, I got up and reached for my camera bag.

"Where are you going?"

"Training."

"Let's watch it on television," he said. "It's easier that way."

We went into the living room, and he slipped a cassette into his video cassette recorder. Celeste brought us coffee and we watched training for an hour.

Their training aid for street fighting interested me most. They had filled stacks of old tires with dirt and made a corridor out of them, representing a street, alley, or hall-way, with openings for doors. Squads of ten were sent down the passageway, a squadleader and three 3-man fire teams. The fire teams leapfrogged down the hallway, while the squad leader covered their back and directed traffic. As a team approached a door, one man lobbed a grenade in; then, with the fire-team leader covering their backs, and watching their squad leader, two men entered the door, one fanning a burst sweeping left, and the other right. They were as smooth as a well-drilled basketball team.

It was Claude's last evening in Lebanon and Sam and Rick asked me to join them and Christine in giving him a rousing send-off.

Since both Rick's and Sam's apartments were right on the Green Line, they and Christine had rented another place a few miles from the center of the city. We were to meet there for drinks before dinner. It was about six-thirty when Sam drove Claude and me to the apartment. Rick and Christine were just getting out of the shower when we arrived. Rick greeted us at the door, wearing old grey cords, his hair still slicked back and wet. Christine ran down the hall to the bedroom in an old terry robe, toweling her hair as she went.

"Fix yourselves a drink," Rick said. "We'll be out in a minute."

I spotted a cassette player and a box of tapes on top of a huge white drawing board with a matching artist's lamp clamped to it, beside the bar. Going over Rick's albums I discovered we had about a seventy-percent overlap in musical taste. I put Jackson Browne's *Running on Empty* on the player, with *Workingman's Dead* in reserve.

Sam, meanwhile, was fixing our drinks. We had all asked for Arak. I took mine and mellowed down onto a stack of big cushions behind a low coffee table.

Rick was dressed and out in a few minutes; Christine took a while longer. While we waited, Sam showed Claude and me his new AK. It was a Czech model, and some parts of the receiver were aluminum. He told me the stock was a laminated plywood that had been test-boiled at 4,000 degrees without coming apart.

"Do you want to see those pictures?" Rick asked. I had forgotten what pictures he meant. "The little girls?"

"Yes."

Christine came in, smashing in a white silk suit and open-collared shirt. She had been hiding great legs under her jeans. She wore heels held on by tiny little straps.

"They're pretty rough," he said.

I held out my hand.

He handed me a flimsy $8\frac{1}{2} \times 11$ envelope. I slid the 8×10 glossies out of it.

"I'm sorry," Christine said, choosing her English words carefully. She had already seen them, and knew what I was feeling. Two little girls, about six and seven, had been caught in a rocket attack. In death their expressions were sweet, as though they were sleeping, but their tiny bodies were ripped and torn in a dozen places. The six-year-old's foot lay beside her body.

"Nobody will print them," Rick said.

"Brown will," I replied. Rick promised me copies, but he never brought them, and I never pressed it. On the one hand, we both wanted every civilized person in the world to have his nose rubbed in the reality of Lebanon. On the other, none of us wanted death junkies drooling over those photos. Let the little girls have their peace.

Rick took the photos back. Sam had put his new AK up and was seated by the window, a drink tilted at a 45 degree angle in his hand, long gone in his thousand yard stare. I watched him for a long time. He did not move. For perhaps the tenth time in the week I'd been there, it struck me that this man had stayed too long at the fair. If he didn't get a chance to go off and get his head straight pretty soon, he was going to zone out in the middle of a firefight, and that would be it for old Sam.

Rick caught my look and winked. He knew what the deal was with Sam; that was why he kept him laughing. It seemed to be one of his major goals, to make Sam laugh every day, reading over his shoulder, jiving in a fake Mexican accent, "I keel for money, Sahm, but you my fran'; I keel you for notheeng."

You had to be there.

We strolled into the restaurant they had chosen for Claude's farewell party. We contrasted unfavorably with the other patrons. The men wore suits, the expertly coifed women—exquisite designer clothes. Christine was the only one of us who looked like she belonged there.

Claude looked like a French Hell's Angel, Rick's pants were ripped about half an inch in the crotch, and a handy-talkie crackled in his right hip pocket. He had shaved off the scruffy beard, however, and looked like the young Turk in the Camel ad. After a week in the same clothes, a khaki safari suit I had picked up at Harrod's in London on the way over was growing a trifle funky. But Sam looked great, obsessively neat, huge eyes, beard and crewcut. He wore sandals, tailored khaki pants, and a loose black shirt with a mandarin collar. He was very quiet, and could have been anything from a mad monk to a tong killer.

We elected to eat outdoors, where chairs and tables had been set up under red canopies, high on a hilltop overlooking the bay. We could see the lights of the city climbing toward the mountaintops.

The view was breathtaking, the crowd around us sophisticated, and the meal one of the best I have ever eaten.

The conversation was U-shaped. Claude and Christine spoke little English. I speak little French. Rick and Sam had to relay any conversation between the three of us. It was embarrassing. Even our waiter spoke perfect French, English, and Arabic.

Claude told a great story about two Legion officers in North Africa who made a bet that they would finish their dinner on the verandah of their club, even though a firefight was raging across it. While each was brave enough to sit through it while they ate, neither was anxious to linger over coffee and a cigarette, and it was only with the greatest of difficulty that the waiter could be coaxed into pouring more wine. They both won the bet, but neither ordered dessert.

Rick asked me what I thought the Americans would do if we were confronted with the same situation as the Lebanese. I replied that we were much alike, and I thought we would do about the same.

One of the things I had noticed was that the cream of Lebanese Forces, including Rick, Fouad, and Christine, came from the same socio-economic stratum of Lebanon which, in America, had furnished most of the opposition to the Vietnam War. I don't think that these folks are any better or braver than their American equivalents; they just face harsher circumstances.

It was fairly late when we finished dinner, and Sam had an early call, so he went on home. But Rick said he had something that Claude and I must see. We drove back down the mountain and into the city. We drove past all the neighborhoods I was familiar with, and closer to the sound of AK fire. Finally we parked about one street over from a firefight. Claude and I both had a difficult time unfolding out of the back of Rick's VW.

Christine was already far enough ahead of us that her white suit was disappearing into the gloom. *"Allez, messieurs!"* she called. Claude and I finally got out, popped the joints in our knees, restored the circulation in our feet and followed.

With Christine in the lead, she and Rick turned the corner toward the firefight. Claude and I exchanged glances. I was certain that Rick would never expose Christine to unnecessary danger, but they had just turned a corner down a street where bullets were actually flying.

We turned the corner. The street bent slightly. As long as we stayed within eighteen inches of the building wall we were okay, but rounds were snapping past our ears in the street. It was sort of like driving in the right-hand lane on a crowded two-lane highway. As long as you don't stray over the line you're okay, but death lies a few inches to the left.

Rick reached in his pocket and produced a set of keys, fiddling with the lock before opening a door in the wall we were pressed up against. We all crowded through, and he locked it from inside. The smell was musty and I could vaguely tell we were in a large room, but what the . . . Rick flipped on the light. At first my view was blocked by a large hanging plant. I stepped around it. To my left a long bar ran the length of the room. Straight ahead were a couch and two chairs facing each other over an Oriental rug and a coffee table. To the right was a dance floor, surrounded by similar conversational groupings of furniture, not standard night-club furniture, but furniture lovingly selected. In one place the coffee table was an ancient, hand-carved marvel, worth many thousands in the States; in another the coffee table was an old G.I. foot locker. The hanging plants were everywhere. The ceiling was an ancient stone arrangement of arches. It looked like what you'd expect to find in the cellar of a monastery. A direct hit upstairs wouldn't even make it quiver.

Rick grinned, obviously delighted. "It's my nightclub," he said. "It's called the Living Room. It's where we used to come to get away from the war, but now the back door opens onto the line." It was interesting to know that the back door opened onto Palestinian positions, and that anyone attempting to leave that way would be instantly gunned down. Especially since we'd had to skulk down the alley with rounds snapping past our ear to get in the front.

Rick zipped around us and turned on more lights. "What'll it be, ladies and gents?" He laughed. "On the house." We gave him our orders and he got busy behind the bar.

He and Christine spoke to each other in French for a moment and laughed. Then Christine, Claude, and I took our drinks and sat down, facing one another across a coffee table. I sank into the comfortable chair with a big grin on my face.

Christine actually understood quite a bit of English, but was not used to speaking it. She sat for a long moment, rehearsing the question in her mind, then turned to me and smiled warmly. "Do you like your life?"

"Yes, very much," I replied.

"You are happee man?"

"Yes."

"Gude." She sank back into the couch and drank.

Rick, meanwhile, had been fiddling around with the sound system. I heard the opening strains of a familiar piece of music that I couldn't quite place. Then I recognized it, the music from the movie musical *All That Jazz.* Just as I recognized it, I heard the *crump-crump* of incoming mortars somewhere upstairs. It was very faint, but with that ceiling it could have just as easily been a direct hit on the building we were in. I really don't think anybody else noticed it. Christine turned to me, smiled and spoke.

Her voice is high, flute-like, and when she speaks French it is difficult to remember it is a regular language, designed for communication, and not simply music. The harsh

Saxon syllables of English do not give the same effect, but her accent was still charming. Just as the mortars slammed in upstairs, she grinned and spoke the line that serves as a signature and recurring theme for *All That Jazz*: "It's showtime, folks!"

It was about four in the morning when Rick brought Claude and me home. Nazih, the bleary-eyed young man who opened the door, looked at me in amazement. "You are going to the range with Fouad at five-thirty," he said. Ah, well, under no circumstances would I have wanted to miss the party at Rick's club, and this wouldn't be the first day of training I had gutted after a night without sleep. I went to shower and change.

As we rode out of town in Fouad's carryall, a few joggers loped through the blasted early morning streets. It had been more than a week since I had run, and I was feeling my chest start to slide down to my belly. I decided to get back into it. I was beginning to be able to find my way around, and I trusted myself to run a couple of miles without fear of turning a corner into a Palestinian position.

The ride to the range passed in a blur. On the way I told Fouad that I was eager to fire the AK. Over the few days I had known Fouad, he had mentioned a long list of mostly Soviet weapons used by both sides in this war—the Soviets supplied the Leftists through Syria, as they did in most Communist insurgencies, and the Rightists bought them from the enemy. I had to confess that, although I had been shot at by most of them, I had never fired them.

"Sometimes it seems as though you have never fired a weapon in your life," he said.

I laughed. "I was an advisor in Vietnam. My weapons were flattery and blackmail."

The range was in the mountains on the way to Michel's position. When we arrived the other car was already there. In it were Michel, who had rotated his platoon back in for a week's rest, Nazih, who was the G-5 treasurer, and Toufik, another young man in the office. Toufik looked like a young Omar Sharif, and played the role to the hilt, smoking his cigarettes in an ivory holder. He was deadly serious, however, when there was a job to be done.

Fouad had brought his own FAL, and an M-2 carbine for me. There was a decal of the Virgin Mary on the stock of my weapon.

Michel and Toufik both had M-16s. Michel had switched to the 16 after he lost half of his left arm at Tall Zaatar. To fire, he laid the plastic guard that covered the barrel over the stub of his elbow. He was deadly accurate.

Toufik professed to genuinely like the M-16, although few others did. Sam had said, "If you think the M-16 is prone to jam in the jungle, wait until you get some sand in it." Nazih had a brand new AK he had bought, and also a P-38 pistol.

The range at first appeared to be an improvisation; in fact, it didn't look like a range at all, but merely a place guys could go to plink a few rounds. I suspect that was how it had started; then it was gradually modified as training required. None of the modifications involved anything like a conventional target, either bull's-eye or silhouette. We stood on a small raised area, a natural platform that looked across a small valley. Some hills formed a natural backstop about 500 meters to our front. Between us and the hills, at 200 meters, a zigzag trench had been dug for defensive problems; at 100 meters were three little hillocks, maybe two dump-truck loads of rock and gravel each. Fouad looked around, found a Coke can, took it and put it on top of one of them. When he came back, we began to fire.

I didn't know if my weapon was zeroed or not, so I started firing aimed shots into the dirt bank. The dirt seemed to be flying pretty much where I was aiming, but I fired six rounds just to make sure. Then I shifted my attention to the Coke can and popped it off the berm on the second round.

"Who hit it?" Michel asked.

"Morris," Toufik said.

Michel looked at me in obvious annoyance. "We were firing like this," he said, jamming the weapon into his hip. "It was a game."

They were all firing either from the hip, or with the buttplate jammed right into the solar plexus, just below the belt buckle. "Oops, sorry!"

They set another can up, and we went back to firing from the hip, to no discernible effect.

I had a run with Nazih's new AK. He had no sling, so I fired it from the hip. It was a great weapon, accurate and easy to handle.

I had not fired a weapon of any sort in about three years, but I upheld the honor of *Soldier of Fortune* and the United States. Only Fouad and Michel outshot me, and then it was close.

"Here, try it with this," Fouad said, and handed me his FAL. I packed it into my hip to fire a three-round burst into the dirt bank, just to see where it might hit.

"Try it this way," Fouad said. His FAL had an extra-long sling. He draped it around my neck. I started to switch the right side of the strap over my shoulder, but he stopped me.

"Here," he said, and jammed the buttplate into my groin. "Let the sling support the weight of the weapon. Just use your left hand to keep it from rising. Don't look at the weapon; look at what you want to hit. Shift your point of aim by shifting your body, not the weapon."

"Okay." I shrugged, and squeezed off a three-round burst. I failed to observe the bullet's strike due to extreme pain, and decided to move the buttplate a couple of inches higher.

The technique was deadly effective. Whatever I was looking at exploded into flying rocks and gravel when I squeezed the trigger. It was as fast, and three times as effective, as firing from the hip, and critical seconds faster than firing a well-aimed shot. For hitting a man out to a hundred meters on full auto, it was deadly.

I was feeling a bit smug about my shooting when Fouad

asked us to cease firing for a moment. As soon as we did he took off running in a zigzag diagonal across the front of those hillocks we were shooting at. Going at a dead run, he crossed their front from about 50 meters out. His first round was about six inches out, but after that he put a three-round burst from the FAL into an area about 18 inches square in the center of mass of each of those little hillocks, firing from the hip. It was the most impressive display of combat shooting I have ever seen.

After we quit firing, the others went back to Beirut, but Fouad wanted to show me something up in the mountains, so off we went.

On the way I asked him where he had learned to shoot like that. He said he had learned at the Lebanese Forces Commando Course, so I started asking questions and comparing that course with the U.S. Ranger School. They are quite different. Much of the Ranger course is designed to put pressure on the student to see how he will stand up under the stress of combat. No one went to the LF Commando Course until he had at least a year of combat.

I mentioned that in the U.S. Army one of the most prized awards is the Combat Infantryman's Badge. Fouad laughed. "I think that in Lebanon everybody would have ten of these medals."

The Ranger School also emphasizes land navigation in all types of terrain, and being able to subsist for days on few rations, while moving in the swamps, or the mountains of Georgia. The Lebanese Commando is operating in his own back yard. His six-week course is all physical training, tactical problems, and range-firing on all types of weapons, under simulated combat conditions.

Fouad pulled the Land Rover into a line of military vehicles parked in front of what appeared to be, and in fact was, a ski lodge. "There is a commando company here," he said, "and some support troops. Would you like to talk to some of the boys?"

Of course, and we went inside. He checked in with the

executive officer of the company, an old friend of his. Actually, he kicked him out of bed. Since it was eleven in the morning I assumed he had been up all night on an exercise of some sort.

We stepped out on the balcony outside of his room and, immediately, I was surrounded by grinning teenagers in fatigues. The one who spoke the best English was an 18-year-old squad leader who had been fighting for three years. He said he was trying to finish high school so he could study electrical engineering in the States.

I asked him how long he had known the boys in his squad, and he seemed puzzled. Finally I found out he had known them all his life; they were the kids he grew up with. He was their leader now because he had been their leader in kindergarten.

Another kid, a tall, smiling boy, wanted to show me his rocket-propelled grenade launcher. On the side of its receiver it had been stamped: "Made by Fateh." Fateh is the largest group in the PLO, Yasser Arafat's group.

"How did you get that?" I demanded.

He shrugged and grinned. "Killed two Palestinians."

Fouad took me to lunch with the command group of the company. The company commander was new, recently promoted from second-in-command of another company. He was a short man with a mustache, built like a fireplug, whose arm muscles stretched the sleeves of his T-shirt. Lunch was informal, in the commander's room, with guys sitting in chairs and on the bed.

There was none of the joking and laughing I'd seen with the kids upstairs. All conversation was in Arabic, so I didn't know what was discussed, but their voices were low and the silences long. Although one or two men were moving in the room more or less continuously, bringing messages or scooping up humus with pita, I never heard a step or a shuffle. This was the most silent group of men I'd ever met. A black T-shirt was part of their uniform, frequently imprinted with their blood type in red over the heart. One wore an exact copy of *Soldier of Fortune*'s Rhodesian Army T-shirt, except the logo on this one read, "Be a man among men. Join the Kataebe Army." I tried to get one, but found they had been made in '76 and were prized possessions of those who had them.

On the way back, when we entered the city, we saw a pall of smoke rising from the center island of the boulevard we were on. "Hmmm," said Fouad, "it looks as though there has been some shelling." He hit the ramp to switch to another traffic artery. There was a long string of cars going the other way. "It is very hot," he said. "Everybody is going to the beach."

The day after he came out of the mountains, which was the day after Claude went back to France, Michel moved into the room with me. "I must get my rest," he said. There was a steady traffic of beautiful women there to see Michel during the day, and most nights I had the room to myself.

Once I got up early for my run, and there was a knock at the door. I opened it and there stood the most beautiful girl I saw in Lebanon. *"Ou est Michel?"* she demanded. She had the face of an angel, and a stunning body. I sighed and went to wake Michel up. They were both gone when I got back from my run.

But he was there a lot during the day. He stayed at the press bureau even though he had an apartment with a live-in girlfriend in town. Maybe that was the problem; the live-in didn't like the nights out.

I had already stayed longer than intended, but I wanted to be in Lebanon when Larry arrived, to brief him. Michel and Larry were already talking over the phone. Michel wanted him to bring some ammo pouches for the "M-seize." He was always fiddling with his gear, trying different placements of ammo pouches, knives. He rigged a hook on his left shoulder harness so he could throw grenades with one hand. He wanted M-16 pouches primarily for the grenade retainer snaps on the side. His Russian pouches didn't have them, so he had to carry another pouch or two, just for grenades. He also wanted 30-round magazines.

Once he got his gear tricked out in a new way, he tried it on and jumped up and down to make sure it didn't rattle. If it did, he took it off, fiddled with it some more and tried it again.

Michel was a great fighter, and although I had sworn never again to go straphanging, I figured he was one guy you could go into the gulf with. You might buy it, but if you did, it wouldn't be because somebody screwed up and left you hanging.

I really wanted to go on a raid. I've been on night ambushes, heliborne assaults, search and destroys, blind stupid charges, blocking actions, encirclements, recons, recons in force, and even a sort of ricky-tick combat jump. But I have always considered the commando raid to be the ultimate military operation. Go in quick, make your snatch or blow your objective, shoot the hell out of everything and everybody, and get the fuck out.

I knew I had passed some sort of test on the range that day, but it was one they had almost hoped I would fail.

"Well, Jim, I cannot go whenever I want. I must go when they order."

I knew that. I knew it probably wouldn't happen. But for a day or so there I actually had myself convinced it might. I got myself psyched all the way up to that very pure adrenaline high. I could almost feel that green paint on my face. Once more I was looking down that long red tunnel, free and at peace.

"Jim, you should know," he said. "If you are wounded in the assault, I cannot carry you out, and I cannot let you be captured. I cannot even let them find your body. We do not want them to think you are *le mercenaire*. I must destroy you."

"How are you going to do that? One hundred and ninety-five pounds of dead Caucasian is difficult to disintegrate instantaneously."

He shook his head. "No, no, no, no."

"Oh, come on, Michel. I'm a big boy. How can you do that?"

He really didn't want to tell me, but I insisted. He looked at the floor, sort of guiltily. "I would put a *grenade* in your mouth."

I must confess that gave me pause.

"It is very dangerous," he said. "You shoot well, but you do not know the terrain, you would not know well your equipment."

There it was. I was a danger not only to myself, but to his patrol, and to the mission. The last thing in the world he needed was an unknown factor.

The real problem, for me, was that, while I had the right to risk my own life, I didn't feel I had the right to increase the risk to the patrol. My own best military judgment was that I should back off. "Besides, I would waste a *grenade*," he said.

I laughed. "Well, Jesus Christ," I shot back. "Will you let me go if I pay for the grenade?"

We finally agreed on a compromise, in which I'd go with his fire-support team, and I'd watch the action, if any, from beside a machine gun on an overlooking hill. If it was a mine-planting expedition there'd probably be nothing to see. Finally, I had three days before my boat left. Not enough time to prepare, even if he got a warning order. Maybe next time I'd have time to go through the commando course, and things would be different.

No action. There had been an Arab foreign ministers' conference going on over in West Beirut, almost from the day I arrived. "I don't like it, Jim. It's too quiet, too quiet." Michel stood on the balcony, beating on his thigh with his fist. I had seen everything there was to see and interviewed nearly everybody in Lebanese Forces who spoke English. Still there was no action. All I was doing was waiting for Larry Dring to arrive, or my boat, whichever came first.

Then came that familiar high, shrieking whistle. I hadn't heard that sound since March 1986, but I wasn't the last guy to hit the deck, in this case the checkered tile under the dining room table. It went over us and killed two women and a man a mile further east. It was in the papers the next morning.

That evening I was alone in the apartment when Youssef, a young man in the political section, ran frantically into the apartment, and stared wildly about the room.

"What's up?" I demanded, bounding from my chair, thinking, *action at last!*

"Starsky and Hutch," he cried, and bolted for the TV.

7
THE BIRTHDAY PARTY

We drove north through Jounieh and along some beautiful Mediterranean coastline, through another town or two, and then into one I had a hard time believing was real. A row of buildings lined the road, but what buildings! If they hadn't been lined up in regular rows, I'd have thought they were caves. They appeared to have been made of brick daubed with mud, centuries before. "Jesus!" I exclaimed.

"This is Byblos," Sam explained. "It's the oldest continuously inhabited town on Earth. The alphabet was invented here, writing as we know it. As in Bible and bibliography . . . Byblos."

I nodded, awed. "The oldest building in Oklahoma, where I grew up, is about a hundred years old." Then I remembered Sequoyah's cabin, a log cabin in eastern Oklahoma, carefully preserved as part of a state park. In that cabin Sequoyah, whom the whites had called George Guess, had devised the Cherokee syllabary, an 87-character alphabet which was so clear and logical that a person who spoke the language could go from total illiteracy to complete literacy in two weeks. I thought of Sequoyah's gentle face, the eyes burning with intelligence, long-stemmed pipe in his mouth, loose Cherokee turban on his head, in my seventh-grade history book, and later the original oil painting in the rotunda of the state capitol.

For an instant, even though I don't know the Cherokee language, and have not a drop of Indian blood, I felt like a connecting link between those long-ago scholars in Byblos and their spiritual kinsman in the old part of the New World. I had, after all, come here to find something to write about.

Sam turned left, off the highway and around a large outcropping of rock. Down past a winding road was a typical Mediterranean resort restaurant, called Byblos-sur-Mer. The sea crashed over rocks on the other side of the parking lot.

Several cars were drawn up by a dock, and families were unloading picnic boxes, ice chests, styrofoam chests, straw picnic baskets. The women were dressed in bikinis, dresses, jeans. The men wore LF uniforms, jeans, or those unbelievably gross European bathing suits. The men also carried a spectrum of light armament, M-16s, AKs, and a variety of pistols. A guy in one of those bathing suits bent over to pick up an ice chest; the outline of the .45 tucked into the waistband of his bathing suit, barrel nestling between the cheeks of his buttocks, was thrust into startling relief. One of the shoelaces on his Adidas sneakers had come loose and was dragging through the dirt in the parking lot.

Sam, who was in uniform, turned me over to a boatload of people, about a family and a half, and went away to do things concerning security. I helped them load the boat, which was long and narrow, sort of like a pirogue, driven by a small outboard motor. One of the bathing suit guys started the engine and we headed out into the Med, spray crashing over the bow. Out at sea the sun was setting and a pastel orange glow lay atop the dark green of the horizon. The boat crashed through the waves for quite some distance, to a small rocky island. I don't know how far it was from shore, but it was further than an RPG could fire. The party would be undisturbed.

I spent a couple of minutes helping unload the boat, but after that I was no help at all. The folks I was with knew what was to be done, but none of them spoke English, and it was more trouble than it was worth to tell me what to do by gesture. I watched for a while, and then wandered over to the sunset side of the island and gazed at all the subtle colors streaming across the sky; cerise, mauve, chartreuse, orangy-pinks, and deep blazing reds that hinted of blood. I sat on a jagged chunk of black rock and watched that Wurlitzer of a sunset, thinking about the sunsets west of Norman, Oklahoma, where it's flat, and there aren't many clouds, and the air is full of dust for the light to reflect from. It's the best show in town.

In all my travels I had never encountered another so vivid until now, but here the air was full of salt spray, not dust. At home the sunsets were more violent, more dramatic. This was peaceful, a musical comedy of a sunset.

This was the first time in about three weeks that I'd had a chance to feel totally alone, to sit down and let my thoughts unravel. I couldn't understand how people as decent as my Lebanese friends could have gotten themselves into the vicious war they were in. Sure, they were a little on the shortfused side, but certainly not without provocation. One thing I knew for certain; these folks were in no moral or intellectual way inferior to Americans. Beirut was very different from Oklahoma City, where I grew up, but no more so than Miami, Florida. In fact, in those pre-Mariel days, aside from language, Beirut and Miami were very much alike, same white buildings and tropical vegetation, a similar European-Mediterranean ethnic mix. The major differences were that Miami lacked a Syrian army of occupation and an unrestricted flow of Soviet arms across the border.

Strange thoughts for a Mediterranean sunset. And what about me? I should be going home soon, but I really wanted to wait until Larry arrived. I wondered about my reawakened thirst for combat. It wasn't blood lust or anything like that. It was just that desire to take chances as far as you could. It was as Stirling Moss had said about auto racing; "you could live ten years on a Sunday afternoon." When I got to Lebanon I felt like I was waking up after a long sleep, but now I didn't just want to be awake. I wanted to rock 'n' roll.

But I missed Kathy very much, and I knew if I got back into all this, I'd lose her; and for that matter, at 44, I wasn't in good enough shape to live through much combat—too slow, not enough endurance.

But the memory of the rising surge of pure energy that comes when you go into an ambush or a hot LZ drew me as nothing else does. I wondered whether I could squeeze in one more, and if so, would I be satisfied with one?

I got up and wandered back to the party. It was dark, but a fire was roaring, racks of shish kebab had been laid out, along with more great Lebanese food than three times the number of people there could possibly eat.

Fouad and Celeste were there, and Michel. Rick was not, but I had no idea why. Fouad loaded me a plate and a glass of arak, and we chatted. I felt no sense of my own foreignness. There was laughter; there was singing. It was great.

Fouad pointed out his brother Teddy, whose birthday it was. Teddy was a shock. I had been told a few things about him. I knew he was Fouad's younger brother, that he had fought at the Battle for the Holiday Inn in 1976 and been wounded badly enough to retire from combat, and he had become a scuba instructor in Jounieh. But none of that prepared me for Teddy. This guy was *messed up*.

Fouad pointed him out, but I never got a chance to meet him that night, because he was always in the center of an admiring group of friends and relatives. The guy was a legend, but he had paid for it. He looked like he'd taken an RPG on his left foot. On land he moved awkwardly on a specially constructed leather boot that partially compensated for his mangled leg and foot. He leaned heavily on a cane. But I could see he'd have no trouble moving underwater, with flippers. One of his eyes was larger than the other, as though a plastic surgeon had been able to repair the flesh, but not the muscle.

By God, I thought, *if my leg was screwed up like that I'd have it whacked off below the knee and replaced with a prosthesis.*

These thoughts were interrupted by a burst of Middle Eastern music from a portable tape player, accompanied by a skinny teen-age kid with a silly grin and fast hands, bopping with great virtuosity on a small drum with a fluted body. By then I was on my third arak and believed the young lady who came out to dance to be the most beautiful I had ever seen.

Remove from your mind any Egyptian belly-dancer stereotype. Such a performance is perhaps a branch of the same tree as this one, in the sense that, say, Jackson Browne and KISS are branches off the same tree, but this was, after all, a family picnic. The girl wore a boutique terry jumpsuit, reminiscent of the belly-dancer's costume only because the pants were full and gathered at the ankle. Aside from the lack of come-hither looks, the moves seemed fairly standard, but hip-shaking or no, this performance was not intended for sexual excitement. It was just for fun. She was shortly joined by a stocky young man in a CAT baseball cap and a Michigan State football jersey. After a while the girl dropped out and was replaced by a matronly lady in her mid-fifties who could really sling it around.

I found myself leaning back and watching the moon, thinking about Kat, how much I missed her, and how much she would have loved this party. I had seen a lot of the world that she hadn't, and this little bit of it I'd have loved to have shared with her, as she had shared her backstage world with me.

Michel came over and asked me whether I'd ride home with his girl, since he had found another one he wanted to check out.

I had too many more araks. I'm not much of a boozer, but arak tastes like licorice, and I hadn't learned to take it seriously. I slipped and fell down climbing into the boat on the way to Byblos-sur-Mer. I have a vague memory of the ride home. I think Sam was driving, but I'm not sure. Michel's girl was in the backseat, but her mood had turned somber.

It was a great evening, but I have one regret. On my one trip to the town where writing was invented, all I can claim to have done was get drunk and fall down in a boat.

A couple of nights later Teddy came up to the apartment to see Fouad. He leaned heavily on his cane and walked with a horrible limp on his blasted, misshapen leg. The one eye that was round and staring gave a contemptuous and angry cast to his face. Or perhaps he was just contemptuous and angry, either toward life itself or toward the circumstances in which he found himself. I left my reading and looked in on the two brothers, talking in Fouad's office. "Teddy, could I talk with you a bit before you leave, about the Battle for the Holiday Inn, for my article?"

He looked back at me balefully and nodded assent.

The television station had gone off for the night when he and Fouad finished their conversation, and so we had that corner of the living room to talk in. He clumped in on his cane, sat across from me, and cocked his head. "Well?"

I grinned. "I've stayed in Holiday Inns all over the south-west United States—Texas, Oklahoma, Arkansas. The idea of a battle in one seems ludicrous. My idea of a battle is hosing down a jungle trail from ten feet away."

He didn't return my smile, but his voice was soft and pleasant. He seemed to regard my comment as a serious one, and he replied seriously. "This one was very strategically placed; three major hotels in a row, on the Green Line, on commanding terrain. One could observe practically the entire city. The hotels were the Holiday Inn, the St. Georges, and the . . . ah . . . Phoenicia."

"It's very hard for me to visualize a battle like that. In my life I've only fought one day in a city, and that was in a neighborhood of one- and two-story houses, during the Tet Offensive of 1968."

"It was very difficult," he said. "I had twenty-four men to defend a 1700 meter front."

That seemed as though it might be minimally possible with commanding terrain, clear fields of fire, good weapons, and an inexhaustible supply of ammunition, but in the end the ammo supply proved exhaustible.

At one point I touched on the issue of atrocities. I wanted very much for my friends to be the good guys. I, and the Americans I have fought beside in the past, have been scrupulous in the matter of handling prisoners.

"With only twenty-four men," he said, "I wanted them to be as afraid of us as I could make them."

I had no reply to that. I was very conscious of the fact that the torture killing of prisoners is pretty much *de rigueur* throughout the Third World, and that the Palestinians had a particularly unsavory record in that regard.

"Why don't you have that leg cut off and get a prosthesis?" I asked. "You could probably get around a lot better."

"Many times they want to take it," he replied. "At my first operation on Cyprus they wanted to take it, but I always say no. I do not believe in . . . it is not a good idea to sacrifice a part of your body when maybe a way to fix it can be found."

I smiled. "Maybe so. In the water I expect you're as good as anybody."

He smiled back. "I like to think I am better."

For all his ferocious appearance Teddy spoke very gently and calmly about these things. I got no sense that he was a man who had never wanted to fight or kill, but that he had been confronted with a situation where there was no choice, and had responded with a cold, intelligent rage. In any case, that part of it was over for him now.

8
BYE-BYE BEIRUT

I took my accustomed sunrise seat on the balcony and dialed the thirteen digits it took to reach my home in Fayetteville. Two rings.

"Hello!"

"Hi, darlin', what's happ'nin'?"

"Well, I've scheduled a wedding on the 27th of June. Think you can make it?"

That was about two weeks past when I'd said I'd be home, but I'd stayed, hopefully, to go on an operation with Michel. Also, I'd wanted to be there to brief Larry when he arrived. But it had become obvious Michel wasn't going out for a couple of weeks, and I couldn't just sit around doing nothing in the meanwhile. And it wasn't actually necessary that I be here when Larry arrived. Mostly I just wanted to show off.

"Sure," I said, "I'll be there, but what changed your mind?" I had been asking her to marry me about twice a week for the preceding two years.

Her husky Southern voice crackled over the phone, "I was talkin' to your mother, and I suddenly realized that if you buy the farm on one of these deals I won't be anything but your ex-girlfriend."

I guffawed. "Okay, I'll be there." I was delighted, no matter what her reasons. Later, she admitted this had been the only way she could think of to get me home.

The morning I was to leave I woke up to realize that I'd better do something about finding a ring. I asked Michel, and he said there were excellent jewelry bargains in Beirut. The gold cost the same, but the workmanship, although excellent, was dirt cheap. "Sounds good," I said. "Let's go!"

He took me to what had been an exclusive shop in a corner location, near the Green Line. There was a lot of black velvet on display, but their stock was way down. I knew exactly what she wanted, however, and they had it, a thin gold circle with a spiral of gold around it; beautiful, delicate, and stylish.

Michel took me back to the apartment that had been my home for three weeks which seemed like a hundred. I was still concerned about the Palestinians. That interview had made it fairly easy to pin down approximately when I'd be leaving. I wanted a weapon, but I couldn't carry one through Cypriot customs. But on a bookshelf in the apartment there was a cedar cone roughly the size and shape of an old WWII pineapple hand grenade.

Not a bad souvenir of Lebanon, that. I figured I'd carry it off the boat and out of the customs shed. If there was someone waiting for me on Cyprus, the sight of it might give them enough pause for me to get away. There was really only a slight chance they'd be after me, but enough of one that Rick was concerned. Rick hadn't lived through five years of this shit by being a fool.

I said my good-byes and Sam drove me to Jounieh, to the

boat. He laid his Czech AK in the seat between us and set off, grim-faced, in Rick's old VW. He looked more and more depressed as we headed north. "What the hell's the matter with you?" I asked. "You look like you could eat a bowl of nails!"

"I don't like to go to Jounieh," he snapped. "I almost hate those people. We're dying every day in Beirut, and they face almost no danger at all. All they care about the war is to make money from it."

I nodded, but what I was thinking was, how can you expect the Americans half a world away to come to your rescue when you can't get the full support of your countrymen twenty miles up the road? But I didn't say it. It would only have made him angry. Instead I took my last Montagnard bracelet off my arm. Once I'd had many of them, but now I had only one. It was just six inches of quarter-inch brass welding rod, with some notches carved on it, bent into a bracelet that turned your wrist green. But it was my most prized possession. It was my badge of membership in another tribe I had loved in another time and place. Another bunch of good folks my government had sold down the river.

"Here!" I said. "This is my good luck. You need it worse than I do."

He slipped it on his wrist and said, "Thanks." His manner was offhand. He lived in a world where these are the things one does.

On the boat back to Cyprus I fell in with a couple of young Lebanese Christians. Roger, the stocky one with the broad grin, was just going to Cyprus for a holiday, catch a few rays on the beach, and hit the discos at night. John, an Errol Flynn look-alike, had a job as a civil engineer in Saudi Arabia. Since both John and Roger were part-time Lebanese Forces militiamen it was quite possible that John had been shot at by weapons furnished by his employers. "They don't care that you're a Christian?" I asked.

He shrugged. "They want engineers."

As we chatted, Roger put a tape in his small stereo deck. It was Middle Eastern music, but with a solid back beat, Middle Eastern music by someone who was also a Beatles fan. It was terrific, the best new stuff I had heard in years.

"This is Marceil Kalife," Roger said. "He is a communist, but his music is good. We all listen."

We listened to Kalife and they told tremendous stories of being teenagers in the militia, making impromptu raids on Palestinian positions after a few too many beers on a Saturday night.

John teased Roger about the trouble a young man could get into on Cyprus. "One time in the Cosmos Disco on Cyprus I meet a girl. She is very beautiful, with long, long hair, and a shape . . . ahh, that shape." He flashed a grin that was pure malevolent Captain Blood. "I ask her out and she say meet her outside so I follow and bump into this guy.

"He say, 'Filthy Arab!' " The Flynn grin was replaced by a grimace of total, focused berserker rage, even now, at the memory. "So I *grab* him, and I *slam* him against the wall, and I say, 'Don't call me *Arab*! I kill you, you son of a bitch! We follow JEESUSS!' "

The next day I left the boat with my bags in one hand and my cedar cone in the other.

9
WHERE'D HE GET THAT BUDDHA?

The wedding was beautiful, the bride was lovely, and the reception afterward was the best party I ever attended. The guest list was a strange mix, though. Kathy had her friends from the drama school, and I had mine from the English department, and we both knew some combat vets with lots of stamps in their passports.

My best man was Paul H. Williams, a former Marine artillery forward observer from Vietnam, and a fellow writing student. He looks like Edgar Allan Poe and writes grim Faulknerian tales about Indians and mixed bloods in Oklahoma. Kathy's bridesmaid was Terry Brustar, her dance instructor. I had known Terry for over a year, and only seen her in a leotard, jean skirt, hair knotted into a bun. For the wedding she looked great, dress clothes, her hair done in electric brillo.

Our ushers were Peder Lund, an ex–Special Forces captain who looks like a killer koala, publisher of my book, *War Story*, and Marty Jordan. Marty is a stocky, blond half-Choctaw who made staff sergeant in one three-year hitch, which included two Vietnam tours. In his ruffled shirt and dinner jacket, he was one of the most frightening-looking persons I had ever seen.

Kat had lectured Lund and Martin on decorum, and they were trying hard. The first guest to seat in the chapel was a young lady, one of my students. "Are you a friend of the bride or the groom?" Lund inquired correctly.

"I guess it really doesn't matter," she replied.

Our photographer, Jim Adair, another former SF man, and an old skydiving buddy, leaned over a pew and said, "Then find your own goddamn seat."

My heart flopped over when Kathy came up the aisle of the chapel. She wore a simple white gown (she says it was "ecru," but it looked white to me) with a modified empire line, her design, and a white gardenia over the right ear, on her shoulder-length dark hair. She is slender and frail-looking, with delicate features and huge dark eyes, and she moves with a gliding grace. But she has Tom's sense of humor and Huck's sense of adventure and none of Becky about her at all.

Music was provided by a friend named Abby, who played, at an appropriate tempo, Willy Nelson's "Whisky River," on the autoharp. It sounded just right if you didn't remember the lyrics.

The ceremony was held up for a moment while I pondered my answer to the question, "Wilt thou have this woman . . ." but I allowed as how I would, and we adjourned to Paul's two-story Victorian for the aforementioned best party ever.

Kathy had pulled out all the stops. Champagne flowed from fountains. There were hors d'oeuvres, and Tequila Sunrises. Larry Dring and the guys from Beirut had sent a gorgeous bouquet of roses.

After the party got rolling my friend David, from the writing program, decided the air was too close, left the party, and was later arrested for crawling against a red light.

The next day we packed a U-Haul and headed for Boulder. Like most of my classmates, I had no viable teaching offers, but Brown wanted me to work for *Soldier of Fortune*.

After Larry got back from Beirut, he came to visit and tell his story for the magazine. He had seen pretty much the same things I had, but, being more technically qualified, he was able to give the Lebanese Forces instruction in vehicle maintenance and advanced demolitions. In return they taught him their anti-tank tactics, and gave him a lot of Russian weapons they had captured, weapons that nobody in U.S. intelligence had bothered to come over and collect.

He and Michel had become fast friends, as I expected they would. They were both super-soldiers, and Larry couldn't talk about Michel without grinning. Once, in a three-quarter-ton truck, Michel had driven them over the side of what appeared to be a cliff, but turned out to be an eighty degree incline, which they slid down in a shower of rocks and dirt.

Larry also laughed about the poor, hash-addled Syrian trooper whom they had captured when he wandered into their camp one night, carefully explaining that they couldn't capture him because he was invisible.

"Do they sell bras in this town?" he asked as we drove through the streets of Boulder, eyeing beautiful U. of Colorado girls in cut-offs and halter tops or T-shirts, riding bicycles.

"Yeah," I said. "They're a prescription item."

Larry loved the hot tub place, because the water was great for his leg. The first day of Tet '68 an NVA trooper had shot six inches out of his left femoral artery. Larry cut him in half with a burst from his M-16, but the damage was done. It always hurt, always. I can still remember him floating on his back under the stars in a hot tub, singing Civil War songs at the top of his lungs, to the extreme consternation of the freaks in the next room, who were trying to smoke a little pot and get into the Moody Blues.

One night we went to a party at Haney Howell's, my CBS buddy from Cambodia, in Denver. Larry was in a suit of Palestinian cammies he had gotten from Fouad. We had taken an AK and an M-16 into the Rockies, which looked just like the mountains in Lebanon, to get some shots of the LF firing techniques.

Having been on his leg all day, Larry was gobbling prescription codeine like popcorn; he was loquacious and charming and brilliant. He fell into conversation with Sandy Sells, wife of George Sells, then anchorman on a Denver TV station. "I had this company of Cambodes and we were having a drink, me Coke, them beer, one night in the cantina after an operation. This one troopie had a Buddha medallion he claimed had been blessed by an extra-powerful *bonze*, and nothing could kill him. Just to prove his point he held his hand over the end of his carbine and pulled the trigger.

"Nothing.

"All the other guys looked at him and marveled. He got so cocky he stuck the barrel in his mouth and pulled the trigger. Blew the back of his head clean off.

"All the other guys were standing around, scratching their heads and saying, 'Where'd he get that Buddha?'" Larry grinned.

10
WAITING
IN
BANGKOK

We found a house in the Capitol Hill section of Denver, a kind of liberal-intellectual-artsy neighborhood, and Kathy found work in the costume shop at the Bonfils Theater.

Over the next nine months I did a series on Lebanon and covered several other stories in the U.S., mostly to do with the POW situation.

Kathy wasn't eager for me to go back overseas, but nine months later, when Brown asked me to go to Thailand, I jumped at the chance. It would be a pleasure to get back to Southeast Asia. Maybe I could even make contact with FULRO and find out what the deal was with the Montagnards. There were plenty of other stories in Thailand as well.

* * *

"Goddamn it!" I muttered. "This is driving me batshit." I took five steps away from Coyne's hotel window, turned and took five steps back. I looked down on what appeared to be a modern city growing out of the jungle. Actually, the tropical trees were neatly planted in rows around palatial villas, but from the tenth and topmost floor of the Nana Hotel you couldn't see the houses, so you saw this jungle, studded with apartments, hotels, Buddhist temples, the spire of the Dusit Thani building, cement factories. From Coyne's room you could not see Sukhumvit.

You're driving *me* batshit," said Coyne. "You're wired way too high for this. Nothing moves fast in this country."

"We've been here ten days," I said; snarled actually, "and I've already spent more time in Bangkok than I did in Saigon in three tours in Vietnam. I didn't come for a good time. I was having a good time in Boulder."

When we first got there, Coyne said, "This is better than Saigon." Truly this was more like Saigon than Saigon had been. But before Bangkok, I had hated Saigon worse than any place I had ever been in my life.

This was, in fact, the first time I'd ever been in Southeast Asia that I was in any particular hurry to get home. Kathy needed me; I had work stacked up to the rafters, and while I was glad to be here, I was desperate to get on with it. I was supposed to be back in Boulder by the end of the month, and nothing was happening.

"I just don't like cities," I muttered. I would not have much cared for this lurid scene, even when I was young and unattached. In Vietnam I had sought the green leafy places, and the occasional firefight, which was what I had hoped to recapture here, but it wasn't happening.

I had liked that life better than anything that went before, and most of what came after. I wanted another piece of it.

Coyne and I both had four or five stories we were working on, the work for which consisted of pestering people on the telephone, and waiting for their reply. Thailand is a *mañana* country; if you pushed these people hard enough, they could simply blow you off—no connection, no story.

But Thailand is an important story, simply because it had not gone down the tubes as expected. The Domino Theory racked up South Vietnam, Laos, Cambodia and stopped at Thailand, then jumped three oceans and started again in Africa, the Middle East, and Central America. Why the Thais were succeeding was important, but nobody was covering it.

The local papers were full of great combat stuff, but nobody outside of Thailand picked it up. It was a very difficult story to cover, unless you had an interpreter or spoke Thai, because the Royal Thai Army didn't seem to have any Public Information setup; we were dealing with colonels and generals, because they had been lieutenants and captains when the Americans were here, and were the only soldiers around who spoke English.

They were very nice and hospitable, but they were running several wars simultaneously—three separate insurgencies and periodic fighting against the opium armies from Burma. Further, they had to keep tabs on the Laotian and Cambodian resistances. If there were any great demand from the international press to cover these wars, they would have come up with some public affairs' officers to handle the influx, but there was no such demand, no demand for success stories.

This merely confirmed my suspicion that the regular press only publishes stories reinforcing the world view of the intelligentsia, which seems only natural since the intelligentsia does most of the world's writing and reading. But that world view screens out a large amount of significant information.

Coyne had been here before and knew the deal. He liked the bush well enough, but he was single, had a girlfriend, and was perfectly content to sit poolside, waiting for a telephone call to confirm an appointment. Of our two attitudes mine might seem more commendable, but his worked and mine didn't.

"What the hell is Brown doing in Chile?" I demanded.

Coyne gave me a helpless look and a wry smile. "Hey," he shrugged, "you know Brown."

Yes, I know Brown; a man crazy enough to think he could make a success of a trade journal for mercenaries is capable of anything. But this was a bit much, even for Brown. Originally, he was going to come with us, but was delayed by an illness in his family. He decided to send us on ahead. Three days later we called the office; his family situation was okay, and he had gone to Washington.

We figured he had gone to see his intelligence cronies about some new development in the POW/MIA issue. That was okay; that was the main thing we were here for.

A week later we called again. Brown had gone to Chile. Chile?

If you could just write Brown off as a screwball, it would make things easier. But Brown is not a screwball: he's a wizard. A wizard is somebody who does totally irrational things that work even though they make no sense. I didn't doubt that there was a good reason for his going to Chile, but I felt like a lion in a closet. No matter what we started, once Brown arrived we'd be faced with a whole new set of priorities.

"I'm going to get ready for dinner," I snapped.

"Yeah," said Coyne, wistfully, "take it easy."

He was, I am sure, looking forward to another evening of my conversation.

Leaving his hotel, I ignored the eight drivers who leapt up and yelled, "Taxi!" I went to the street and bellowed, "Tuk-tuk!" Immediately a Honda motorcycle with a passenger chassis, a sort of motorized rickshaw, sputtered to a halt at my feet. "Windsor Hotel, twenty baht." A regular taxi would want forty for the same ride. Coyne had taught me about tuk-tuks. I climbed in and propped a Tony Lama up on the railing between me and the driver. The tuk-tuk sputtered off.

Emission controls are unknown in Thailand. A blue mist of monoxide hung over Sukhumvit, a major traffic artery, like a smoke snake, its bloodstream the honking, snarling traffic. I blocked off my nose, breathing as shallowly as possible through my teeth.

At the hotel I bathed and was just changing into a khaki safari suit, every correspondent's first purchase in Bangkok, when a naked general charged into my room.

Brigadier General Hiney Aderholt, USAF (Ret.) is self-described as "one of those rough old sonsabitches." He was our only high school dropout general. When I first met him at the Stapleton Airport in Denver I wondered how this crude bastard ever got past lieutenant colonel. He talked tough and butchered the English language like a construction boss, but in the days we traveled with him he switched effortlessly from good-old-boy camaraderie to diplomatic polish to brilliantly reasoned analysis, as required. I saw him blister the ears off a deputy assistant cabinet secretary, and heard him charm the socks off a nun, over the telephone. "Crude bastard" was but one of his many personas.

When I first met him I spelled his name "Heine," and thought he had German ancestry. Later I learned Hiney was a childhood nickname that stuck, earned when he was three years old because his ass was always hanging out.

He was in Thailand, representing a POW-family group from Tampa called the Forget-Me-Nots, to pick up the remains of a fighter pilot who had crashed in Laos. The deal had been set up by a retired Air Force colonel named Donovan, who had lost his son in Laos. "Donovan's spent more on POW/MIA's out of his own pocket than the whole goddamn United States government," Hiney said. "I figured with my connections I could save him a few bucks."

"Goddammit!" said General Aderholt, standing in the connecting door of our rooms, G.I. glasses down on his nose, a newspaper in his hand. "Have you seen this?"

He referred, I hoped, to the newspaper. Normally Hiney wears a towel, as a sarong, Thai style, in his hotel room, but it tends to come loose when he lies down to read.

"What, sir?" I inquired.

He referred to Hill 508 at Surat Thani, where the Thais were waging a marginally successful battle to take an entrenched Communist Party of Thailand guerrilla base. The Thais fight like they do everything else, cleverly. They fight to minimize casualties, and who can blame them for that? There's no end of tour and rotation home in the Royal Thai Army.

"Here, read this!" he concluded, and padded back into his room.

I sighed and looked around the room. Hiney had chosen this hotel before the rest of us arrived. Coyne had come late, through Hong Kong, and checked immediately into the Nana, where he had a top floor room, an FM radio, and a great view. Probably the reason most military decor is so drab is that the other generals have taste like Hiney's, which runs to Early Dayroom. Also, he is convinced that the best thing which could happen to the younger generation is to live through the Depression, like he did, and I believe he chose our rooms in an attempt to replicate that experience.

Downstairs in the lobby, going out, I passed an old American who had obviously been in the Orient for a long time. He looked like something that had been sculpted out of mashed potatoes and left out in the sun a long time ago. I repressed a shudder. *Got to get out of this place*, I thought. I remembered the line at the beginning of *Apocalypse Now*. "Every day Charlie stayed in the jungle he got stronger, and every day I stayed in this hotel room I got weaker."

We ran into Coyne's girlfriend, Som Kit, coming out of the elevator as we started down. She had a paper bag of street-stand food in her arms. "Where you go?" she said to Coyne.

Back in Boulder, Coyne was a kind of easygoing, happy-go-lucky jazzbo, but when he speaks bargirl English he goes squat and growls out monosyllables like Sessue Hayakawa, always with a bit of a smile playing around the corners of his mouth. "We go Oriental for drink. You want come?"

She thought a second, then shook her head. "My sister come later. We go movie." When Kit thinks, you can see the synapses connect behind her eyes. When she sits down and puts her feet in the chair, her rail-thin body folds up like a carpenter's rule. She is very bright and more than once saved us a lot of trouble by correctly identifying some person we had to deal with as a phony.

"Why he laugh?" she demanded, looking at me.

"He make fun of way we do," said Coyne.

She aimed a desultory kick at my kneecap, gave us from her sack two ears of roasted corn on Popsicle sticks, and went off down the hall.

The Oriental Hotel in Bangkok has been voted the world's best hotel by the International Bankers Association, or some such organization, and is a high-class joint, indeed. You can't just arrive there in a tuk-tuk. We rented a white, air-conditioned taxi.

Dismounting at the Oriental, we left our corncobs neatly wrapped in Kleenex in the backseat of the taxi, and walked through the plush, spacious lobby. At the Oriental it is virtually impossible to light your own cigarette, because they employ too many uniformed flunkies.

We walked out back to the verandah, where a cool breeze blew across the muddy expanse of the Chao Phrya River, which reflected a lurid Asian sunset behind the slums on the other side, two hundred yards away.

"All that construction we passed, the freeway, all new since I was here last summer," said Coyne.

"Another significant difference between Thailand and Vietnam," I replied. "In Vietnam nothing was made out of anything but bamboo and sheet tin from the time the

French left until the Americans arrived. Things move at their own pace here, but they do move."

Four *farang* women, who looked sort of frizzy and heavy after seeing only Thai women for a couple of weeks, sat at the next table. A couple of them were nice-looking, although it seemed strange to hear the assertive cadences of American women's conversation. Their laughter was throaty and confident.

"Ah, Jim," said Coyne, sweeping them with a glance, "I want them all."

"Yeah," I said. "Right now! I know the feeling."

Coyne ordered a German white wine with a five-syllable name, mostly consonants. "The last time I was here," he said as we sipped our wine and the last cerise line of the sun faded from the horizon and barge lights drifted by like squadrons of fireflies in formation, "this depressed Japanese businessman chose that moment to take a high dive out his window on the eighth floor. They were having a wedding reception below . . . champagne, seven-tier cake. Somebody took a picture just before he hit. There were all these people laughing and talking, raising their glasses in a toast, and these blurred feet, just at the top of the frame. It was a very surreal picture."

The breeze ruffled the hair over the ears of the American women at the next table.

"They go in big for omens in this country," I said. "That's not a good start for the marriage."

"The hotel management thought the Japanese had jumped from the seventh floor and broke the door open with an axe on a guy from the *Times* who was boffing a hooker. 'Thank God you're alive,' they exclaimed. 'Get the fuck out of here,' he screamed; it was a tremendous hassle."

After finishing our drinks we left the Oriental. Out front, ignoring the pleas of white-uniformed flunkies, wearing matching topis, that we hire another air-conditioned limo, we strolled to the street and rented a tuk-tuk.

"Tiger's?" Coyne inquired. "I got a Jones for Tiger's

beans." Tiger serves a bowl of homemade beans and ham that is the best cheap meal in Bangkok.

Later Coyne and I steered a meandering path down Pat Pong, winging between the outstretched palms, fruit carts, good-looking shills offering some combination of drink, haircut, massage, steambath, and/or blowjob. I stepped around a dead dog, keeled over in its own vomit.

Coyne pushed open the door of the Grand Prix Disco Bar and walked into the dark and the noise.

Behind the circular bar, on a raised platform, ringed by circus lights, three young ladies in sequined bikinis ground away, with varying degrees of skill and enthusiasm, to Bob Seger's *Nine Tonight*.

We wound our way around the bar to the back where the big screen TV was showing *The Towering Inferno* for the handful of people who listened to the soundtrack from headsets at the bar.

Back in the corner was a smaller bar, presided over by Rick Menard, an ex-G.I. who had come to Bangkok on R&R, liked it, and had come back to stay. He looked and talked like a younger Phil Foster, a Brooklyn comedian of the Fifties.

Facing him was the man I was looking for, Alan Dawson, a columnist for the *Bangkok Post*. A Canadian by birth, Dawson made the mistake of dropping out of school in the U.S. and got drafted. If ever there was a guy with good reason to skip to Canada it was he; instead he went to Vietnam and stayed on as a reporter after his enlistment. He even stayed for six months after the fall of Saigon, which he chronicled in his book, *55 Days*. In the dim light at the little bar, with his cadaverous cheeks and lank hair, Dawson wore the bemused and wary expression of a vampire, who, unable to get back to his coffin, had chosen to ride out the daylight hours at a Bugs Bunny Film Festival.

The reason I wanted to see Dawson was that he had been contacted by FULRO, the Montagnard underground in Vietnam, to see whether he wanted to make a run into the Central Highlands. He had declined on the grounds that he would have to go through Khmer Rouge territory. Dawson will not voluntarily stay in the same room with a Khmer Rouge.

If there was any way possible, I wanted to make that trip.

"Hi, honee!" A small brown girl in a sequined bikini, with a tight, shapely brown body, stood under my armpit. A slender arm went around my neck, and a fine brown hand ran up the inseam of my trousers. "How long you stay Bangkok?"

"Excuse me, ma'am, but your hand is on my wazoo."

"You work Saudi?"

"I'm here on business," I insisted.

She looked puzzled for a while longer while I talked to Dawson; then she went away.

Dawson shook his head. "No possibility of a trip," he said. "Too much activity on the border."

"Are they in town?" I asked.

"I'll call you," he said.

I looked for Coyne. He was in animated conversation with an American couple at the other end of the bar. As I approached them I realized he was talking only to the blonde, while her husband stared transfixed at the go-go girls. Coyne leaned forward intently. "Sure, you can get away for a couple days," he said. "We'll go to Penang; we'll have a great time."

She looked as though she were considering it.

Tuesday morning I woke with a chill and sat bolt upright in bed. It dawned on me that all this grab-assing around was lulling me into a false sense of security. One phone call and I could be on an airplane, and in an hour or two I would be in another world, a world of jungled mountains and armed, angry people. I rolled out of bed and checked my gear, checked the wrist strap on my camera. For the hundredth time I cursed my civilian status, cursed the fact that when I went into one of these deals, I had to borrow whatever weapons and ammo they gave me, if any.

In '73, before I was doing this for *SOF*, the Cambodes had given me an M-16 and four, count 'em four, 20-round magazines. That was all they had apiece, and there was no reason why I was so special that I should have more. What I really wanted was a Galil SAR, which is basically an Israeli-made AK that shoots M-16 ammo. Rare indeed is the customs official who will let you through with one.

My next chore was three laps around Lumpini Park, which is about a mile and a half per lap. Even at seven in the morning I was soaked with sweat after five steps. But it was fun to lap the park and see the Chinese ladies practicing their Tai Chi Chuan, and Thais practicing some kind of weird sword fighting—little ladies and gentlemen whirling across the grass, flashing their chromed scimitars—and other runners.

One was a slender, muscular Thai lady in great shape. Every time I went around, she passed going twice as fast the other way. I tabbed her for a marathoner, which I later learned she was. After that came the fitness center and an hour or so of pumping chromed iron.

The life of a writer is primarily sedentary, and if I wanted to keep humping the hills with teenage troops, I had to work out. The older you get the quicker you get out of shape, and the longer it takes to get back in.

After my workout I shared the sauna with a sweaty, towel-wrapped Brit, and another sweaty, towel-wrapped American.

"How's old Gordon?" the Brit asked the American.

"Son of a bitch's still taking 'em on two at a time every day. He gets one with a tight pussy and one that gives good head and takes 'em both upstairs. Sixty-five years old. The son of a bitch is amazing." I knew Gordon; he was an Australian who had forsaken booze because of a heart condition, and had become addicted to sex instead. He was in great shape and very dapper in white shorts and knee socks and a white shirt.

Back at the hotel I worked on my notes for a while, and then went down to breakfast. No point calling anybody before nine-thirty. Some would consider it rude even to try. I went back upstairs, made five telephone calls and struck out five times. Seventeen minutes. I never got through a day's work so fast in my life.

I looked through the window and sighed, then checked my other set of gear, trunks, towel, lotion, flip-flops.

At the conclusion of tanning activities that afternoon, I returned to find a note to the effect that Lt. Gen. Tenchai Sirisumphan, the originator of Thai Special Forces, had agreed to give me an interview that Friday, two days away. Thank God. It wasn't an action story, but General Tenchai had one of the greatest names in counterinsurgency; an interview with him was a real coup.

As soon as I got to my room the phone rang. It was Coyne. His friend, General Pichitr, had cleared us to go to Surat Thani, down south in the peninsula where the Royal Thai Army was battling guerrillas of the Communist Party of Malaysia. Great!

Now we were lined up for two good stories, only I didn't want to leave for Surat Thani until after the interview, which was still three days away.

Blam! Blam! Two knocks on the door. When I opened it, Colonel George Goetzke, Chief of the Army section of JUS-MAG Thai, turned his shoulders sideways to enter the room. Goetzke was a huge man, blond, with a crewcut and G.I. glasses. He wore jungle fatigues, with both U.S. and Thai master parachutist wings. To avoid frightening normal people, Goetzke had cultivated a pleasant expression and a soft, soothing tone of voice. "You and Coyne are making the Mitrapab jump Saturday," he said. "You'll fly into Haad-Yai on a Thai C-130 Friday."

Friday, that was my interview. Jesus! But I really wanted to make that jump. Not only was it a good story, but we'd be awarded Thai wings, the most gorgeous military decoration known to man. I had coveted a pair for twenty years.

Col. Goetzke went to the map of Thailand taped to my wall. Haad-Yai was way down south on the peninsula, in Muslim country, almost in Malaysia. Insurgent country. I'd have to try to postpone with General Tenchai.

"You want to join us for a drink downstairs?" Goetzke asked.

"Yessir, I've got to make a couple of phone calls first."

The "us" he wanted me to join was the U.S. Special Forces Advisory detachment from Korea, here for the jump; the crew of their U.S. C-130; and Col. George Marechek, now operations officer of the Green Beret headquarters at Fort Bragg, former commander of U.S. Special Forces, Thailand, when there was such a thing. Indeed I would be delighted, be crazy not to.

I got General Tenchai on the phone. He understood. Certainly we could do it later. When? Oh, week after next, maybe the week after that.

I called Coyne and told him about the jump. "We've got two days before we go to Haad-Yai. You want to go to Surat Thani tomorrow so we can get it in before the jump?"

He actually laughed.

The next morning at eleven we were at the pool. No sense rushing things. Over on the other side of the pool, on a chaise on the grass, a young American groped the tawny thing in the wet bikini beside him. The several couples around them paid not the slightest attention. Directly across from us a German hausfrau, who strongly resembled a boiled Alex Karras, also in a bikini, doused herself with lotion. She had a great-looking redheaded daughter, also boiled, and unfortunately, what appeared to be a son-in-law as well.

From our right I caught a snatch of conversation from two men, one a businessman in a size 44 swimsuit, the other a rough type in a safari outfit.

"As I see it," said the businessman, "he has two choices. He can either be silent or be silenced. This must be made clear to him."

Sunlight shimmered as the blue water of the pool dappled and rippled, making instant little troughs and valleys, forming and vanishing in an ever-changing, never-repeating pattern. It was marvelously soothing.

11
BUDDHA ON THE DROP ZONE

Our first clue that all was not wonderful came when somebody said, "Helmet," and I realized neither Coyne nor I had one. We were in a hotel coffee shop in Haadyai (or Haad-Yai, Hadyai, Hatyai or Haatyai, Thailand, depending on which sign you read). The restaurant had been done in a Moorish motif, appropriate since Hatyai was Muslim country. Under an awning in a white Moorish arcade, parachutists sat around us in a strange assortment of gear: fatigue uniforms, skydiver suits, coveralls, jogging outfits.

Coyne and I wore the tiger-striped camouflage fatigues that were sometimes our work clothes. Since we were going to be jumping MC 1-1s, a military parachute, out of a Royal Thai Air Force C-123, we had, in our own minds, classified this as a troop jump, and the helmet as something we should be issued.

Coyne was deep in breakfast-table conversation.

I immediately sprang up and went to the next table. "Anybody got an extra helmet?" Col. Goetzke, a bull with a crewcut looked up.

He was a skydiver with 1,600 jumps. Beside him sat Major Mark Smith, cocky little wiseass commander of the Special Forces advisory detachment in Korea. Smith had the distinguished Service Cross, and had been a POW for 364 days. He boasted of being the only field-grade high school dropout in the U.S. Army.

Another jumper was a young, olive-complexioned guy with coal-black hair. He wore a bright red camouflage suit, which would fit into no known background on this planet. Next to him sat a beautiful, very blonde, very pregnant lady in blue jeans. The guy in the Martian cammies immediately reached down into his kit bag and pulled out a gleaming white Bell helmet. "Just happen to have one here."

"When you go jumping it's customary to bring a helmet," Goetzke muttered, his eyes over a coffee cup inspecting me for signs of mental incompetence.

"Where'd ya get the red cammies?" I asked my benefactor, hoping to make somebody else look dumber than I did.

He grinned. "Maid washed 'em in Clorox," he said.

I thanked him for the helmet and went back to our table, where Coyne was deep in conversation with two men; Jack Phillips, a retired Special Forces lieutenant colonel who had spent his last six years in the Army in Thailand, learned to speak and write Thai fluently, and stayed on as an oil company exec, and Jack's friend, later identified as Dr. Sivavudh Devahastin Ayudha, advisor to the deputy prime minister for economics. His Ph.D. is from Claremont College in Orange County, California.

"This first time you make jump?" Coyne asked him, speaking slowly and carefully.

"Yes," said Dr. Sivavudh, "it's something I've wanted to do for a long time, but I only recently made the decision to proceed."

"You better get yourself a helmet," I said to Coyne, as I sat down.

He gave me a look of annoyance, since I had procured only one and kept it for myself.

"There's bound to be one on the flight line," he said, and went back to his conversation.

This part of Thailand is on the southern peninsula, which had not one but two insurgencies going at the same time, one from the Communist Party of Thailand, theoretically backed by the Chinese, although the Chinese had largely pulled the plug on them, and the other from PULO (Pattani United Liberation Organization), a Muslim separatist group, mainly trained and supplied by Libya.

For that reason the jump we were making was in every sense operational. It was part of a joint Thai-U.S. Civic Action project to build a school at Tambon Pang La, Sadao District, Songkhla Province, the 230th such school financed by the Mitrapab (Friendship) Educational Foundation in the 21 years of its existence, all paid for by selling tickets to jumps like this one.

What made the program significant was that it was a valuable tool for national stability; what made this jump possibly significant was that it was the first to be made from U.S. aircraft since the United States pulled out six years before. Maybe it signified closer military cooperation between the U.S. and Thailand; maybe it only meant that Mark Smith, his team, and the Air Force flight crew had wrangled a free trip to Thailand, a Hollywood jump, and ten days *per diem* from the U.S. government.

Mitrapab began in 1961 on a field training exercise near a village called Ban Yang. During a sudden tropical downpour, Lt. Col. Prathip and his counterpart, a Capt. Carver, took shelter in a nearby one-room schoolhouse. To their surprise there was just about as much rain inside as outside. It was a mystery to both of them how any learning could take place there during the rainy season.

They decided to get a bunch of their jump buddies together, put on a demonstration, and charge admission. They hoped to raise enough money for a new schoolhouse.

There's not much to do in a Thai village on a Sunday afternoon. The night before, some villagers had walked a block and half to watch me eat noodles in a restaurant; what would they give to see a whole flock of Thai and *farang* paratroopers falling through the air under clouds of bright nylon?

At the Haad-Yai Airport, Coyne and I went our separate ways, I to shoot pictures of pre-jump activities, he to scrounge a helmet, which after much cursing and not a little apprehension, he did.

It's natural to be scared on a jump, and paratroopers have a number of rituals to minimize that. But they have to be done right. Nothing builds confidence less than getting the MACO (marshaling area control officer) briefing in a foreign language. Even so, the Thai major who served as MACO had an excellent chart of the DZ (drop zone); it wasn't that hard to follow, the symbols and numbers were the same as ours, even if the alphabet wasn't.

Col. Goetzke came up and said, "Coyne just told me he's never jumped a steerable before. Tell him how it works, will you, so he won't land in Malaysia."

"Okay, sir," I said. No problem there, a steerable is the easiest thing in the world to operate.

"Face into the wind and hold at 150 feet no matter what," he shouted over his shoulder as he walked away.

Oh, yeah, I forgot.

Stateside, as a safety factor, the army requires paratroopers to take a day of refresher training before a jump if they've been off airborne status for as little as six months. This was Coyne's first jump in sixteen years. If I had realized that, I'd have had him doing PLFs (parachute landing falls) off the dresser in his hotel room. It wouldn't have hurt me to do a few either. I hadn't jumped in two years.

Glen Gamble, a former U.S. Army captain, vice president

of the Mitrapab Foundation, had organized this jump. He was geared out with a jumpsuit but walking with a limp.

"You gonna jump on that?"

"Yeah, it's twisted a little. The ankle's wrapped so tight it won't bend, that's all."

I didn't say anything. It was his ankle, his ass for that matter.

If you haven't jumped in a long time you forget too many things. Before chuting up I put my notebook and pen in my left breast pocket, which turned out to be a mistake.

Finally everything was ready; everybody chuted up, rigger checked, standing around hunkered over, bound up tight in seventy-five pounds of parachutes, in loose formation, watching the airplane sit on the runway, showing no sign of going anywhere. I sighed, about to do this thing that had been the greatest joy of my young life. This was about the hundredth time I had done this exact same thing, in almost exactly the same way.

Mark Smith, bound in his heavy gear, waddled up from behind and slapped me on the shoulder. "What are you thinking?" he asked.

"I'd like to do something for the first time again," I said. "It's been about twenty years since I did anything this much fun for the first time."

The loadmaster waved us aboard for the 50-klick flight to Tambon Pang La.

Five minutes after we took off, seated in red nylon bench seats along the side of the aircraft, Goetzke stood and took the jumpmaster position by the tailgate. He lifted his arm and blew across the face of his watch, then held up three fingers, the sign for a three-knot wind.

On the first pass, Mark Smith was to jump with the Thai flag, while a Thai colonel jumped with an American flag from the other aircraft, a U.S. C-130. From a journalistic standpoint, either Coyne or I should have been on the ground to photograph this moment, but screw it, we were both paratroopers long before we became journalists. Neither of us would pass up this jump for a couple of lousy photographs.

Smith stood crouched in the door for a long time, his static line whipping in the windstream, and then the green light flashed. Presto, he disappeared.

The first stick of jumpers was made up primarily of petite lady parachute riggers from the Royal Thai Army, in cute gold and black jumpsuits and oversize white helmets. They were the only demure parachutists I have ever seen. Then it was our turn.

As we stood hanging onto our static lines like New Yorkers on the rush-hour subway, I was surprised that I had none of the usual pre-jump flutters, no frantic gulping for air, no butterflies in the stomach. That *really* frightened me. This was a Hollywood jump, no rifle, no pack, no 120 pounds of gear in a griswold bag, and it was from a skydiver's altitude, 3,000 feet, as opposed to the 1,000 from which paratroopers drop, which meant that in the event of a malfunction we'd have a generous thirty seconds to repair the damage, instead of nine, but there is no such thing as a casual parachute jump.

When it goes it goes like a freight train. Quickly, one by one, the jumpers ahead disappeared as their static lines went taut from the anchor line cable to the door. Then I had both hands in the door, one toe over the edge, hundred and thirty-knot wind in my face, a glimpse of blue sky, wispy clouds, a rice paddy in the lower third of my vision. Go!

Up and out, feet together, hands on the reserve, but my elbows weren't in right and the prop blast turned me face to earth as I felt the tug at my back that pulled my trash out. It billowed and inflated, stopping me rather abruptly in mid-air.

No sweat, maybe one twist in the lines. I kicked it out as the sound of the airplane droned away and I was left alone in a clear blue sky.

Then I heard Coyne's eerie cackle as the olive-drab hemisphere of his chute drifted under my feet. Below I could see paddies, some kind of off-the-wall industrial plant, not a sign of a DZ.

Swinging under my olive-green canopy, turned blazing lime by the sun behind it, I pulled the toggle on my right riser, turned right, swinging out, and ran with the wind. There it was, maybe two-fifths of a mile ahead, 2,500 feet below, a great scar of earth with a canopied reviewing stand, right center on a rectangle about the size of six football fields, little dots of people all over it, coming toward me with a velocity more appropriate to a balloon race than a jump.

I looked for grenade smoke on the ground to mark the wind direction, but instead there was a smoking brush fire. The smoke was flat to the ground and streaming. This was no three-knot wind; more like thirty. I turned and held, even though I was still at 1,200 to 1,500 feet. This rig should have about a 10-knot forward speed, and I was still going backwards at a good clip. Even so, from where I had turned I should come in pretty close to the skydiver's target.

Time to take some pix. Only, whenever I took my hands off the toggles to shoot my wrist-mounted camera, the wind turned me around to run with it. All my shots were only half-aimed, and I was blown way off course and way over the target, over halfway to the far edge of the DZ.

Fuck photography! I turned and held, still moving like I had driven a motorcycle off a second-floor ramp, backwards. I cursed every ounce of the eight pounds of Singha Beer and restaurant food I had put on since Boulder, knowing from previous unhappy landings that it could make the difference between an okay fall and hitting two sides of a garbage compactor. I got my feet and knees together and my toes involuntarily curled upward. I held, caught one glimpse of the earth racing in a streaming blur backwards beneath my feet, then locked my eyes fixedly on the horizon while my entire reproductive apparatus withdrew into the perineum cavity, for I did not want what I knew was coming.

SLAM! I felt something snap in my chest. It felt like I'd been speared; intense pain spread from a point near the heart. Compared to that the bashing my thigh and back took as I completed my PLF—a maneuver sort of like turning oneself into one rocker of a rocking chair, bent over, feet and knees together, elbows in to the sides, hands on the chest pack reserve parachute—was as nothing. Good training pays off again. I tried to move around and encountered no difficulty. But the pain in my heart was incredible. I got to my feet and pulled the quick release on my bellyband. Seven Thai kids already grabbed and collapsed my chute. They and I took it off.

I withdrew the notebook and pen from my breast pocket. I had been stabbed; what snapped was the spine of my notebook. If I could still breathe this easily no ribs were broken, but I had bruised them badly.

A 10-year-old girl in a scout uniform came up and extended a tray filled with cold glasses of ice water, easily the nicest thing which has ever happened to me on a drop zone.

"Thanks!" I grinned like an idiot to excuse my inability to exchange pleasantries.

Airborne pride made me take my kit bag, filled with seventy-five pounds of main and reserve parachute, from the Thai kids, and lug it to the turn-in point myself.

"Congratulations!" Mark Smith yelled at me as we came in. "You're one of six people who hit the DZ."

"Where's Coyne?"

He pointed. Mekong Jimmy stood two hundred feet away, in front of the reviewing stand, shooting photos, laughing. "I did a perfect PLF right in front of the reviewing stand," he said.

Were I a more generous-spirited man, this news would have pleased me, but it did not.

Glen Gamble turned too low and augered in. He broke an arm and his pelvis. The next day they put him on the airplane on a stretcher, moving very carefully. At every abrupt movement he clenched his teeth and his body tensed, but he said nothing. He did not look happy.

One of the Thais broke his pelvis also.

Dr. Sivavudh landed in the trees a long way from the DZ, but he was okay. He came in grinning, talking real fast about his next jump, about maybe getting into freefall. We all smiled, remembering our own first ones.

As we came off the DZ, we were led under the saffron canopy over the reviewing stand, before an ancient, wizened, saffron-robed and shaven-headed Buddhist monk. His look was enigmatic, but amusement and compassion were in his eyes. As I knelt before him, he placed a medal of the Buddha around my neck, hanging from a saffron ribbon.

12
KHAO
KOR

Being in Thailand gave me an opportunity to work with Thai Special Forces, something I had wanted to do for a long time. An assignment to the U.S. 46th Special Forces Company, which had advised Thai Special Forces before the American pullout, had been one of the most coveted in the Green Berets, one that I never achieved.

Thailand was especially fascinating to me because it was so close to Vietnam. The nature of the threat was similar, and yet the Thais had survived and the Vietnamese had not. I wanted to lay Mao's principles, and my own experiences and conclusions, over the Thai situation and see how it varied from the Vietnamese experience.

Toward that end I asked Colonel Rut Komalvanich at the Royal Thai Special Warfare Center to set it up for me to visit an active Special Forces group. He was happy to oblige and sent me to the Fourth Group at Pitsanulok.

The country on either side of the car looked like the Central Highlands of Vietnam. Exactly like the Highlands. Green hills stretched off into green mountains in the distance. Fields close to the road were cut short for dry rice farming, and on the other side of the fields stood ranked rows of thatch-roofed houses on stilts. Occasional clumps of stooped brown people in tribal dress, baskets on their backs or handmade hoes on their shoulders, shuffled along the side of the road. They grinned blasted betel nut smiles as we drove past.

Eighteen years before, such a scene would have been an everyday thing. But this was Thailand in the '80s, not Vietnam in the '60s. The road ahead was a curving ribbon of new blacktop, and our vehicle a pale green '78 Valiant with the Beatles' *Good Day Sunshine* blasting from the radio.

An RTA motor pool sticker on the dashboard and a locked and loaded CAR-15 that leaned against the bench seat between me and the driver, Colonel Udom Ketprom, were other reminders of the old life. We were on our way to visit one of his "A" detachments, deep in what had recently been terrorist country, a place called Khao Kor.

Udom, slender and wiry, with a tough but good-humored face, idly bopping the steering wheel with the heel of his hand to the beat of Ringo's drums, wasn't dressed like a colonel. He wore matched faded denim pants and shirt, slick white loafers and a golf hat. I had been amazed when he came out dressed like that this morning. "Not good wear camouflage if draw fire," he replied sensibly when I asked him about it.

When the U.S. pulled its large advisory force out of Thailand in 1976, at the Thais' request, it was widely believed that Thailand would be the next domino to fall, after Laos and Cambodia. This never happened.

Thai Special Forces has basically the same mission as

ours: to organize, train, and direct indigenous forces in the conduct of guerrilla operations, with a secondary mission of organizing counterguerrilla operations. Their public success has been in the latter. They are quite willing to express gratitude for the help of the U.S. Special Forces in getting started, but their success has equaled, and in many cases, surpassed ours.

They may have run guerrilla missions in Laos and Cambodia, but if so, they don't admit it.

By now it should have occurred to our deep thinkers in the Pentagon that those of our client states who have succeeded against the "War of National Liberation" strategy have, at some point, had to do so on their own. Many examples come to mind; Guatemala, Venezuela, Bolivia, but the most striking is Thailand, which squelched not one, but three insurgencies simultaneously. They used principles learned from the now-departed Americans, animated by a peculiar genius of their own.

The day before, reviewing a graduation parade for a company of black-uniformed paramilitary rangers who had been trained by his group, the Fourth, he invited me to join him on the reviewing stand, with a three-star general and the inevitable saffron-robed Buddhist monk.

In Thailand, where our advisors had pulled out in 1976, the people who knew the Americans best are now colonels and generals. If you turn up as an ex-G.I. and correspondent for a U.S. military magazine, you find yourself hanging out with important people.

This means you get the VIP tour, which has its good points and bad points. You see things it would be very hard to see otherwise, and you usually have the situation explained by the most savvy person around. On the other hand, nobody wants you to get shot at on a VIP tour. It's difficult to explain to a man who's giving you the best he's got that your real job is to sleep in the rain like a dog and try as hard as possible to shoot and get shot at.

The new rangers looked very sharp as they goose-stepped

past the reviewing stand. The Thais have had German as well as American military training, and they have learned a type of precision that we never attempted to teach in Vietnam.

Later we went over to his little "O" Club for a beer. He was delighted by a visit from a former American Special Forces person. We knew a couple of people in common, including Larry Dring, who had done a tour there.

As a young lieutenant, almost twenty years before, Udom had been executive officer of a joint U.S.-Thai "A" detachment. His best memory of that experience was a night HALO jump. Twelve of them, six Americans and six Thais, had spun off the tailgate of a C-130 at 30,000 feet, at night, on oxygen, and fallen at 125 miles per hour for two minutes, straight down into the darkness. Then they deployed their parachutes. This is a way to get in under radar.

Another reason Udom was glad to see me was that he had been working twelve-hour days for more than two weeks straight, and protocol demanded that he knock off and show me the sights.

When we got to town he took me to the temple of the Golden Buddha of Pitsanulok. Almost a thousand years old, this Buddha was the premier attraction of the town. The ancient temple lacked the jukebox look of Thailand's newer *wats.* The reverence of the common people kneeling before the Buddha, the incense, the great gold Buddha itself, gazing with transcendent compassion out over the open interior of the temple, filled me with deep respect.

This Buddha was a most potent defense against communism; people need it to give their lives meaning, and the Communists don't have anything like it.

Udom invited me to his favorite restaurant for a few beers and some dinner. We drove across a bridge and down along the river. Across the wide, flat expanse of red-brown water was a fair-sized town of maybe 100,000 to 150,000. A few modern buildings shot up out of the jungle maze of Thailand, but most of the city was unpainted grey wooden houses on stilts. The city was clean, people appeared well-fed, and a big smile was the most common expression.

He braked to a stop along the river and we walked down a long wooden gangway to a little, flaking-green wooden houseboat restaurant bobbing at the edge of the water. In my memory it has a rusty Coca-Cola sign on its side, but maybe that was the one in Louisiana.

We bounced down the gangway and across the swaying deck, taking seats on folding chairs, beside the water. The river was wide and beautiful, lined with palms and banana trees on either side. A few small boats plied the river, narrow and graceful with upturned bows and sterns, piled high with wicker baskets of fish or fruit. The boatmen stood and poled, their faces shielded by conical straw hats. A goodly breeze blew across the river.

The waiter brought us two huge bottles of Kloster beer and a tray of tiny green peppers. I have been known to munch hot peppers like popcorn, peppers so hot that other Americans can't smell them without crying. People have tried to ambush me with hot peppers from Mexico to Lebanon. It's my one macho trick.

"Hot, very hot," said Udom.

I smiled condescendingly and popped a couple of them into my mouth.

Pain, very intense pain, raced along the blood vessels on the underside of my tongue. Tears sprang to my eyes and the lingering traces of a sinus condition disappeared instantly; the top of my head felt as though a stake had been driven through it. I immediately chugalugged half a quart of beer.

Udom carefully controlled his smile.

I finished that beer and half another before I could talk again.

I asked him how long he had been in the army, and he said twenty years. I asked him how long he had been in Special Forces and he said twenty years. Score one for the Thais. The U.S. Army had consistently refused to make SF an officer's career field. I asked how long he had been in Pitsanulok and he said he was born there. Score another one for the Thais. They seemed to have learned not only from our successes, but from our mistakes as well.

Just as Mao's model for revolutionary warfare is organized in three sets of threes, counterinsurgents also use a three-pronged strategy; military operations to combat the enemy, civic action, as it is called—the use of army assets to build roads, dig wells, treat illnesses, and other actions to win the support of the people—and a public-relations campaign to spread the word that this is going on. Obviously being a hometown boy is a big help in such an effort.

There was no way a Green Beret could have arranged to be born in Pleiku, but it was powerfully discouraging to spend months building up that rapport without which it is impossible to operate effectively with paramilitary troops, or to build a good intelligence net among the local tribes, only to be pulled out on the eve of major success because of the army's personnel rotation policy.

This dedicated man sat at ease in his favorite restaurant, but his lines were out everywhere. He knew the people; he knew the country, and he knew his stuff. For the Communist terrorists to try muscling in on his territory was like a cat trying to scratch its way inside a bowling ball.

The restaurant owner, a high school classmate of Udom's, brought our food. He was a laughing man, wiry and strong. He introduced himself as Sam Long.

Our dinner was hot seafood soup. I dug my spoon in, and out came a little squid, tentacles dangling four inches down from the spoon. Its beady little dead eyes stared past. I mashed the tentacles off on the side of the bowl and swallowed him. He was delicious, but very hot. It required several more beers to get through the meal. The pleasant afternoon turned into a long crazy night.

We were halfway to Khao Kor the next morning before my brain engaged.

Khao Kor had been a Communist Party of Thailand guerrilla base area, a region of thickly jungled mountains, very difficult to probe. General Pichitr (pronounced peach-it) Kullivanijaya had elected not to probe it. He dozed it off. He lashed logs around the Cat operators for protection and ran operations up to battalion-size around them. "A year from now we'll be putting up hotels and schools," one of his officers had said. Now it was a year later and we were going back for the victory celebration.

Colonel Udom's Fourth Group had provided reconnaissance elements for the initial operation. Some of his "A" detachments were now deployed in a role very similar to the Strategic Hamlet program in Vietnam, developing hilltribe villages and dry rice farming on mountains that had hidden hundreds of guerrillas. Many of those guerrillas were still hidden in the mountains around, and they seriously didn't want those villages to succeed.

When we arrived at the Khao Kor headquarters there were no hotels in evidence yet, but there was a terrific-looking school, which had been let out for the occasion.

There was a raw frontier quality about the place. The headquarters building was sheet tin and there was an awful lot of red dirt and earth-moving equipment. Two green and white agriculture department Bell Jetrangers were tied down across the road below.

Udom had to go immediately into the headquarters for a briefing conducted in Thai; I elected to nose around outside. There were a few TV crews and print reporters from the Thai press there for the occasion.

Udom wasn't the only one in jeans, but a lot of it wasn't jean cut. I saw one denim business suit. I was at a loss to understand it, and there was no one to explain it to me.

Another chopper came in, an army Huey, and out jumped General Pichitr in a denim safari suit, and Jim Coyne in a khaki safari suit similar to my own.

I shook hands with General Pete, his West Point nickname, and he disappeared into the briefing.

Coyne and I strolled down the raw, red road, past the earth-moving equipment. "How come everybody's in jeans around here?" I asked.

"This operation was run by a joint command that is strictly a Thai innovation," he replied. "CPMU 1617, Civil-Police-Military Unit. Everybody was under General Pete, the Ag department, the Border Police, everybody. He thought the people in the headquarters ought to have the same uniform, and he hit on the idea of putting everybody in jeans."

I grinned. "He unifies his command and at the same time makes his staff identify with the people."

Coyne lit a cigarette and took a deep overhand drag. "Pichitr is an authentic military genius. When I was up here last year the German military attache was along and we were up on this mountain, looking down on this whole brilliant operation, which was like nothing anybody else had ever done. This goddamn German was simply overcome with admiration. He grabbed Pichitr and hugged him and exclaimed, 'You . . . you're another Hitler!'

"Then he gave me a kind of sheepish look and said, 'You know what I mean.' "

"Did you know what he meant?"

"No!"

After the ceremonies and congratulations were over, and the last helicopter had taken off, Udom took me out to visit one of his "A" detachments. Split into four sites, each on a mountaintop, all within sight of at least one other, each separate site detachment had one company of paramilitary rangers, and each company provided security for a large hilltribe village. We toured a couple of these. The villages were much like Montagnard villages in Vietnam, with the houses off the ground on poles, except that they were single-family dwellings, and instead of thatch they were roofed with sheet tin.

We paused to visit with one family sitting on the porch of

their house. In Vietnamese Montagnard villages, Vietnamese officers had not been welcome. The people clammed up and averted their eyes. The man of this family, strongly muscled and obviously delighted to see the Thai team ser-geant who was taking me and Udom around, grinned around his crooked pipe. His wife held up a fat healthy baby for us to tickle and cluck over.

The houses were laid out in neat rows and the rice fields around were beginning to show a crop.

We left that site and headed for the one under direct control of the "A" detachment commander.

Udom pointed out the tallest mountain in the area as we drove. "Khao Kor," he said, "mean Grandfather Mountain. I lose twenty men on Khao Kor. Recon." His face was stoic, but I looked deep in his eyes and saw that he was prey to the worst occupational hazard of the combat infantry, grief.

The new two-lane blacktop highway ran right up to the villages, tangible evidence to the villagers of their government's concern. It caused me to flash back almost twenty years to the South Vietnamese officer in our province who defected to the VC rather than do Civic Action among the "filthy Montagnards," to the district chiefs who had kept their areas in a constant state of turmoil, because every time a family was relocated it was allocated 1000 piastres in USAID money (about $10.00) and the district chief was pocketing 800 of it.

The Thais aren't like that. They are very smart people, they have guts to spare, and they love their country.

The road to the last camp stopped at the bottom of the hill. We left our car and walked to the camp. When we reached the crest we turned and looked back at the hills, and the village we had come from, the black ribbon of road leading to it, and a small local security patrol that crossed an open area at the foot of the hill.

Further up the hill was a wonderfully laid-out mini-A camp, with an excellent defensive perimeter and neat thatch-roofed rattan buildings. The camp was immaculate. The young CO reported in jeans and a white T-shirt. He was Captain Sootom Sriklon, about 5'10", maybe 180 pounds, a big man for a Thai.

He took us on a brief tour of the camp, and I asked, if possible, to accompany his troops on a local security patrol.

They readily agreed, but it didn't turn out exactly as I expected. I can imagine what the sergeant's instructions to the patrol were when he got the men in the hootch. "All right, men, this is for a big-time international magazine, so wear your best uniform. I want everything to go perfectly. That's the Group Commander out there, so whatever you do, don't fuck up! And act natural."

He had a squad fallen out five minutes after I made my request. They looked good. The sergeant was sharp, calm and serious. The point man looked a trifle addled, but they all do. There were a couple of kids among them, one looked very earnest and watched the older guys to see whether he was doing it right. The other kid was a cocky little shit, the kind who makes a champion warrior, if he lives long enough. He let the corner of his mouth smirk when I took his picture, looking hard over his weapon.

We moved into the woods on a short patrol. There was no noise and no grabass. The troops kept their interval and watched the patrol leader's hand and arm signals. Each one had an assigned area to watch and kept alert. When the leader held up his hand everybody stopped without bunching up. When he pushed his hand down they went into a low squat, their weapons ready. They were supposed to be paramilitary troops, but they moved very professionally.

The one thing that sticks in my mind the most about that trip was a casual remark by the "A" detachment commander. "Well, Captain," I said, "you've built yourself a pretty nice little empire here."

The young captain gave me a reproachful look. "Is not for me," he said. "Is for the people."

13
AVERAGE
DAYS

In Thailand, with the jungle and Vietnam so close, I began dreaming about my days in Special Forces; not the bad days, not days when I had done something especially brave and/or stupid, the days on which I got shot. I had already come to terms with those memories in dreams, and they didn't haunt me anymore.

There were a couple of other recurring dreams I'd been dreaming for years. In the first I was in an alley in Saigon, in the present day, with the city under the NVA. I was in an alley, unarmed, in a tiger suit, with my Caucasian face, running and hiding. In the other recurring dream, I was sitting next to a bunch of Yards camped in the jungle. They wore rags, and carried old weapons. They were eating a meager dinner, and they were thin and grim. I knew they were FULRO, and I knew they were still fighting the Vietnamese, but I wasn't armed and they couldn't see me. I was like a ghost.

I wondered whether there was anything to astral projection. I was sure I wasn't the only guy dreaming that dream, and I wondered whether they could feel that we were still with them, that we were now the *yang* of the forest, lying in our beds in the States with our souls still roaming the jungle.

But here in Bangkok I was dreaming about average days, the ones that stuck in memory as everyday life. It was some life.

Once, after I got out of the Army, I visited my friend Tom Kiernan, who had done two tours with the Forces and one with MACV as an advisor. We were spending an evening with some of his law school classmates, shooting the breeze, telling a few stories.

One of his classmates mentioned that Tom had two Silver Stars. I hadn't known that, so he must have earned them with MACV. "How in the hell did you get two Silver Stars?" I asked. The only guy I knew with two Silver Stars was Larry Dring, and the stories of what he had done to earn them made my hair stand on end. But criteria for those medals vary from unit to unit.

"You remember what an average day was like in Special Forces?" Tom replied.

"Yeah, sure."

"We had two days like that."

I dreamed of average days.

In early 1964, in the northern part of Phu Bon province, the VC weren't active within a day's march of our camp, and we made no contact the first day. We made camp beside a stream, close to a Bahnar Montagnard cornfield and banana grove, and slept all night under a creaking bamboo tree. The next morning we were up and off early.

Our Jarai Montagnards shuffled noisily through large dry leaves, called elephant ears, which lay under the trees. I halted the company and told Kpa Doh, our interpreter, to have them quit kicking the leaves. This was very early in the war and most of our equipment was WWII stuff. A couple of months later we got the first M-79s and AR-15s, issued on an experimental basis.

But even then we were the most heavily armed force in these woods, eighty-five Yards with M-1 carbines, one hand-held sixty-millimeter mortar, and four Americans with M-2 automatic carbines.

That early in the war the most we could expect to encounter was a squad of VC-controlled Bahnar Montagnards with maybe one automatic weapon between them. But they'd be gunning for the Americans. We were obvious targets, and there was a price on our heads. It was only about twenty-five bucks, but that was big money in the Central Highlands. The Special Forces "A" teams were losing about eight percent a year killed in action at that point.

Our Yards expected to frighten the VC away by making a lot of noise. I didn't want to frighten them; I wanted to kill them.

It took three more halts to get them to quit shuffling through the leaves, but finally they moved silently.

We were in unusually open terrain for Vietnam. We were able to keep on the trails, with flank security in sight, and still make good time.

Since we had no fixed objective, but were just out looking for a fight, and since, if we found one it was likely to be us getting ambushed, we had devised a combat formation that consisted of three parallel columns, each platoon with three files of one squad each, abreast, about twenty meters apart. If they ambushed us from close to the trail, we already had a squad behind them. If they ambushed from further back, we could lay down a base of fire and flank them easily. For that terrain, and with those troops, it was a great formation.

We found one bare footprint and spent the rest of the morning running down that trail, finally coming into a valley surrounded on three sides by low, forested mountains. A pretty little stream came down through a cut in the hills to the right.

I spread the company out in a skirmish line and we went through the valley looking for the owner of that bare footprint. We found a small Bahnar village clustered under tall trees. They had individual family houses instead of the multiple-family longhouses of our Jarai. But, like Jarai houses, they were up on log-size stilts, with the same rattan porches in front, and a notched log leaned against the porch for stairs. Some of their fires were still warm. The villagers had gotten out just ahead of us.

It seemed very likely that they'd send somebody to tell armed VC we were in the area.

Dappled light through the trees made a pleasant, shady place of the village.

I walked over to the nearest house and pulled a handful of thatch out of the roof, then dug around in my pocket for a lighter. I set fire to one end of the clump and shoved it into the roof. "Burn it!" I said, thinking wryly that this was probably the first touch of civilization these people had ever seen.

The concept of operations we were using was to bring the Bahnar into lightly fortified villages along the main highway, and train them to defend themselves against the VC, thus denying access to their food to North Vietnamese passing through the province to become replacements in VC units further south. This concept didn't work, because the Bahnar weren't going to leave their hills no matter what anybody did. But we didn't have a better plan then, although later we did, so we stuck to the old one.

Armies are not precision instruments, and every time they go to work innocent people get hurt.

It was easy to understand why the Bahnar didn't want to leave these hills. Their houses had been built with care, each strip of bamboo split by hand, each of their wicker baskets painstakingly woven by their women, each water gourd grown and fashioned carefully into a dipper.

With the last of the burning clump of thatch, I lit a Parliament, and, with the filter a cool quarter-inch away, watched flame and smoke billow around the fourteen houses in that village.

"Sir, sir," Nay Re, the company commander, called. "We find buffalo, many buffalo." We moved quickly through the woods to an open clearing where the buffalo were boxed in on three sides by low hills. We closed the box on the other side.

They were large peaceful-looking beasts, their enormous grey-black bodies topped by a hump, the weight of their flat-topped, back-curving horns keeping their heads low. This herd most likely was the entire wealth of this village. With these gone and their crops destroyed, maybe, theoretically, they'd be desperate enough to pay attention to our psy-ops messages and leave this backcountry for the strategic hamlets. I had to believe that, but even then it didn't feel right.

I stood with a blade of grass stuck in a corner of my mouth, reached up and cocked back my hat to let the breeze cool my forehead and pushed my shades back up on my nose. Slowly my three Americans arranged themselves beside me and the Yards spread out until we formed a solid wall of armed men. I put my carbine on single shot and carefully took aim at the head of an old cow.

I squeezed off a round and a small red dot appeared in the center of her forehead. She stood there and looked at me stupidly, as though she had been bitten by a mosquito.

The rest of us opened up on the herd. There didn't appear to be any effect. Then they started lowing a little and walking around in circles. We moved in closer.

I put the switch on full auto and moved in on the old cow I had shot first. She looked at me quizzically as I fired a six-round burst into her neck and shoulders. She dropped to her knees and went, "MOOOOOOOO!" blood streaming from a half-dozen holes in her huge slab of a body. I fired another three-round burst into her and something in there must have broken because a great gush of blood came out of the holes in her chest. She rolled over on her side and lay there panting, trying to get some air into her lungs, only they wouldn't hold it anymore. I put a round into her brain and she lay back dead before her head hit the ground.

Now the buffalo were milling faster, lowing louder. One calf tried to run out of the box. I picked her off in mid-stride, went over and fired another round into her brain. Then I changed magazines.

It took about half an hour to kill them all. It was hot work in the sun.

I took a long cool pull from my canteen and lit another cigarette. I allowed the Yards thirty minutes to cut off what meat they wanted from the buffalo. Minutes later they ran by with great red hunks in their hands.

More meat was slung on poles or tied to the backs of their packs where it hung dripping down the canvas and some-times onto the tigerstriped seats of their pants.

Then we spread out again in a skirmish line and combed the entire valley. All we found was an almost dry creek bank with many footprints running down it, and wicker baskets where the Bahnar had dropped them.

"It looks like they went up that creek," I said. "We'll run that out and see what we find."

I moved the company a little way up the creek and stopped in the shade. It was going to be a long climb. The Americans came up and we sat there on the boulders in the middle of the creek, smoking and refilling our canteens. The creek bed was fifteen or twenty feet wide, all grey, worn rocks. Now, in the dry season, the stream only flowed in a foot-wide trickle, and there were many small stagnant pools trapped in little depressions in the rock. All around were abandoned wicker baskets and gourds that the Bahnar had left behind, crushed and broken on the ground. Nay Re, the company commander, and Kpa Doh, the inter-preter, came up and I offered them each a cigarette.

There was one small wicker basket left behind that contained a litter of puppies. Their eyes were barely opened and they tumbled over each other in the basket, small bundles of soft flesh and hair.

"I hope the momma dog comes back," Augie DeLucia, our medic said. "They sure are cute." Augie was a short, blond, good-hearted farm boy, an E-6, and about my age, twenty-five.

"She probably will," I said.

Nay Re saw us pointing and talking about the puppies so he reached in the basket and picked one up. He looked at it for a moment as it squirmed in his hand, then dashed it against the rocks, smiling good-naturedly.

Maybe it was our fault. He'd just helped us kill fifty or sixty animals, but I didn't think of that. To me the difference was self-evident.

"You son of a bitch," I said.

DeLucia became so angry that John Watson, our weapons man, reached out and took his carbine away from him. John was nineteen, a rangy E-5. He looked like a classic frontiersman.

"Now you've broken its back," said George Stogdill, our intel sergeant. "Go on and kill him. But leave the rest of the litter alone," he said.

"Tell Nay Re," I snapped, "that Americans do not kill for fun. Only for food and for enemies."

I was never able to work effectively with Nay Re after that. I couldn't help hating him, maybe because of the killing I'd done myself that day. He knew I disliked him, though he probably never figured out why.

When the break was over we started off again, climbing steadily upward. The grade steepened until finally we were climbing straight up, a hundred feet or more, over dried waterfalls. Craning my neck upward I could see the first platoon stretched out above, clinging to bare rock. And far below, partially obscured by trees, Augie skipped from rock to rock, his rucksack bouncing on his back, carbine gripped in his right hand as he grabbed for rocks with his left. I had to sling my carbine to climb over an outcropping, and for a moment my feet dangled over a sheer, forty-foot drop as I hauled myself over the next shelf.

It took two and a half hours for us to climb to the top. We could see thirty kilometers or more across the valley below. Through binoculars I could make out our forward operational base, a small camp that we had left two days before. Beyond that, six or seven klicks further, the Song Ba snaked its way down toward Cheo Reo. The valley was crisscrossed with Bahnar rice fields.

We went down the reverse slope of the hill and that night made camp beside another stream.

We spent all the next morning moving east up a gradual slope. We had almost crossed the line into Pleiku province and were halfway out of chow anyway, so I gave the order to start looping back toward the FOB. It was either cross that mountain or go back down the same valley we came up, and there was no point in that. Anytime you go back the same way you came you run the risk of ambush.

But going down the steep reverse slope of the mountain after a lunch of cold rice balls and C-ration cookies was not the easy job that walking up the gentle forward slope had been. It was a nearly straight drop down.

The three columns moved parallel to each other, reaching, grabbing for handholds, gradually gathering momentum until we were falling down the hill a foot or two at a time. I swung from tree to tree, feet constantly slipping out from under me, reaching for trees seen from the corner of my eye, sometimes pulling a hand back just in time to avoid grabbing a grey trunk covered with three-inch thorns.

It was a mad scramble to the bottom and when we got there we lay on the ground, except for the security detail, heads cradled on our rucksacks; we panted and smoked and gulped some of our water and smoked some more until finally I just couldn't put it off any longer.

"Okay, saddle up. Let's get out of here."

It was easy walking on the valley floor, and the center of the column couldn't move fast because the flanks guiding on us were slowed by brush. Strolling was pleasant and my mind started to wander. We were on the way home and still hadn't made contact, and I was eager for action.

Behind me Kpa Doh whispered, "Sir! Sir!" and I looked in the direction he was pointing. At first I didn't see anything. Then I walked quietly over to the right flank security squad and peered through the trees. Another village lay open in the sunshine. It appeared deserted. I gave the first and third platoons thirty minutes to move around in an encirclement. While they were getting into position, the second platoon spread into a skirmish line. When the half hour was up we moved into the village.

Ksor Yul, leader of the first platoon, had been a corporal under the French. He watched me curiously out of the corner of his eye. We were still sizing each other up. I liked him very much. His moves were sure and skillful, and his gaze was steady. He was fair to his troops, but allowed them little slack.

The village was empty.

I slung my carbine, propped one foot up on a paddy dike and lit a cigarette. Then I mopped my face with my patrol cap and slapped it back on my head soaked with salty sweat. Waving Re and Kpa Doh over, I dropped my rucksack. The minute my ruck hit the ground the Yards shrugged out of theirs and started hacking down sugarcane with their knives, but the ones on the outer edges still faced outward with their weapons ready.

Kpa Doh and Re hacked off stalks of sugarcane on their way over to where I stood. Kpa Doh got two and gave me one.

"Thanks," I said.

I unsnapped the kaybar knife from my harness suspenders and slowly peeled the outer skin from the cane stalk. "You think Bahnar work in fields now?" I asked.

"Yes, I think maybe so," Kpa Doh replied.

"Maybe they know we here," I said. "But if we burn house they know for sure."

Kpa Doh nodded and told Re what I had said. Re nodded.

"I think maybe we no burn house, then might make contact. Better no burn house, kill VC."

They conferred in their harsh tribal language. "Re think that good idea," Kpa Doh said.

While they nodded again I bit down on the tip of the sugarcane; sweet juice ran down my throat and coarse, tough fibers caught between my teeth.

I glanced at my watch. "Okay, let's form up and get back on the trail. We got a long way to go before dark."

It took too long to get the company squared away. Our formation had gotten scattered in the encirclement. Finally we got back on the trail and marched down the valley toward the creek. It was smooth, easy walking and I had started to enjoy the scenery when a burst of automatic-weapons fire snapped my head around.

I knelt, carbine chattering sixty rounds into the foliage across the river as fast as I could change magazines. It was stupid to waste the ammo, but if we were going to have a firefight I wanted my share. A hard charge of adrenaline blew me straight into another plane of existence, where everything is serene and stands out sharp and brilliant.

They were firing from our left, from maybe thirty meters away. We didn't seem to have taken casualties, so I stood up and gave the hand-and-arm signal for skirmishers. Down the line with the first platoon, I saw John Watson stand up at my signal and give the same command to his troops. The whole company was standing now, as far as I could see. We spread out in one long, thin, straight line.

I shouted, "LET'S GO!" and started moving forward. All up and down the line the Americans moved forward, tall, lonely targets ten meters ahead of their troops. We were all firing, but in my heightened state I couldn't hear. I could see little puffs and the high shiny arc of ejected shells, crystalline in their exactness.

Ksor Yul came up beside me. "Punjis," he said and pointed at the sharpened bamboo stakes hidden in the grass, angled to about fourteen inches, shitsoaked and ready to infect. "Fuck a bunch of punjis," I muttered and promptly took one through the toe of my boot. I couldn't feel it and kicked it away. It went flying off in the grass. "COME ON! COME ON! LET'S GO! LET'S GO!"

Yul looked at me happily and said, *"Oui, mon capitaine."* I knew then that I had passed his test. It was a good feeling, for he was an old soldier and I was a very young one.

"Un groupe traverson la fleuve," I said to Yul and motioned that I wanted one squad to cross the creek and swing back toward the center. We came to very tall grass and thick brush and couldn't see where we were moving. Our forward movement started to bog down. "All right," I yelled, "LET'S ROLL!" and gave the move out hand-and-arm signal.

"Capitaine," Yul said, *"le mortier, le mortier."*

"Huh?" I said. "Oh yeah, you want to mortar in there. Okay, good idea. Go ahead. *OUI! OUI!"*

The mortarman came up, unwrapped the red scarf from his neck and used it as a potholder on the tube of his little 60mm mortar, firing hand-held and getting good accuracy. The mortar is an indirect fire weapon that lobs a shell in a high arc, good for getting to men in holes and behind cover. Crump. . . . . BLAM! Crump. . . . . BLAM! Crump. . . . . BLAM! White puffs of smoke drifted out of the bush across the river.

Before we could get up to get the attack moving again, Augie DeLucia, our medic, and George Stogdill, the intelligence sergeant, ran up panting, their faces smudged and dirty. "They bugged out," George said. "We found a little firing platform on the other side of the creek. It had maybe two or three guys with a submachine gun and a couple of carbines." I hadn't realized that either of them had gone across with the squad I'd sent. Later I found that they had crossed even before I gave the order.

"Any stiffs?" I asked.

"Maybe so," DeLucia said. "There was some blood on the platform. We got one old man took a round through the arm; we gotta get him back. And maybe eight or ten guys with punji wounds. They'll infect fast."

"Yeah, I know," I said. "Got one myself."

"Let me see it."

"Look at that old boy with the wounded arm first. This isn't anything."

He told me to take off my boot while he looked at the old fellow with the arm wound. I watched. It wasn't a bad wound; he was just grazed on the upper arm. But he was almost fifty years old, far too old to be on a combat patrol. We would have to weed these old guys out and put them to work around the camp.

My punji wound was a small puncture between my left big toe and the one next to it. My boot had taken all the damage. Augie put some merthiolate on it, and a Band-Aid.

"That's a Purple Heart for you, sir," he said.

"For that? I've cut myself worse on the edge of a piece of paper."

"The regulation doesn't say how bad. It just says wounds resulting from enemy action."

I didn't argue; I wanted a medal badly. I was afraid the war would soon be over and I'd never get a chance for another one. No matter, I would earn the next three in spades, after the NVA arrived.

Some of the Montagnards with punji wounds did not get off so easily. It took another half hour to bandage them all, and then three of them required help to walk fast enough to keep up.

In the morning when I remembered this dream that had really happened, it occurred to me that I was now about the same age as the old guys I'd wanted to get out of the field and put in administrative jobs. I pushed this thought aside.

14
AT THE HOT L
CHAING RAI

I had been told we'd only be in Thailand for three weeks, and more time than that passed before Brown arrived. Finally he got there, after having been diverted to an air show in Chile. While there he'd concocted a scheme to bomb the main Russian air base in Kabul, Afghanistan, from ultra-light airplanes. None of us even pretended to take him seriously.

Three weeks after his arrival, during which time we accomplished little or nothing, and appeared to be no closer to finishing, I told him flatly that Kathy and I had been married less than a year, and either she came over or I went home. Then I made a serious pitch to bring her over. Why not? She's a terrific administrator, great hostess, good photographer, pretty good writer, and has great charm in social situations, something the rest of us were lacking. He bought it.

When she arrived two weeks later, his welcoming present was a weekend in the Hyatt in Chaing Mai, the northernmost city in Thailand, a beautiful place. But while we were there he also wanted us to buzz on up to Chaing Rai, further north, and make contact with Khun Sa, the so-called "Opium Warlord" and his Shan United Army, to arrange for *SOF* to go into Burma. I figured for Kat it would be a good introduction to our "method"—if that is indeed the term— of operation.

At sunset, three *samlors*, the Thai version of the bicycle-rickshaw, carrying Kat, Chan, and me arrived at our tiny, hidden-away hotel in Chaing Rai, the northernmost city in Thailand large enough to have a hotel. The people we didn't want to know we were there would, theoretically, be staying at the luxurious Wiang Inn on the other side of town.

Dr. Seuss, who had set up the meet, was a stickler for keeping a low profile, so he had chosen this out-of-the-way place. Dr. Seuss was a former CIA spook who had been cashiered for excessive drinking. Now he was off the sauce totally, and worked for Brown very professionally.

But I don't think he ever appreciated the difference between a magazine and an intelligence agency. As a magazine, we couldn't just dazzle each other with bullshit, graphs and charts, endless intelligence reports that never led anywhere. We had to tell stories to sell the magazine and pay for all this. I think Dr. Seuss thought we were a rogue detachment of the CIA, with a weird cover.

The low profile was part of the reason Kat was along. Two men, one a farang, and the other looking like an account executive for a Chinese ad agency, would draw unwholesome attention. "If they're not here to buy dope, jewels, or women, what the hell are they here for?"

But if the redheaded joker is seen to follow a foxy farang lady from jewelry store to jewelry store, then all the Chinese has to do is sit at his favorite cafe, glance at his watch, order a drink, and all is explained.

The diamond-shaped muscles of my *samlor* driver's calves relaxed to a halt. I dismounted awkwardly from the springy rickshaw seat behind his bicycle saddle and escorted Kathy into the lobby, while Chan fumbled for the fare.

Four Orientals sat reading papers in the tiny lobby. "That's Mr. Loy," Chan muttered from behind, as we picked up our bags and headed toward the stairs. "I think they are already here." I muttered a curse, and checked my watch. It was seven o'clock. The deal was that they would show up any time after eight. We had come back this early specifically to avoid this encounter. But it did reveal that they were even more antsy about this than we were.

"Well, so much for your plan not to let them know I'm here," Kat said. I had expected we would be settled into our room when they arrived in town, from whatever torturous route they had followed from Burma. Their mission was theoretically friendly, but they were known to be hard boys, and our liaison was built on a transitory mutual interest; we had no history of friendship or trust. This was the first contact between the *SOF* staff and agents of Khun Sa.

I had wanted to bring Kat on this trip. She'd arrived in Thailand only two days before, after a seven-week separation, and this jaunt into hill tribe country was the best chance I would ever get to show someone I loved why I kept going back to Vietnam. But I didn't want her involved with these people in any way.

The way I had it figured, the opium-growing Shan tribesmen had much to gain and nothing to lose from cooperating with *SOF*, and much to lose and nothing to gain from assassinating a reporter. But I did not want to test this theory on Kathy.

The idea was that Brown, Coyne, Reisinger, and I were going into bandit country to interview Khun Sa; Brown and me for the magazine, Coyne to do video. This was the meeting to set up that trip.

Khun Sa's version of the story was that his organization, the Shan United Army, was a legitimate revolutionary movement, at war with the socialist government of Burma, and that their relationship to the opium trade was roughly analogous to that of the North Carolina National Guard to the tobacco industry. They wanted to use *SOF* as a vehicle to sell this version to world opinion, and also wanted to get a message to the CIA and the DEA that they'd be delighted to get out of the drug business if they could come up with another way to finance their operation.

Of course, there was no chance that Bob Brown's magazine would endorse dope runners.

And the U.S. government, I was quite sure, would not bankroll a revolution against a non-Communist government in Southeast Asia, even if by so doing they could take 60% of the Golden Triangle out of opium production, especially since organized crime could cover the shortfall with purchases from a half dozen other places. Even if, by some magic, Khun Sa could be induced to stack arms, no junkie would miss a fix.

I hoped we could get in, cover the story, and get out before they figured that out.

Kathy and I went upstairs, into our room, locked the door, and flopped down on the twin beds. Kathy returned to her *Newsweek* and I to a bloody fat file on Khun Sa.

I figured Chan would come get me in about a half hour, but that half hour crawled by, then another, then another.

Clouds outside closed off the sun even before it went down, and there were long ripping peals of thunder. Lightning flashed in the mountains. One moment it was dry and still, and then there was rain, as though one enormous bucket was being continuously dashed on the town. Air came into the room, cold, muggy and sodden; heavy enough to make the rice-paper Far East edition of *Newsweek* swell and wrinkle.

Our lights flickered and went out. There was an enormous crash, which was never explained and a peal of hysterical farang laughter from down the hall. It sounded like a lady passenger from the tourist bus, booked here by a greedy and sadistic travel agent in Bangkok.

"I guess that's it for the hill tribes fair," Kat said, lifting her head from her magazine. We had thought we might go see some Yao handicrafts after the meeting.

"At this rate there wouldn't have been enough time anyway." I suppressed a smile at the thought of those poor tourists who had traveled for three hours by bus from Chaing Mai, only to spend the night in the muggy darkness of these spartan quarters, then to ride the same bus back the next day.

We lay on one of the two narrow single beds in the room, talking for a long time, catching up on what had happened to our friends and families after I had left the States.

We talked for more than an hour after the lights went out, and never did mention our friends down the hall. Then there was a knock at our door and I jumped like I'd been stuck with a cattle prod.

Opening the door a crack, I saw Chan's scholarly face, gone all weird over a white flickering candle. "They are ready," he said.

I followed him to the end of the hall, one room down from ours and across. He knocked and the door opened. The tallest Chinese I have ever seen, his face made fierce in the candlelight by a Fu Manchu mustache, looked out. He bowed us in.

Then the lights came back on and it was all changed. There was an untouched basket of green grapes and bananas on the table. They stood and looked at me with a trace of desperation in their manner. There was no threat there.

But they were known killers. I examined their eyes to see what kind of killers they were. The guy on the left was a short man, in his forties, in businessman's slacks, a starched, ironed white shirt, and flip-flops. His smile was genuinely warm and friendly, but there was a hardness in his eyes. This man would not kill unless he had to, but if necessary he would do it as efficiently and unemotionally as he would change the oil in his car.

The one in the middle was the galoot with the Fu Manchu. he was about my height, six-two, maybe 165 pounds. He grinned delightedly, and he was no killer at all. He handled himself like a man who's been in a couple of firefights and done all right, but who really likes the girls and the cafes. He was not a man to be dismissed lightly, however. He would do what was necessary.

Understand, if we went in, we would be completely at these people's mercy for at least four days. I was not giving them the once-over-lightly. Nor was I dealing from limited experience.

The one on the right was an old man in a thin, white, collarless Chinese shirt and grey slacks. He wore the high-topped crewcut I associate with the NVA. He had the face of a man who believed in nothing and would do anything, but he was old and tired.

They were introduced to me as Mr. Lee, Mr. Young, and Mr. Lee. We all shook hands and sat down.

The Mr. Lee on the left, looking very sincere under his straight, swept-back hair, smiled a warm smile and began speaking in a language full of quiet "sch" sounds. Mr. Young translated. "We are very happy that you have taken an interest in our movement. Much has been written about us, but no one has come to see what they are writing about."

I smiled. "To be honest," I said, "I must tell you that our magazine takes a generally favorable view of revolutionary movements against socialist governments, but an unfavorable view of the drug trade. You must expect me to ask hard questions."

Conversation through an interpreter is always difficult, and many shades of meaning are lost in the process. Mr.

Young pondered my statement for a moment before translating for the two Mr. Lees. The elderly gentleman soaked it all in with no sign of response. The younger Mr. Lee pondered the translation of my statement for a moment, then composed a diplomatic reply, which I feel sure Mr. Young further diluted in translation.

"We are glad that you support revolutions against socialist governments. Nobody wants the name of a drug trafficker, but we cannot let the Burmese conquer our homeland."

I nodded. "We know from our study of revolution that no resistance movement in history has succeeded without outside help. We know that no government has offered to help you; your only source of aid has been the opium trade. But most Americans have never heard of the Shan states. All they know is that their families are subject to attack by junkies needing money for dope. What can I tell such a person?"

This was buzzed back and forth for a while, but no satisfactory answer was found.

"Your missus is with you?" he replied, tactfully changing the subject, and almost causing me to jump six inches off the chair.

I hesitated, but they had seen her, and the worst thing I could do at this point was get caught in a lie. "Yes."

"Will she be coming to Burma with you?"

I laughed. "No. I think she likes the city too much for that."

There were smiles all around. Nobody wanted the extra work that having a western woman in the jungle entails.

"Do you think you might like to try a country girl while you are there?"

I laughed again. "No," I said, "but my friends will have to speak for themselves. I will probably have two other people with me, Colonel Brown, our publisher, and Jim Coyne to do television." I handed them Polaroid shots of the three of us. Brown had asked me to get a shot of our SUA contact in case for some reason I didn't come back up with them, but I didn't want to throw them into a fit of worry and doubt about security, so I didn't bring it up.

"Colonel Brown looks much younger than he did on the cover of your magazine," Mr. Young said in English. We had sent two copies of different issues, and as we talked I began to realize that in Mr. Young we had created an instant hard-core *SOF* fan. Before the meeting was over he was pushing hard for a complimentary subscription.

I laughed at his remark about Brown. That cover photo with the Lao resistance was shot after an all-day straight-up-the-mountain climb to their camp. Brown was dead tired and it showed; he looked like a man coming out of the anesthetic after a lobotomy.

"I want to interview your leader," I said, "but there are always leaders. As soon as one is gone another takes his place. You can tell much more about a movement by talking to average soldiers."

"It would take a long time to do that."

I smiled. "Just a few; I don't have to talk to them all."

The younger Mr. Lee spoke earnestly for quite a spell. Mr. Young looked slightly pained as he translated. "This is very hard to arrange. We are all in Burma now. We are on a war footing; we have to change our location constantly. We must have horses for you, and soldiers to guard the route. If we arrange all this you must promise to come."

We had been forced to cancel a previous trip to visit these folks because the Lao resistance was supposed to be bringing two American POWs over the border, and we had made arrangements to be there when they did it. Brown had figured that there was maybe one chance in three that it would happen, but after working on that story for two years we couldn't afford to take the chance that it wouldn't. Of course the POWs didn't come, and we missed our first chance to interview Khun Sa. I explained that we couldn't just wait for them. We had to be free to cover other events.

We finally hammered out a deal whereby they would give

us two weeks notice before they were ready, and we would give them 48 hours notice that we were coming. As I said, they wanted this story.

Toward the end of the conversation, Mr. Young asked me what I knew about their movement. I replied that I had read everything printed about it in the past six months.

"Trash," said Mr. Young without hesitation. "All trash."

My experience with Vietnam, the war in Lebanon, and other stories in which I had been an observer/participant, had given me no reason to reject that claim out of hand.

"We had some reporters come to see us two or three years ago," said the younger Mr. Lee, "but when they left they wrote stories like the others. They called our leader an Opium Warlord. We are hoping that a soldier magazine will tell the truth."

I nodded. "We are soldiers of truth," I said. "I promise to report what I see as fully and accurately as possible.

"But you must understand that to change someone's mind you have to start where they are. I might start my story with a lead like, 'I am not an Opium Warlord, says Khun Sa.'"

"It would be better if you said, 'I am a revolutionary, says Khun Sa,'" said the younger Mr. Lee with a smile. I find it difficult to dislike a quick-witted, humorous man.

There was no use trying to explain to them that no journalist is going to relinquish his "Opium Warlord" story, the term itself is too colorful. If Khun Sa were not an "Opium Warlord," no one outside Burma or Thailand would have heard of him, and I wouldn't be doing the story. There were three other Shan revolutionary armies, but none so colorful. They get no publicity.

The Nationalist Chinese 93rd Division, which went South into Burma in 1949, when the Communists took over China, and muscled into the opium business, occasionally gets a mention, but its circumstances are weird enough to make a good story. The hill tribes of Burma—Shan, Karen, Kachin, Lahu, Wa, all of whom fought with the American

OSS or with the Brits—are in revolt because the Burmese have reneged on the terms under which the tribes joined Burma in the first place, treating the tribes like conquered people. But these conflicts are ignored.

The Karen had a charismatic leader named Bo Mya, who looked like a mahogany Jackie Gleason in British-style fatigues and a green beret, but no one had heard of him in the West—not without a spiffy tag like "Opium Warlord." Khun Sa has as much chance of shaking that description as Ringo Starr has of becoming something other than a "former Beatle."

"We live in a world of misunderstanding," said the humorous Mr. Lee. "I came to speak the truth about our movement, and my wife thinks I have come to Thailand to see the girls."

We all had another good laugh at that.

There was no question that these guys considered themselves the aggrieved party in their dispute with the Thais. "When the Thai Border Police raid our headquarters at Hin Taek," said Mr. Young, with a kind of innocent, injured outrage, "they loot, they smash things, they urinate in the kitchens." I tried to look sympathetic, but it was obvious that he knew nothing about young troops, psyched-up and mean for battle.

The essential business of the meeting taken care of, we relaxed, munched a few grapes and shot the breeze. "Well," said Mr. Lee, "now that you've seen we're not junkies, what do you think?"

"You seem like pretty good guys to me," I said.

"We want to tell the CIA and the DEA that we are ready to get out of the drug business. Is there any way you can help us; can you get the message to them?"

I shrugged. "I know they read the magazine, but I don't know them. I have no way to know how they'll react."

We talked for an hour or so. I was comfortable in their company, and looked forward to the trip.

* * *

The next morning, when we awoke, Kat said, "Black coffee. I can't move before I have black coffee."

I was responsible for this situation. At home I liked to get up early, make a pot of coffee, read the paper over a cup, then write for a while, or run three or four miles. Then she got up and we drank coffee and shot the breeze until noon, then I worked from lunch until between ten p.m. and four a.m., depending on deadlines. Neither of us suffered much jet lag coming over. The world just adjusted itself to our schedule.

I picked up the phone and a voice said, *"Sawadee, krap,"* and went off in a long string of Thai.

"Room service," I said. "ROOM SERVICE!"

"Ah, you want restaurant?"

"Yes, restaurant please."

A moment later I got a young lady who spoke no English at all. I bellowed, "Black coffee!" and our room number several times, and hoped for the best.

Kat lay in bed, waiting for her caffeine injection while I went into the bathroom to brush my teeth and shave my neck.

"How'd it go last night?" she called.

"Pretty good," I replied. "I really like those guys. They'd kill you in a minute if it suited their purposes, but shit, everybody I know is like that. This one guy, Mr. Lee, is really funny. You know what he said . . ."

"These are the people who killed the DEA agent's wife?" she asked, a slightly shocked tone in her voice.

"That's what it says in the papers," I said sheepishly.

If this were a novel, this chapter would build from this atmosphere of intrigue into a stunning denouement during which Brown, Coyne, and I go into Khun Sa's camp with a homing device cunningly concealed in our gear. We would bring the Royal Thai Border Police in on a raid that ends the dope trade forever, and we kill Khun Sa and his hench-men in a thrilling shoot-out.

What actually happened was that the Border Police got on Khun Sa's ass and he had to cancel because he was running. We never went to Burma, and we never met him.

Fortunately, we shortly got another chance to get in with a guerrilla army, one more important to the U.S. strategic defense posture.

15
PUBLIC RELATIONS IN CAMBODIA

The Khmer People's National Liberation Front, led by remnants of the old Lon Nol government, was waging guerrilla warfare against the Vietnamese-backed Heng Samrin regime and against our old enemies, the Vietnamese. We wanted to do a story on that for the magazine, and if possible get in some combat against the Vietnamese ourselves.

The original idea was for the four of us, Brown, Tom Reisinger, a former Special Forces medic who was our business manager, Jim Coyne, and me to go into Cambodia, essentially the same way Brown and company had gone into Laos the year before, armed, sneaking through the jungle in cammies.

But the Cambodian situation was entirely different from Laos. Thailand is shielded from invasion through Laos by rugged mountains and the broad, flat expanse of the Mekong River. But where the highway crosses into Cambodia, near Aranyapathet, the terrain is flat, and during the dry season it turns hard. This is tank country, and a perfect invasion route for the Vietnamese. So the Thais had built a mile-wide swath of tank traps, moats, heavily armed patrols, guards, and searchlights on the Cambodian border.

It is theoretically possible to crawl across this barrier in the dark, but highly dangerous. It seemed like there should be a better way to get into Cambodia.

As it turned out, there were two better ways, both with problems. One was simply to apply to the Thai government and go in as journalists. Son Sann, president of the KPNLF (Khmer People's National Liberation Front), had announced tentative plans for a press conference, but he could hold it only if the Thais allowed journalists to cross their border.

The purpose of the press conference was to discuss plans for a proposed coalition of the three Khmer anti-Vietnamese resistance movements.

On January 7, 1979, the Chinese-sponsored government of the Khmer Rouge had been toppled by the Vietnamese, who installed their puppet Heng Samrin regime. As refugees, the Khmer Rouge fled west to the Thai border, already dotted with the camps of refugees who had fled from the Khmer Rouge.

Cambodia was occupied by Vietnamese troops who were and are draining the country of food, raw materials, manufactured goods, and national treasures.

In the liberated zones of Cambodia, three main resistance factions had established themselves. The Khmer Rouge was led by a committee, formerly chaired by Pol Pot. Because of his international reputation as the man who committed genocide on his own people, he had been replaced by Khieu Samphan, but they were both still members of the same committee. The KR was by far the strongest rebel group, with 25,000 troops, and the richest, since they received plentiful aid from China.

The Sihanoukian National Army (Moulinaka), led by Prince Norodom Sihanouk, had a force with a reported strength varying from 800 to 5,000 troops. Their real strength was Sihanouk's international reputation; this was also their greatest drawback. Sihanouk was by no means universally admired.

The Khmer People's National Liberation Front, led by Son Sann, had, at the time of our visit, a reported military strength of 3,000 to 9,000, depending on whether you listened to critics or supporters. The KPNLF's main strength was its free-world ideology and its growing ability to spread that ideology into the interior of Cambodia.

Its main problem was to feed the growing population of 115,000 refugees in the civilian camps, through sometimes cantankerous aid organizations, and to equip its military by scrounging whatever it could from wherever it could.

The political leader, Son Sann, a seventy-one year old economist and former minister under Lon Nol, was tagged early on as the most important anti-Communist leader. Living in exile in France until 1979, Son Sann, in spite of poor health, had returned to the Cambodian jungle.

The KPNLF's military leader, General Dien Del, 50, a brigadier under Lon Nol, had the reputation of being one of the few honest generals in that army. He had risen rapidly and been given command of the 2nd Division in the early '70s.

Of the three things necessary to fight a revolutionary war —secure areas from which to operate, outside support, and support of a significant portion of the indigenous population—the KPNLF and the Khmer Rouge each lacked one major factor.

The Khmer Rouge had alienated half the population of Cambodia by murdering the other half. Since the Vietnamese and their quisling flunkies, the Heng Samrin regime, were almost as bad as the Khmer Rouge, almost every Cambodian with a choice in the matter rallied to Son Sann's KPNLF. However, without an outside source of resupply, the KPNLF could not arm and train new fighters very quickly.

The Thais allowed humanitarian aid, but they were not about to provoke the Vietnamese by providing arms, ammunition, or the radios that are indispensable to modern warfare, not without the concurrence of their allies in the Association of Southeast Asian Nations (ASEAN). The United States was forbidden by law to provide such aid.

Many Thais were embarrassed by their failure to help the KPNLF, and as usual when you're embarrassed the temptation was to blame the other guy. One of their complaints about the KPNLF was that it didn't fight much.

But without radios, much less ammunition, it would be suicidal to initiate conventional operations against the Vietnamese.

The KPNLF (Khmer Seraika in Cambodian), at least according to the theory of revolutionary warfare I learned at Fort Bragg, was doing exactly what it ought to be doing, which was sending armed propaganda teams into the countryside to broaden its base of support. Ho Chi Minh kept his cadres in this stage for twelve years before he launched so much as a platoon-size raid.

There was pressure on Son Sann's general, Dien Del, to go out and kick ass. But the pressure came from people who denied him the means to do so. Dien Del wisely used his main force units to defend KPNLF settlements.

Meanwhile the Chinese were pouring in military aid to the Khmer Rouge. But the Khmer Rouge had no popular support whatever. They had an army and they had slaves. Many of the slaves were children as young as eight, delighted to escape a life sentence of hard labor by joining the army at age fourteen.

It was an army of what my friend, Alan Dawson, called "teenage robots," an army which was, among other things, almost totally illiterate. In fact, literacy outside the party appeared to be an offense punishable by death under the Khmer Rouge.

The Khmer Rouge had an army at least twice as large as that of the KPNLF, since they could arm anybody they could shanghai. They seemed to have a policy of not letting their soldiers live long enough to think up any embarrassing questions.

Khmer Rouge defectors were one of the KPNLF's largest sources of arms, ammo, and recruits.

ASEAN had promised a measure of aid if the KPNLF would form a coalition with the Khmer Rouge, uniting the popular support with the outside aid. Also included would be good old Prince Sihanouk, who had a deft hand with the press, even though he had changed his political stance as often as Fleetwood Mac has changed guitar players.

But there was resistance to the coalition within the KPNLF. Mme. Suon Caset, their press officer, for instance, was against it. Her reason was that the Khmer Rouge had tortured her husband to death. He had been director general of the agriculture department under Lon Nol. Before the Khmer Rouge took over, she grabbed her children and left for Paris. He didn't want her to leave. "They won't harm us," he said. "I am no politician; I am a technician. We can work together for the Khmer people."

He had misjudged them.

For what it's worth, neither Reisinger nor I was in favor of the coalition either. We both had legitimate bitches against the Khmer Rouge. Mine was that I thought they had executed my Montagnard friend, Kpa Doh, along with his wife and three little boys, in front of the French embassy the day they took over Phnom Penh.

In Reisinger's case, a company of Cambodians from the Loch Ninh Strike Force, which his team advised, had been transferred to the Cambodian Army after the Americans pulled out. They were presumed to have been killed in the final days of their war with the Khmer Rouge. One of the main things he wanted to do was to see whether he could find any survivors.

Neither of us felt it would be wise for Son Sann to form a coalition with the Cambodian Reds.

Those urging that course of action insisted that this was no time to be sentimental; this was a time for hard-headed pragmatism.

It seemed to me that a hard-headed pragmatist would consider that every Communist revolution since the Indochina War, whether Soviet—or Chinese—backed, has begun by forming a broad coalition against a repressive oligarchy in a third-world country, then, when the time was ripe, the Communists co-opted and/or murdered outright the effective leaders of the other factions. This is not an optional extra. It is a standard feature of the "War of National Liberation."

The Cambodians have an example within their own experience of this tactic. Sihanouk was in coalition with the Khmer Rouge until they took over. He barely escaped with his life, and he lost four members of his family to them. He plays footsie with them now, but he has taken care to get on the good side of the Chinese first. Whatever one can say about Sihanouk, he is the most accomplished skater in Asia.

The ASEAN policy was to deny Son Sann supplies until he agreed to a coalition with the Khmer Rouge, but he required guarantees of his own movement's survival.

Even if the Thais allowed Son Sann to go ahead with his plans for a press conference, there was a strong possibility that SOF would be denied permission to attend. Many Thai officials were convinced that SOF was a U.S. intelligence operation, using the magazine as a cover.

The fact that we ran agent nets from our apartments, through Dr. Seuss and Chan, did nothing to dissuade them. The only people in Thailand who knew for sure we weren't spies were the real U.S. intelligence organizations.

Mme. Suon had another idea. It was for a couple of us to volunteer as relief workers with some of the international agencies working with Cambodian refugees. The Thais let a lot of these people across every day.

Coyne and I immediately volunteered and were immediately turned down. Mme. Suon explained, "Both of your pictures have appeared in the magazine. You would never be cleared. They know who you are. Tom and Kathy are the only ones who could get through."

I sighed.

16
KAT'S CAMBODIA STORY

While I was fighting the war in Vietnam, Kat was demonstrating against it. She had been with me and the *SOF* crew long enough to have serious doubts about the rightness of her stance during the Sixties. This expedition offered a firsthand look at the results of the student demonstrators' handiwork. Maybe that's why she was so eager to go.

When I first got out of the Army I came to know and like the student demonstrators at the University of Oklahoma. I told them that if all I knew about the war was what they knew I'd be against it too.

"I'm willing to accept that you guys are decent people acting from decent motives, if you're willing to give me the benefit of the same doubt; then, at least maybe, we can establish a dialogue."

But I'd always secretly wanted to rub their noses in it a bit. I lost more friends in Vietnam and Cambodia than I had remaining. I believed Kpa Doh and his family had been executed by the Khmer Rouge. Once, in Vietnam, I helped load a truck full of bodies of the wives and children of men I had fought with, killed in an ambush, thirty-four in all. Other friends had died in re-education camps after our government abandoned them to the NVA.

None of this had made me a happy man or an easy one to live with. No matter how close Kat and I grew, I often wandered into jungles in my mind where she could not follow. I felt that in pulling out of Vietnam, we had betrayed friends who had risked their lives for ours. For that, and perhaps for other reasons, from the time I left Vietnam until I met her, I was indifferent to life. She was not my only reason for living, but she was the only reason I liked it.

I kissed her good-bye in the parking lot of our apartment complex in Bangkok. She was excited to be setting off on her adventure with T.R. and Mme. Suon. I grinned to see her adrenaline up like that, even higher than it was on an opening night. I told her to be careful, and I told her I'd pray for her, and I told her not to take chances.

She told me not to worry. Their van pulled out of the parking lot, and I waved as it disappeared around a corner.

You fool, I thought. You have put her in range of Vietnamese mortars.

On the drive to Aranyapathet she flaked out in the back of the Nissan van, trying to keep the afternoon sun off. The steamy green countryside rolled by. Every once in a while a pair of Thai feet appeared from under a bush. Everything alive was trying to avoid the afternoon sun.

Kat was apprehensive. She and Tom were with two people they didn't know very much about: Mme. Suon Caset, the slender, charming, and irascible KPNLF press liaison officer, who had served as Princess Monique's secretary under the old regime, and the driver. They had to trust them to get in and out in one piece. The driver, who had yet to say a word, looked like Oddjob, the Oriental hitman in the James Bond movie.

They drove along a two-lane blacktop that was in much better repair than many in Arkansas or Louisiana. Farms and farmhouses zoomed by. The only difference between Thailand and home was that the houses were on stilts and the people plowed with water buffalo instead of John Deere tractors.

Temples gleamed white, blue, and gold in the sunset. She wondered whether Vietnam, Cambodia, and Laos were like this before the wars. They pulled into a Shell station for gas. The station offered a free blow-up beach ball with a 90 baht purchase.

The next day they drove across Cambodia via a rickety bridge, switching immediately from the left to the right-hand side of the road. The Thai road system had been set up by the British; Cambodia was a former French colony. They made their way to Shrok Srang village, a collection of low bamboo huts, laid out with military precision and kept carefully clean. There they toured the military training camp and interviewed Son Sann.

Over the next three days they watched this elderly, wispy gentleman move among his men. He appeared to inspire respect bordering on reverence.

Over tea, in an open-sided bamboo hut, he said of the proposed coalition, "If I am to go into the tiger's cage, I must be given full power to do so, because to do otherwise would deceive our friends, the ASEAN countries, but most of all it would deceive the Cambodian people."

The men of the military camp were the same as G.I.s all over the world. They stared at Kat boldly and flashed big grins, or cast sidelong glances and smiled sheepishly.

The civilian camps got rice from international aid agencies once a week. The people there didn't stare at foreigners the way people in rural Thailand do; foreigners were frequently seen here—relief workers, nurses, doctors. The children rushed to a camera, delighted to have their pictures taken.

Nearly every household in these villages had a two-year-old toddler. Under Pol Pot, marriages had been forbidden unless arranged by the government, and couples were allowed only one night a week together. Lovers caught together were executed. Everywhere Tom and Kat went, mothers proudly held their healthy, beautiful babies up for inspection.

Each woman and female child above the height of 3'5" was given 2.7 pounds of rice and 10½ ounces of fish per week. Each woman was allotted enough food to feed three members of her family, including herself. But none of this was supposed to go to combatants; i.e., the husbands and fathers. The women were faced with a serious dilemma every day: which children do I feed, or does my husband need the nourishment today?

Five kilometers away from the Vietnamese, so highly did they value their culture, the KPNLF had built an arts center for teaching classical Cambodian dance, complete with elaborate costumes, to talented children.

The next day Tom and Kat visited Rithisen, a refugee camp that had just joined the KPNLF in July 1980. Older men and women stared at their air-conditioned bus, with eyes that had seen too much pain. Some had allowed it to break their spirit. There were black-market goods there, which had not seemed to be the case in other camps, but only in small quantities—soap, candy, gum, soda, bicycle parts, and ratchet wrenches.

Several people had motorcycles or bicycles. There was an affluence in Rithisen that didn't exist in the other camps. Funny, she'd suddenly tagged as "affluent" the owner of a half-dozen bottles of Fanta Orange, a couple of boxes of soap flakes, and a bicycle.

The new buildings and huts put up since the camp joined the KPNLF had the same appearance of cleanliness and efficiency as Shrok Srang. The older parts of the camps had bottles, cans, and undefinable pieces of litter scattered about.

She asked to see the military camp first, and apparently took them by surprise. The deputy commander had just finished Sunday lunch with his family. Tom and Kat were served tea and chatted politely as though they had just dropped in to have a Sunday afternoon gossip with an old friend. As discreetly as possible, the deputy commander dispatched a young man in fatigues, an AK slung over his shoulder, on a yellow Yamaha Enduro, to warn the troops of the VIPs' impending visit.

Presently he screeched up in a shower of fine red grit, and after a five minute conference, the deputy commander climbed on the back of the bike and motioned for them to follow in the van.

Along the road to the camp men emerged from their huts, buttoning camouflaged shirts, slinging rifles, and buckling on ammo pouches. They had interrupted lunch. Kat saw men melting into the bushes on side trails to beat them to the camp.

These men defended themselves from the Khmer Rouge, their ostensible allies, who were camped a few kilometers away. The Rithisen camp also had a problem with the Vietnamese; at night they slipped people in to poison the wells. Every time a well was poisoned, a family died. Samples of water were taken and the well sealed. The samples were turned over to local intelligence agencies, and the International Committee of the Red Cross sent people to look at the bodies. Neither organization had responded to requests for results of the analyses.

At the entrance to the military camp a sharp-looking honor guard had been turned out. Weapons were spotless, as they had been the day before. The area needed to be picked up, but the soldiers wore clean uniforms. They took obvious pride in their organization.

The last day Kat spent in Cambodia, things were tense.

The Thais had denied journalists entrance to Ampil military camp for the scheduled press conference with Son Sann, diverting them to another camp instead.

Dr. Guffar, a high-level officer of the KPNLF, who had formerly taught poli sci at the University of Michigan, was furiously typing when they arrived at headquarters. Dr. Guffar and the people around him appeared to be evaluating the new proposal for coalition and formulating their plans. Kathy asked him about the chances of the coalition being formed. Wryly he replied, "We are determined to form a coalition."

"On what terms?"

"On terms acceptable to all three parties; on terms acceptable to the Cambodian people."

They departed for Nong Chon, their third and last camp. They were to go on a patrol to the front lines. They had also been to the front the previous two days, but by the time they had arrived the sun was so hot that neither side moved. The Vietnamese made their attacks in the morning.

A motley assortment of press had managed to get passes to this camp. But since there would be no conference, the press corps opted for a three-hour stroll in the merciless sun. Mme. Suon told them they would walk twelve kilometers to a Vietnamese camp the KPNLF had recently taken. They were assigned a platoon from Battalion 219. Kat hated being with the other correspondents. Unlike the cat-like and all-but-invisible Cambodian soldiers, they stomped through the jungle like the city people they were.

Thirty minutes out she started having chills from sweat drying on her skin. She was neither trained for this nor in shape for it. Artillery thundered in the distance; gunshots sounded from the right.

She turned around to discover that their driver had followed. He wanted to see where they were going. The Cambodians had to send two men back with him anyway, and she decided to accompany them.

She felt bad about leaving. She knew she'd be razzed unmercifully when she got back, but thought she might become a burden if they got into serious combat. I had told her many times that the only weapon a correspondent has is the ability to back off if things don't feel right.

She came back through the jungle with one soldier. The fat driver had quickly fallen behind with the other men bringing up the rear. The quiet of the trek was broken only by the sound of sneakers crunching on sand, an artillery barrage, and gunshots.

Back in the camp she sat watching people work in the offices. It was the same as administrative work anywhere. A secretary brought file folders full of papers and gave them to Colonel Chea Chhut, the commander of the camp. He sat reading, asking questions, and signing something every once in a while. Several men, obviously part of the hierarchy, sat around a rough lumber table with a green oilcloth cover. Occasionally the commander asked a question or dispatched somebody with papers.

One of the soldiers sitting at the table of officials pulled out a grenade. "Buy Vietnam," he said, gesturing with the grenade. It had been bought from the enemy; most of the soldiers were carrying them.

Later they took a break and she sat with them in their open, thatched restaurant, listening to gunfire in the distance. It started to pick up, becoming louder and more frequent. There were dark clouds in the sky and a strong wind came up. At first she thought the rumbling in the distance was thunder. Unfortunately there was no one there who spoke English, except, of course, for the phrase, "I do not speak English."

There was one Cambodian soldier who spoke Thai. The driver, with a lot of effort, translated questions and answers for her.

The phone buzzed. "Hello!" came over the line. Commander Chea listened for a few minutes, muttered a few works, turned to the men, who, a minute before, had been concerned only with city sanitation and whether to dig a well near the front entrance.

They quickly scattered. Commander Chea disappeared into his house. Men who had been lounging in the shade in sarongs suddenly reappeared in camouflage uniforms, complete with yellow kerchiefs tied in perfect square knots. Men and boys she had thought were just hanging around slapped loaded magazines into the receivers of their weapons.

A platoon leader came double-timing from the village, yelling two indecipherable words. Men fell in behind him from the huts and alleyways. The leader stopped and yelled two new words. The men dressed right and covered down.

Commander Chea emerged from the hut in full camouflage uniform, boots gleaming and pants bloused perfectly over their tops. He carried a short, carved riding crop that he used to punctuate his sentences.

The men were briefed by a captain. A beat-up blue Toyota truck pulled up in the yard and the twenty or so men started trying to wedge their equipment and bodies on board. A few minutes before, she had been jiving with these guys, trying to trade her bush hat for one of their yellow scarves. Not one would trade a thread of his uniform for her hat or for anything else. As they pulled out she saw the faces of the young boys, some with fear in their eyes, or maybe a reflection of her fear for them.

She smiled and gave them the thumbs up; a few managed a smile and one returned the gesture.

She asked the location of Tom and Mme. Suon. The driver inquired and came back with a confused answer. He also informed her that two hundred Vietnamese were attacking three kilometers away.

My God, she thought, *two hundred Vietnamese!* She asked him to verify the information; he asked again and came back with the same information. She told him to move the van closer to the restaurant, and to load all their gear.

He argued that the van would get too hot in the sun. She

surprised herself when she turned around and in a low, commanding voice said, "Do it! Now!"

The driver scurried away.

She was determined to stand in that restaurant until Tom came back or the Vietnamese rolled over them, whichever came first. But she saw nothing wrong with having the van two seconds away.

Soon a man in a green and black print shirt came in and sat down behind the head table. Here was a man who was in charge, and he spoke excellent English. She waited for him to consult with another man carrying maps covered with plastic. She asked him about Tom. He said, "Oh, they're on their way in. They engaged ten to fifteen Vietnamese and are very tired. We're sending motorcycles out to pick them up because they had to circle way around to get out."

"Ten to fifteen!" she exclaimed. "The driver told me two hundred."

Their laughter was broken by the arrival of a kid with a rucksack. He placed it on the table and snapped to, then unloaded the contents onto the table; a blood-splattered helmet, two plastic water bottles, a hammock, and a mosquito net. The man in the green and black shirt, Colonel Bory Chhut, said that this stuff had just been taken by a patrol. The helmet was the only thing that wouldn't be recycled for field use.

Relieved to know her friends were safe, she sat down and visited with the colonel. He, like Colonel Chea Chhut, had been a successful insurance man in Orange County, California. They had left their safe jobs and lives in the States when called back to fight for their country. Both men told her they had men who served under them in Lon Nol's army, living in the States, who would come when called.

In the meantime the men in the States were waiting for the time when rice, boots, and arms became available, working and sending what money they could.

Two motorcycles roared up and deposited their exhausted loads. Two journalists staggered in, gesturing for something to drink. After downing a glass of warm Fanta Orange, one Japanese reporter told her about his walk in the woods.

The patrol had gone six kilometers with no contact; they decided to push on. A couple more straphangers, including this reporter, had to be left back because of their light-colored, highly visible clothing. Four men were left to guard them and bring them out. The journalist told her they had been sitting on a bare hilltop. "The four men are around me, guarding me. Then *Boom! Boom!* and then *dat-a-dat-a-dat!* They pushed me in the bunker." He wiped his face. "Very exciting, very exciting!"

By this time another load of journalists had been deposited. Still no Tom. Finally two more bikes appeared in the distance. At last, Tom. Special Forces, first in the field and last out. She quickly checked him over for signs of blood, then took a picture of his filthy, tired, but smiling face.

As they drove out of the camp, they passed a boy in a wheelchair, wearing a fatigue cap. His legs had been blown off about twelve inches above the knee.

A toddler playing in the dirt looked up at the air-conditioned van cruising by and mouthed the word, "Okay."

17
TOM'S STORY

Even though T.R. and Kat were together for much of their trip into Cambodia, Kathy was seeing things for the first time, and she noticed small details that Tom took for granted. Conversely, as a former SF trooper he was looking for militarily significant details that she was unaware of. Perception of this shared experience was very different for each of them.

The first thing Reisinger did on their trip was start searching for his missing Cambodians. He had made many friends on patrol with that company. They had shared cigarettes and rice, coffee and tea. The lack of a common language had been no barrier to friendship. They weren't supposed to talk on patrol anyway.

Tom had kept in touch with his Cambodians for a couple of years after leaving Vietnam, but after the Americans pulled out, it was almost impossible to get mail through. In 1970 most of the Cambodians in Special Forces camps were pulled out and sent to Cambodia. They formed the 7th Division of the Cambodian Army and had a reputation as the best fighters in that war.

The Company from Loch Ninh fought as part of the 47th Infantry Brigade. Kim Long, who had commanded the company in Vietnam, was Brigade Commander.

They fought in the final defense of Phnom Penh, and Reisinger later heard that Kim Long had led them in a last minute punchout through the attacking forces. He lost track of them completely after that.

There was not much chance that many of them had made it, but maybe a few had, and the logical place to look for them was with the KPNLF.

The first place they visited was Camp Ampil, the military headquarters, a part of the Shrok Srang refugee camp, a huge city of bamboo houses, laid out like barracks on a dusty plain.

The troops at Camp Ampil were a very different kind of Cambodian from the troops he had led at Loch Ninh. For all that the Loch Ninh Cambodes had been super field soldiers, they had cultivated a scruffy image, even in camp.

Compared to them, the KPNLF kids looked like an ROTC drill team. The KPNLF troops were perfectly turned out in brand-clean cammies, their weapons spotless, and they could fall in, fall out and present arms like clockwork. These skills are not as highly prized today as they were in, say, the War of 1812.

Still they were obviously well-trained, within the limits of what Reisinger saw them do.

It became clear that what Tom and Kat were seeing was a canned demonstration. The KPNLF leadership was well aware of the precariousness of their own situation, and good press was essential to their very survival. They weren't about to let our people nose around at will.

It was that way for the first couple of days of the trip.

Even so they were only five klicks from Vietnamese combat units. There was always firing in the distance.

We knew two Americans in Thailand who might legitimately be considered experts on revolutionary warfare. Both had visited the KPNLF camps. One was a senior U.S. Army officer with Special Forces and Vietnam experience. The other was Dawson.

The colonel liked the KPNLF people, and wished them well, but he didn't think their officers had done their homework. "They haven't read their Mao," he said. "They haven't read their Giap. They'll introduce you to their armored cavalry expert. They're living in Never-Never Land."

Maybe he was right. On the other hand, maybe they showed him their dog and pony show, and he saw through that, but did not perceive the reality behind it. Dawson claimed that they were sending out armed propaganda teams, and that their conventional troops were to defend their safe areas and cover the evacuation of those hundreds of thousands of civilians, should the Viets launch an attack.

Shrok Srang had been overrun and rebuilt once, and Nong Chon twice, so there was plenty of defending to be done.

The picture that emerged during Tom's and Kat's visit was halfway between those two versions. The Khmer admitted to a propaganda school, but Reisinger didn't get a look at the curriculum.

He learned, however, that they were graduating six hundred people every three months. He didn't know where they were going, but they weren't hanging around Shrok Srang. They had an advanced course that graduated one hundred every three months. Even our doubting colonel admitted that somebody, and he didn't know who, was waging effective guerrilla warfare in the interior. We thought it might be those cadres.

Reisinger and Kat didn't meet the armored cavalry expert, or if they did he had learned to keep quiet about it. Several officers asked *SOF*'s help in getting guerrilla war-

fare manuals, and said they were seeking Special Forces
training from friendly Asian countries.

There was a military academy at Camp Ampil, with about
two hundred and fifty students, both cadets and company-
grade officers. They also had a basic training camp and an
NCO academy.

Except for courtesy titles for officers who served in the
Lon Nol army, they had no rank; they used job titles.

After two days of inquiries, Tom was finally introduced to
a survivor of the 47th Brigade, but he wasn't from Loch
Ninh. He told Reisinger that the remnants of the 47th had
fought their way into eastern Cambodia. There they were
trapped by a superior force and annihilated. This man had
gotten away, but he didn't know anyone else who had.

Later that day Tom and Kat linked up with some other
journalists—an NBC-TV crew, a man from the London
Times, and a stringer for UPI. The correspondent with the
NBC crew was Neil Davis, a huge blond Aussie who had
been a legend in the Saigon press corps for courage and
journalistic professionalism.

They were given an escort of what was described as a half
company of the 219th battalion, about fifty troops, and set
out to film a recently captured Vietnamese camp.

Reisinger observed the troops carefully. They worked
very smoothly together, kept a good interval between men,
and looked alert. There was no kidding around. There was
a squad on each flank and a small point element. The journalists accompanied the command group, behind the first
squad of the main body. They set off on a small trail
through fairly open, flat terrain.

After a while Kat felt faint, and went back with the
driver. Further on they found the remnants of a few huts, a
bloody poncho, and a few empty tin cans with Russian writing on them. The TV crew had not shot a single foot of film,
nor did they rise to this bait.

The KPNLF were no fools. They knew that if their movement was to survive it must have outside support, and to get

that they must have publicity. It was decided to go another four klicks and attack a Vietnamese battalion outpost, so the TV crew would have something to film.

Despite the show-biz aspect of this operation, it was carried out in a smooth and professional manner. Its purpose was neither to take territory nor to kill the enemy, although if that happened it would be fine. This was a propaganda mission.

Finally they came upon a small Vietnamese outpost. Our guys lobbed in a few B-40 rockets and fired a few bursts. The other guys responded with B-40s and mortars. It lasted only about a minute, long enough to look like a furious battle on television.

Reisinger was impressed by the fact that there was no bitching and no clowning. The lowest private seemed to understand that this was necessary. It was a business situation.

18
GENERAL KHANH'S COUP

The days passed in false starts. Stories were developed and then pre-empted by other stories that never happened. My frustration mounted. Tom and Kat had their moment, but nothing brought us intrepid correspondents closer to the field, or to guerrillas, or to the adrenaline rushes of old. I continued dreaming of Vietnam and my glory days. Maybe because of the false starts, I dreamed of General Khanh's coup in early 1964 and the events it had set in motion at our forward operational base in northern Phu Bon province, another adventure in frustration.

"Why no patrol?" Cowboy demanded when he came into the shack, sweeping off his cowboy-rolled bush hat and wrap-around shades. He and Ksor Yul, now in command of the company at the FOB, who had been a corporal under the French, came in and seated themselves on some C-Rats boxes.

"They had another coup in Saigon," I replied. Their expressions remained unchanged. Clearly they saw no connection between our war and events in Saigon. "Anyhow, the big headquarters in the sky doesn't want us to run any more patrols. I guess until they find out if the U.S. is for or against the new regime."

Cowboy told Yul what I said, and they both shrugged. "Okay."

"We'll run local security patrols until this is over. Maybe we can scare up one of these snipers firing into the camp." I picked up my map and turned it over to the white side, drawing diagrams with a grease pencil.

"We use all three of Yul's platoons and run three local patrols a day. One platoon will run a close circle, about one kilometer out from the camp. One will go north and check out that long ridge line overlooking the FOB, about two kilometers out. The other can loop around south three or four kilometers.

"I want the one that goes along the ridge line," I said. I'd been wanting to check it out for some time. "Augie can take the close one and Hank will go with the one south. You all got any ideas?"

They didn't. I had not yet learned the trick of asking for suggestions before giving our plan. They would never offer a change for fear of hurting our feelings.

The next morning Cowboy, Yul, and I set out with the first platoon. We splashed across the little creek running just north of the camp, and entered the woods on the other side, cutting down a trail which led to the western end of the ridge line. Golden light filtered through the canopy of trees, turning them to a translucent, shimmering green. The trees were tall and stately. For Vietnam this was open terrain.

It took the better part of two hours to gain the top of the ridge line, all hard climbing. It was flat and grassy up there, pockmarked with 81mm shell holes from rounds fired by the FOB to discourage observation.

We took a break, and the Yards flaked out under the trees. I lit a cigarette, and Cowboy, Yul, and I took a look around. A walk of the perimeter of the flattop we were on revealed that it was not a part of the main ridge line, something a study of the old French map had not indicated. That early in the war our maps were English-language copies of old French maps, one over 100,000, compared to the standard U.S. map ratio of one over 25,000, and grossly inaccurate. At our in-country briefing I had seen a wall map on which a river jumped ten kilometers going from one map-sheet to the next.

The main ridge line hooked south so that the hook faced our FOB. It was joined to the main ridge line by a small saddle. We were standing on the end of the hook. You couldn't tell from the map that this wonderful little observation post was up here, and as far as I knew, the team we replaced had never patrolled the ridge line. Like us, they tried to go as far out as they could before they ran out of chow.

Our local security patrols were usually squad size and didn't come out this far.

"Man!" I said, pointing back the way we had come. "Look at that." We were looking right down into the FOB. I got out my binoculars. Through them, the camp looked twenty meters away, but standing in a curiously flat depth-of-field. I looked down at the back side of the commo shack. Ken Miller, our comm chief, came out, walked over to a lister bag hanging from a tree limb and filled his canteen.

He turned and walked back to the commo shack, bare-chested as usual, a slender, well-made, middle-age man with the face of a presidential candidate. I could make out his homemade rosary, a knotted cord, one knot for each bead, with a crucifix on the end. His lips moved as he spoke to someone, and for a second I wondered why I couldn't hear him.

I handed the binoculars to Cowboy. "You can pick out the mortar positions, the commo shack, the Americans' shack. You could just sit up here and pinpoint your targets." He passed the binoculars on to Yul. Their looks were grave.

We formed the company up again and started down off the edge of the hill, into the saddle that led back to the main ridge line. The way was steep, grassy and slick and stubbled with grey rock.

The climb up the hill was arduous; I could feel the strain all the way down the backs of my legs. I grabbed at rocks, tree trunks and clumps of grass, anything to haul myself up that bloody hill.

Just as I was about to reach the military crest of the hill, one of the squad leaders went by me like a rocket, to be the first man to arrive at the top. A moment later I arrived beside him, breathing hard. Bubbling out of the rocks was a pure stream of clear water. Not a big one, but enough; a clear, steady stream, and around it in the mud and dirt were the marks of tire-soled sandals. I called down, "Hey, Cowboy! Yul! Come here!" A moment later they hauled up beside me. "What, sir?"

"Look at this."

"Un Croupe! Securite!" Yul called, and the lead squad went the rest of the way to the top. We followed them up and found the tracks and cold campfires of at least one company of VC. The fires were one day old.

Later I questioned Cowboy closely about the squad leader who had passed me going up the hill. We normally assumed that up to fifteen percent of our strike force was made up of VC infiltrators, and I thought maybe one of them had just given himself away. Cowboy assured me that he had known him for years, that he was just a very straight, ballsy guy. I still didn't trust him, though. He must have had some idea what was on that hill.

I turned on the radio and put the handset to my ear. "Bolen Alpha, this is Bolen Handy. Bolen Alpha, this is Handy, over."

Ken came up, and I told him what we had found.

"Roger, Handy. Kildare reports spotting estimated VC squad in vicinity Bravo Quebec 249580." Kildare was Augie DeLucia, our senior medic.

"Roger that, Alpha," I said. "I figure that's part of the company that passed through here. I think they split up into small groups when they left."

"Roger, I agree. Alpha out."

"You know what, sir?" Cowboy said.

"What?"

"VC always have spy in camp. They know you plan to leave for patrol with only small force to guard FOB. They have company here for attack. Plan to hurt us, get weapons, kill Americans."

"You're probably right," I said. I turned and faced in the general direction of Saigon and muttered, "And thank you, Major General Nguyen Khanh." It was Khanh's coup, after all, that had saved the FOB.

We hadn't come equipped for an overnight stay, and the ridge line proved too long to cover in one day, so we returned to the FOB. The next day we set out to come back up the ridge line from the other end. Since the VC company might have moved only a kilometer or so down the ridge line and holed up again, I took two platoons with me.

It was a long, hot, dry walk. I stuck with the company headquarters. Hank Johnson, our junior weapons man, and Augie each took a platoon. All we found on top of the ridge line were rocks and trees. We sat down on the rocks, in the shade of the trees and ate lunch.

I twisted my ankle on the way down, which may have saved our lives, because I couldn't walk fast.

As long as we were on fairly level, fairly open terrain, it was fine. We held a good formation. Flank security was good, and the three parallel columns cut through the brush ready for action. Then we hit some thick brush and a small stream, and in less than thirty seconds my command changed from a disciplined force, moving as fast as terrain would allow, to sixty separate guys trying to get home as quickly as possible.

"Hold it," I said to Yul in a calm, reasonable, friendly voice. He looked at me, then looked helplessly at his troops. All Jarai like to be liked, and he didn't want to make a scene.

"Halt the company," I said again. Yul looked around at his men and held up his hand, but they were too far gone now, heading for home.

"ALL RIGHT, GODDAMMIT!" I bellowed. "ALLA YOU SONSABITCHES STOP!"

They stopped.

"Now," I said to Yul, "get your company back in a secure march formation and we will go. But only as fast as we can maintain march discipline. Got it?"

He nodded his head.

We moved out again slowly. But soon the pace picked up again and the formation started to fall apart. I halted them again and ranted some more. Then I moved up right behind the point man so I could control his pace. We moved out.

I kept about ten meters behind the point. If he went too fast, I told him to slow down. Five minutes after we moved out he turned and came screaming back toward me, yelling something that sounded like, "Say ton mean! Say ton mean!"

Finally I understood: *"C'est un mine!"* It is a mine. I grabbed him by the wrist and said, "Okay, babe, calm down!" He tried to jerk loose and run off again, but I held fast and said, "Show me the mine. I want to see it."

Yul, Hank, and Augie came up. I made them stay back twenty meters, and together the point man and I went up to look at the mine. I expected something like one of the U.S. Army's little hockey puck antipersonnel mines, so at first I didn't see the fine nylon string stretched across the narrow trail we were on.

It was connected to a cast-iron grenade, shaped like a tin can, but with the edges serrated into squares like the U.S.

World War II hand grenade. Apparently the idea was for us to trip over the wire and set off the grenade. The top was stoppered with a bamboo cork, sealed in wax. From this a string loop was tied to the trip cord. It would have taken me and the point man both out if he hadn't seen it. I told the point to get back, and DeLucia to come in a little closer.

"Augie," I said, "keep the company back. I'm going to try to disarm this thing."

I traced the string to the other side and gingerly, slowly, knelt and pulled out the peg that held the other side of the string. Then I went back over and examined the grenade again. It was fixed in place by a stake hammered to an iron ring protruding from its bottom. I took out my knife and started digging around the stake.

"Don't pull it out, sir," Augie said. "Sometimes they put another one underneath that goes off when you try to disarm that one."

"Good point. See if you can rustle up about thirty feet of suspension line off somebody."

He had line in his pack so I tied one end to the stake. Then I ran back over a small fold in the ground that furnished protection if we lay down flat, and motioned for everybody to get down.

"Okay, pull the line," I said. Augie pulled it slowly at first, then hard. Nothing happened. "The line is fouled somewhere," he said.

"Okay! Let the slack out." He did, and he and I went out and unfouled all the kinks and places where the line had caught on rocks and twigs.

"Okay, one more time." We both took hold of the line this time and tugged all the slack out. Then slowly, very slowly, the line budged, and budged some more, and then sprang free. We lay there and waited a moment, panting a little. Nothing happened.

"Okay," I yelled. "Everybody stay down." I got up and tiptoed over to the grenade. It lay in the dirt, the stake still through the ring, with little clods still clinging to it.

I explained to Yul in bastard French that I was going to carry the grenade in and wanted everybody to stay at least thirty meters from me. It didn't require much explaining. They gave me lots of room.

The big question in my mind was whether it had an instantaneous fuse, or whether I had a couple of seconds to get rid of it if I tripped or something caught on the loop.

It took about two hours to get back to the FOB, and by that time it was an hour after dark. Ken was kind of mad when we got in.

"*Sir*," he said, giving it that particular inflection only an old NCO can. In some fashion it changes the meaning of the word to "you stupid bastard." "If you can't get back before dark, the *least* you can do is call in on the PRC-10."

"Tried," I said. "Couldn't make contact."

"Too bad," he said. "Then I could have told you about this." He handed me another message. It read, "MAKE NO ATTEMPT TO DISARM VC MINES OR BOOBY TRAPS. TOO MANY CASUALTIES FROM THIS PRACTICE. BLOW ALL IN PLACE." Later I found that this message was the result of some poor guy having done exactly what I did about two days before, and blown himself all over the map.

Augie took the grenade down to our main camp in the truck the next day. He and the Old Man and Slattery, our senior demo man, took some pictures of it for a tech intel report and then took it out past the perimeter and blew it. It had an instantaneous fuse.

I awoke lathered in adrenaline and ready for action, only to realize I was in a king-size bed with Kat, under an air conditioner.

19

BLOOD MOON OVER BANGKOK

Our air-conditioned bedroom was huge. As usual I awoke early and pulled on a pair of athletic shorts and a T-shirt.

Working for *SOF* you accumulate a certain number of macho T-shirts without trying. This Special Operations Association T-shirt was at least fairly discreet, sporting only a small crest on the left breast, a bereted skull on a red shield, blood dripping from its mouth.

I looked at Kathy's slender, sleeping form in the bed.

She had a fair number of those T-shirts herself. Once, traveling cross-country alone at night, she gassed up our black Firebird in Dalhart, Texas. She wore jeans, boots, and a tight "AIRBORNE: Death from Above" T-shirt, which sports a skull superimposed on parachute wings.

An outlaw motorcycle gang pulled in just as she was

hanging up the hose. They looked at her with a strange shock of recognition, and gave her the thumbs up as she roared off into the night.

The sauna serving as Bangkok's air hit me as I left the bedroom. Brown thrashed on the floor, already out doing his exercises. He has a long waist and lower back problems. Once his back went out at a major gun show, and he was carried out in a wheelchair.

But an old girlfriend had shown him some exercises that kept him limber. She had wisely not told him they were yoga. Brown did stretching exercises, had quit drinking except for an occasional white wine, and ran three miles a day. He lived like a new-age guru, and for his age, 51, was in fantastic shape.

I dropped down and pumped off thirty-one push-ups, rolled over and started the half-sit-ups Brown had shown me—as hard on the gut but easier on the lower back. Brown did a hundred every day. I was up to sixty-five. I got up and did some stretchers for our run.

Bangkok is not laid out in blocks. Major streets have narrow half-mile alleys off them, called *soi*s. Homes front on the *soi*s. Brown and I ran up and down the *soi* beside our apartment building for three miles. Then we stretched again.

After breakfast, Kathy and I joined Hiney on the balcony for coffee. Something he said had got me to thinking, and I wanted to pursue it. I led the conversation to his experiences in Laos. He had said that he loved the little people but could barely tolerate the big people. Once a Lao general had told him, "You Americans are creating monsters that we will have to deal with after this is over." He was referring to those people the U.S. had insisted be promoted on merit rather than family connections. Perhaps if they'd made a few more monsters those generals wouldn't be in exile now.

Hiney said the best fighter pilot he had ever seen was a Hmong tribesman they had trained to fly T-28s. "Flew four or five missions a day, and crewed his own airplane," he said.

I took a sip of coffee. "Whatever happened to him?"

"Fifth mission of the day. He was tired; he'd been flying for years. After that he couldn't go back to the village, and there was no place else for him to go. He flew that T-28 right into a Vietnamese anti-aircraft gun that was shooting at one of our fighters."

I tried to get him back to the sociological implications of guerrilla warfare. At one point he had ventured the opinion that one of the reasons Thailand had not been the next domino was that the American presence had created an active middle class. There had been a way for poor people who were sharp to make money without overthrowing the government. After the Americans left, the new middle class had found ways to sustain itself.

Kathy and I both sucked in our breath and sat up straight as See, our Wa tribesman houseboy, came around the outside ledge of the building, sweeping the ledge. The Wa are a hilltribe, reputed to be headhunters, who live their lives on narrow mountain trails. The ledge was only a foot wide and had no corner. For a moment, as he came around the edge of the building, he was suspended over the courtyard and the pool below. He grinned as he passed us and swept on. He was just showing off.

We went back inside. Coyne was reading the first draft of my Mitrapab jump story. "No getting around it," he said ruefully. "You are good."

I smiled with no attempt at modesty. Coyne is the most naturally talented storyteller I know. I always told him, "Jimmy, any story you tell me, and don't get into print in sixty days, is mine." He thought I was kidding.

We went back into our bedroom. Our dirty clothes from the night before were gone. See would have them washed, ironed, and back in the closet by one o'clock.

A half hour later Brown walked in unannounced. Bad

timing again. "Uh . . ." he said, and closed the door behind him.

"Be out in a few minutes," I bellowed.

What he wanted was for me and Hiney to go over to Hiney's old headquarters that afternoon. Hiney had completed his POW business, at least for the time being. He had secured the remains of one American airman, and was going home. I already knew Colonel Goetzke, Hiney's replacement, but this would give me a chance to get in solid with what was left of the American advisory effort, under the best possible circumstances.

On our way back Hiney got into a conversation with our driver about his recent six-month stint as a laborer in Saudi Arabia. "Six month, no fucking," the driver said. "Very bad. I never do again."

"Do ye drink the blood?" Hiney asked.

"Say what?" I interrupted. Hiney explained that vendors came to Lumpini Park in the morning and sold cobra blood. They hang a live cobra upside down, slit its throat, and you drink the blood as it dies. "Makes ya horny," he summed up. I think he meant virile.

When we got back to the penthouse, I told Brown about the cobra blood and he got all excited. He wanted the four of us, Brown, Coyne, T.R., and me, to go down to Lumpini Park the first thing in the morning and drink it. "C'mon," he insisted. "We can put our picture in the magazine. It'll be real macho."

"Not me," said Coyne.

"Bob," I said, "it's not macho to do something you don't want to do, just to prove to somebody else you've got the guts to do it."

He raved on for a while, but finally saw we were adamant. "You could do it by yourself," Coyne suggested. He would shoot it, and I could write it up for the magazine. But Brown didn't want to do it by himself.

* * *

After lunch Dr. Seuss showed up with his girlfriend. He brought her because their Thai hotel room was too spartan to leave her there, and he could not throw her into the city. Dr. Seuss lived up country.

Dr. Seuss, chunky and fifty, had worked for the Agency but had been fired for drinking on duty. He had the booze under control now. The girl was seventeen, but she looked fourteen, a Thai Brooke Shields, but with the brains of a gnat and an inexhaustible supply of chewing gum and Siamese movie magazines. It seemed to me that his pedophilia carried within it the seeds of its own punishment.

Kathy detested him, even before she met the girl. She said she didn't trust any man who carried a purse. For myself, nothing I ever did with the man came to any good.

Brown, T.R., Dr. Seuss, Colonel Boon Lert, and I sat around the conference table, which was also our dining room table, and plotted revolution against the Vietnamese, the regional sport of Southeast Asia.

After we had finished our scheming for the day, it was time for Kathy's exercises, which she took in the pool.

We hit the highly chlorinated water in our fairly good-sized pool about six or six-thirty. She did twelve lengths a night. Usually so did I. I floated on my back and watched the soot from Sukhumvit drift down onto the water.

"Fuckin' pollution!" I muttered.

Kathy splashed water on me. "What's the matter with you? You don't like the pollution; you don't like Bangkok; you don't like anything."

"Yeah, well, I'm really cranked," I replied.

"You've been acting like an asshole," she said. "What's your problem?"

I stood on the bottom of the pool and leaned against the rope that separated the deep and shallow ends. "My problem," I said, "is that this is my last chance to relive the greatest adventure of my life, and it's so close, but it's not happening."

"It's like you're not happy unless you're trying to kill somebody or somebody's trying to kill you," she snapped.

I shrugged. I guess it did look like that, but there was more to this than simple adrenaline addiction. Even to Kathy I couldn't seem to explain that I had found more than war in Vietnam; I had found peace. I missed the solitude and the jungle. I didn't want to kill anybody, and I sure didn't want to die. I just wanted a couple of weeks of bush time.

She splashed water full in my face. "This is a good place," she said. "Lighten up."

I splashed her back and dived for her. "Don't tickle me," she shrieked. "Jim! Don't *tickle* me!"

After dinner we dressed to meet Dawson, my Bangkok *Post* buddy, and Tuk, his Thai girlfriend. Kathy had bought a gold lamé spacesuit, not the NASA kind, but the skin-hugging Buck Rogers kind, and a pair of shoes that were two thin gold straps on four-inch heels, so we were going dancing.

The disco was extravagantly lurid, but the Thai preference for bubblegum music drove us into the street after an hour.

The four of us pub-crawled Pat Pong. We hit Rick Menard's Grand Prix, which featured a videotaped movie at the back bar, with earphones for those who would rather listen to the movie. The music was played by a Thai D.J. in a booth at the front. Rick's dancers were not the best on Pat Pong, but my favorite worked there, a tough-looking tawny woman with hair to her ass and thigh-high purple boots.

We ricocheted across the street to the King's Castle, and waded into the press of the crowd: squareheaded Americans, foxy young Thai girls, and a few American or European women. Some of the Thai girls wore street clothes, but most, dancers who worked there, wore high-heeled shoes, pastel bikinis, and red plastic buttons with numbers on them.

For most of these girls this life was their only way out of the paddy. For some, life was a party that went on too long; for others, it was just a gig, and for some lucky ones, a steppingstone to something better.

Up on the stage one of the more beautiful girls thrashed listlessly to Steve Miller's "Livin' in the U.S.A." while picking her nose.

In Thailand a homosexual transvestite is called a *katoy*. The eyes of the one who hangs out at the King's Castle lit up when he saw Kat's jumpsuit. I knew this particular, avid little creature from the night when, successfully dressed as a girl, he had tried to pick up Coyne.

He was dressed like a tough street chick, in a tight black skirt and a newsboy cap. Big-eyed, he squeezed up to Kathy, and his mouth formed a silent "Oooooh!" He reached out and caressed the shiny smooth fabric on her shoulder, turned his limpid eyes to me, and murmured, "Beautiful madame; madame sexee!"

After one drink we went on to the Superstar. This club had the best sound system in Thailand and the most beautiful girls. Many of them could actually dance. It was the most tastefully flashy of all the clubs; the girls were more raucous and more daringly suggestive in their dancing.

Once Dawson and Tuk went with Kat to the Superstar while I was on a story with Coyne. They table-hopped, and for a while she was alone at the table. One of the girls, seeing she had no date, invited Kat to share noodles with all the girls after the club closed. We both thought that was pretty decent.

The music thudded and slammed and lifted us along to our table; we ordered our drinks and sat back to enjoy the tableau.

There weren't many Americans living in Bangkok, aside from tourists, but almost to a man they were Vietnam veterans. The room was suddenly filled with the *whop-whop* of helicopters right down on us, and for a moment we all felt that exact degree of apprehension you get going into a hot

LZ. Then the sound segued into the Doors, and we realized the D.J. had once again ambushed us with the music from *Apocalypse Now*.

After the bar closed we said good night to Dawson and Tuk and grabbed a tuk-tuk. It roared off into the night, up Silom Road, through the traffic circle at Lumpini Park, and along Embassy Row. The night Bangkok air, jungle smells through motor exhaust, poured over us. I propped my boot on the frame of the tuk-tuk and leaned back. The moon over Bangkok was the color of dried blood. It's the pollution.

20
BROWN BLASTS BALLOON

From the balcony of our penthouse, traffic noises from
Sukhumvit were frequently so loud, even on the eighth
floor, that all conversation had to be conducted at a bellow.
When agitated, Coyne screamed, "I'M READY TO JUMP
THE FUCKING BALLOON!"

Coyne and I had first learned about the balloon on the
Mitrapab jump when a couple of guys from Mark Smith's
SF advisory team-Korea showed up wearing weird wings
such as we'd never seen. "They're Thai balloon jumpers
wings," Mark had said, chuted up, one foot propped on the
tailgate of an RTAF C-123.

"They have a barrage balloon on a thousand-foot cable.
They winch it down; six jumpers climb in the gondola and
hook up. They run it back up to about eight hundred feet

and go out on individual tap-outs. Jump school trainees make their first two jumps from it."

"How was it?"

He shrugged. "There's no wind blast. You just float out of the gondola. It takes a six thousand count to open, which scares the shit out of you, and by the time you open you're at five hundred feet. I've got more than three hundred and fifty jumps, and this was the worst."

Coyne and I had the same thought simultaneously. *Brown!* Brown has to jump the balloon.

As soon as Brown got to Thailand I called Colonel Rut Komolvanich, Operations Officer of the Thai Special Warfare Center. Col. Rut would do anything he could for the Special Forces old-boy network. He put us on the manifest for the following Wednesday.

But that jump was pre-empted by the first of our long-range strategy sessions.

When we canceled that first drop, Brown decided we'd do the jump last thing before we closed out in Thailand, so as not to take a chance of missing a combat patrol because of a broken leg.

We used up two months skulking in alleys, holding secret meetings over sputtering candles in hotel rooms cooled by ceiling fans, making anxious, coded telephone calls. We accumulated enough secret information to get a military intelligence detachment an increase in budget and personnel; but, aside from Tom and Kat's jaunt to Cambodia, none of it was anything we could print in the magazine without getting people killed.

With each new disappointment Coyne yelled, "I'M READY TO JUMP THE FUCKING BALLOON!" This became the *leitmotif* of our expedition.

Brown became morose. He spent hours locked in his room with a book on commando operations. I took him aside and gave him a little lecture on how it's always darkest just before the dawn.

"Don't worry about it," he said. "I'm not going over the

rail." I was not cheered; he was the only one who had mentioned suicide. Brown abandoned his commando book and moved to the living room, where he sprawled across the arms of an easy chair in his sprung Jockey shorts, chewing his mustache and staring at his feet. Finally things got so bad he went four days without even screaming, "You're fired, asshole!" at Coyne. Something had to be done.

"I'M READY TO JUMP THE FUCKING BALLOON!" Coyne bellowed in frustration.

I called Col. Rut.

"Sure," he said. "Come tomorrow. In the morning we jump the balloon, and in afternoon you can jump C-130 if you want."

"Good, we'll do them both," I replied.

The next morning I rented an air-conditioned taxi to take Brown, Coyne, T.R., Kat, and me to Lop Buri and back. Coyne decided to take his video camera, a large, heavy, professional model. Kat had been a news and sports photographer in Little Rock, so she shot the stills. We had six people, including the driver, and a lot of gear, in the car. It was a squeeze.

"Should have got two cars," Coyne muttered.

"You fuckhead," I sneered. "You got an air-conditioned limo. You used to ride out to jump in a two-and-a-half-ton truck."

"I was nineteen," Coyne muttered. "I didn't know nothing."

There was a consensus that Coyne had been spoiled by his association with the motion picture business.

"I'm hungry," said T.R. Although he ate very little, Reisinger seldom stopped. "Could we stop for breakfast?"

"No sweat," I said. "We'll stop at the next Dairy Queen." T.R.'s stomach rejected everything but basic Cheeseburger-in-Paradise American cuisine. I often wondered how he'd made it in Vietnam, but he had.

For miles, Thailand shot by outside: flame trees, houses

on stilts, entire families on small motorcycles. I said nothing, lost in my pre-jump funk.

Skydivers wonder why paratroopers feel fear, but skydivers pack their own chutes and open at three grand. Paratroopers jump rigs packed in a speed shop, by somebody else, which open at a thousand feet.

Further, the military reserve parachute has no pilot chute. A rip cord must be pulled, and then the canopy must be grasped and shaken out like a sheet, and this must be done with the wind. If it is done against the wind, the reserve will be sucked into the main canopy, in which case the jumper has two malfunctions to correct in what's left of his nine seconds. This requires a cool head and an enormous jolt of adrenaline. The adrenaline starts on the ground; the cool head is something you have to put together for yourself.

The paratrooper's sky is filled with other paratroopers, and frequently with falling objects as well—rifles, rucksacks, jeeps, 105 millimeter howitzers. Small wonder paratroopers tend to be tightly wired.

Brown was very quiet on the drive. He was fifty-one and had a bad back. Coyne and I had set up this jump as a joke, to test his macho image. A major factor in the success of his magazine is that Brown puts his ass on the line two or three times a year, on camera. I got a quick mental image of him being taken out of the S.H.O.T. Show in a wheelchair when his back went out.

I don't know whether he was afraid or not, but he was damn serious.

At Lop Buri, Colonel Rut placed us under the guidance of a suave and intelligent young staff captain, Kitti Patummas, only recently returned from the States, where he had attended the Ranger and Special Forces Officers' courses. His English was better than Coyne's. With a confident saunter, he led us into the balloon hangar, where it bulked and bobbed against the ceiling like a fat, friendly fish on a dozen lines.

A tightly muscled, very short Thai sergeant, with a young, tough face and excellent English, gave us gondola training. He taught the difference between a balloon exit and an aircraft exit. "You just step out of balloon. If you jump up and out, like on airplane, you might hit cable," he said, referring to the quarter-inch steel cables that suspend the gondola from the balloon.

A two-and-a-half-ton truck with an enormous winch on the back towed the British-made balloon out, while we did refresher parachute landing falls from a wooden platform into sawdust. We jumped off from about six feet, practicing the various landing positions; front, left-front, right-front, left and right rear. I did them fairly well, but hit a lot harder than when I went through jump school in 1962. Twenty years later and thirty-five pounds heavier, what the hell was I doing here?

But I loved it—the ritual of procedure, the comradeship of shared risk, the risk itself, and the adrenaline jolt that went with it. I shared that with Brown, which is why he never held our joke against us, or even recognized it as such.

We drove to the drop zone where the balloon was parked, etched low against a pale blue, cloudless sky. A huge Thai word was painted on the side, but since the Thai alphabet is a derivation of Sanskrit, I could neither read nor pronounce it. Alongside was parked a two-and-a-half-ton truck loaded with parachutes. As a stick of six Thai jumpers boarded the gondola and was winched into the sky, Coyne strapped into his video rig, and Kat started shooting stills. The balloon's cable drooped in the direction of the wind.

I could see the value of the balloon as a training device. It was much cheaper than flying students on their first two jumps, and provided an excellent vantage point from which to grade them on canopy work and PLFs, but was absolutely useless for practicing door exits.

It took only a couple of minutes to winch the balloon to altitude. Very shortly the jumpers dropped out, one by one. Unlike a C-130 jump, where the speed of the aircraft snaps their chutes open before jumpers have fallen four feet below the flight path, these jumpers were almost halfway to the ground before their chutes fully extended, billowed and inflated. By then Brown, T.R., Coyne, and I were chuted up, ready to board the balloon, which was quickly winched back down. Single file, we waddled around to the front of the gondola and boarded.

The jumpmaster moved us into position and hooked our static lines to a cable above us. We stood there for a moment, looking at each other in our bulbous helmets and parachute gear. The gondola swung free and the ground dropped away. Then it was so quiet and the breeze so pleasant that I couldn't believe it was dangerous. Our jumpmaster or "dispatcher," as he was called, said they had never had a malfunction.

Our dispatcher was the same tough young sergeant who had given us refresher training. He wore Thai, U.S., and British jump wings. "How often you jump balloon?" I inquired.

"Almost every day," he said. "It's my balloon."

As we rose, the horizon extended further and further, until it became a haze blending sky and ground, miles away. The sky grew enormous, and the people and cars below shrank, but never so much that they became dots, or even toys. It was like looking down from the fifth floor of a building, only there was no building. Then we stopped, and swayed. The cables creaked, and the wind hummed faintly around them.

The dispatcher nodded and dropped the safety bar from the entrance to the gondola. He gestured Brown into the door. As soon as Brown had a good door position, the dispatcher tapped him on the ass.

Brown yelled when he went over the edge. He claims it was a battle cry, but it sounded like terror to me.

Then it was my turn. I wheeled into the door and assumed a standard door position. The DZ was way down there, almost like a sand table.

"Ready!" said the dispatcher. I came to something like attention, grasped my reserve at the sides and took one step forward, like a little tin soldier.

It wasn't like skydiving, where you don't feel weightless until you get away from the aircraft. There was a feeling of instant buoyancy, like the Moonwalk or Big Slide, only longer and better. My legs sort of floated up so that I was sitting midair in an L position, then I felt the first soft tug at my back, then three more; my trash streamed out and ever-so-slowly billowed and inflated.

I reached for the right toggle, even as I checked my canopy. The plan was to hold against the wind and save myself a long walk to the turn-in point. It worked pretty well. For a while it looked like I was dropping straight down on one of the two trees on the DZ, but I drifted away without correction. Then the ground got close and I locked my eyes on the horizon and got my feet and knees together.

Crump! No sweat, good one. I was up and running to collapse the chute, but two little boys who were hanging around the DZ beat me to it.

Meanwhile, in the air, Coyne could not find his toggles. He still swears he jumped an unsteerable T-10. He got his feet and knees together and crashed in for a right front fall, moving at about ten knots, hitting his left heel and twisting his ankle. No more jumps that day. All the better for him to tape the C-130 jump.

A little over an hour later, engines roared and we were airborne. Brown, T.R., and I sat on the incline of a closed tailgate on a C-130, staring out at a sea of eager young faces. We were jumping with a class of junior cadets at the Royal Thai Military Academy, for whom this was the fourth of five qualifying jumps.

Smaller and lighter than Americans, the Thais put about a hundred jumpers on a C-130 that would hold sixty Americans, but to do it they leave the seats up and everybody sits cross-legged on the floor.

I was the first man in the right door, then T.R. right behind me. Brown was first in the left. I love being first man, and what I love most is that moment the door is opened, the wind grabs you, and paddies below go by, close below.

The light went green. The jumpmaster didn't tap me out. Once, over Okinawa, a navigator's sleeve triggered the green light by accident, and if the jumpmaster hadn't grabbed my harness I would have led an entire stick into the East China Sea. I took a quick peek. The third man was going out the left door.

Bye-bye.

Out and open, I grabbed my right toggle and pulled, turning into a surprise; the entire stick from the right door was drifting right toward me. The cadets were jumping T-10s. They had no directional capability, and the forward thrust of my directional chute drove me into them. Too late to turn. I held into the wind as a ragged but solid line of olive-green parachutes headed my way.

I drifted into the glistening green dome of a canopy. It billowed as I bounded across, sinking further and further into it, finally breaking into air on the other side before either canopy collapsed, wondering what the kid below thought when he saw the imprint of my size twelves sprint across.

Brown and I landed well, but T.R. sat flat on his ass and did mischief to his spine. Nothing serious, several days of twinges and awkward motions, plus a football-size bruise on his hip. I think it is no coincidence that the two old farts who ran every day got away clean, while our two young *bon vivants* were mangled.

"Well, we finally did something," said Brown as he came striding in, wearing a big, evil grin, still in his helmet, parachute kit bag slung across his back.

* * *

He was in an expansive mood at our very late dinner in the apartment over Sukhumvit that night. "This is good fuckin' shit," he said through a mouthful of spaghetti.

I laughed. "The Bob Brown equivalent of 'My compliments to the chef'?"

Brown gave me an injured look. "Well, it is good shit." He called out to the kitchen to See, our Wa cook, "See! Hey, See!"

See padded barefoot in from the kitchen, wearing a concerned frown. He wore warm-up pants and an *SOF* T-shirt. Brown grasped his arm, grinning. "Good shit!" he bellowed. "Good fuckin' shit!"

See went back to the kitchen beaming, walking like a pouter pigeon.

Brown belched mightily and wiped his mouth with the hair on his arm. "Well, guess I'll hit the rack," he said. He slid back from the table and walked to his room. Covered with wiry brown hair, in his sprung Jockey shorts, Brown had a helluva build, incredible for a man his age. He looked like what a papatrooper ought to look like.

"Ah, sweet mystery of life, at last I've found you," he sang as he padded away, flip-flops flapping on the floor, arms waving wildly to the meter of his croak. He began to yodel as the door closed behind him.

21
THE
LAOTIAN
RESISTANCE

Brown and Coyne took off for Afghanistan with the video camera, looking for a little more action before we closed out. This was my last chance to really do something here; I wanted to get into Laos.

"You do not understand our customs," said Chan, the intelligence agent. "You must spend money to gain face, so you will be respected." He looked at me earnestly over the dining room table in the penthouse. Across the table with Chan was Colonel Boon Lert, allegedly a big wheel in the Lao resistance. All we had was Dr. Seuss's word for that.

Actually, I do believe he was fairly important. He carried himself like a Lao colonel, was a man of simple dignity with an active, if limited, intellect. We had seen pictures of him with a column of troops moving through the jungles in Chinese-style uniforms and with Chinese weapons. The Chi-

nese will support anybody they consider likely to stick a
thorn in the side of the Vietnamese. Chan was also intelligent and likeable.

He looked at me astonished as I pounded the table and
snarled at him. "Look," I bellowed, "I have just about had it
with this bullshit. I wanta go into Laos with the resistance.
You say they're willing to take me. Great! They say they
don't have weapons. They have to rent them from the Thais.
Fuck that!

"They want money. Okay, I understand that. Fine, but no
money up front. They get the weapons, we go in, they get
the money. It's that simple." We had spent almost four
months putting up front money for things that never happened. Enough already.

"But we must have some money first," Chan said earnestly. "Otherwise they will think you are not men of importance."

I smiled broadly, and said nothing. Chan gave me a look
like a puppy that didn't know why it had been whipped, and
Colonel Boon Lert sat hunched over, cowed.

"You know, I understand your customs a lot better than
you understand ours. One of our customs is that anybody
who lets himself get ripped off repeatedly is an idiot. We
have a word for such a person. It is 'sucker.' If they want to
take me in, fine. We've backed Dr. Seuss and Boon Lert to
the tune of many thousands of dollars.

"Now you wanta talk about face. What do you think it's
gonna do to my face to go back to Boulder and tell them
that my wife got into Cambodia, and I couldn't get into
Laos, or anywhere else? So I lose face if I give you money
up front and this thing falls apart, and I lose face if I don't
go in.

"So you guys get me in if you're so fuckin' hot. Get me in
or so help me, I'll do everything I can to insure that Brown
shuts down your entire operation. No more bucks from the
looney magazine."

Two days later T.R. and I were on our way to Nakon

Phanom to prepare to go into Laos. Kathy stayed in Bangkok, manned the phone, and worked on some reports for Brown.

Contemplate this scenario: two Americans come to town in a rented car, which drops them at the hotel and leaves. They check in with a smattering of Thai and a great deal of gesticulation. The astute observer, one who had seen both American military and civilians, would take these two for Vietnam vets by age and demeanor. A true connoisseur of walks and mannerisms would not have much difficulty placing them under a pair of green berets.

So these two check in and don't do anything. They don't phone anybody, except for two calls to Bangkok. They don't see anybody.

Oddly enough, nobody seemed to pay it much mind. I would assume the cops kept tabs on us, but they did it discreetly.

It was about two-thirty in the afternoon when we got there. We were supposed to be contacted at six. So we dropped our gear and went for a walk.

We had driven straight in from Bangkok and hadn't eaten, so we set out to explore the town. We'd been there once before, with Hiney, but he had been commander at the now-closed U.S. airbase, knew the town, and just took over. We had followed him around and not learned the town.

Most of the NKP was along the river. The town stretched for about three-quarters of a mile, maybe three blocks deep, along the Mekong. There was a hotel at one end of town and a semi-fancy restaurant at the other.

We left the hotel and walked to the restaurant, passing row after row of flat, fake-front stores on the way, open front food and hardware stores jammed with goods, and several bell, bangle, and Buddha shops for religious artifacts. The Thais not only worship Buddha, they love him.

They give a lot to their religion, and have every appearance of getting a lot back.

We passed a group of young men at an intersection, teen-agers taking a break, playing a game with what appeared to be a soccer ball woven from bamboo plaits.

The game they played was simple in concept but difficult in execution. The idea was for a bunch of guys to stand in a circle and keep the ball in the air with their feet. In Lumpini Park I have seen rings of young men who were wizards with their feet, but these lads were just fair. Two of them were playing in flip-flops, and when one of those boys saw Tom and me coming, his foot connected at an angle and the ball spun off into the street, sending him chasing after it.

Several of the old buildings were of concrete construction, like a rough stucco, usually painted a dirty pastel, with the old signs from when G.I.s were here; Bar Butterfly, O.K. Corral. We finally came to the restaurant and went inside. We sat at a rickety table on red vinyl seats in the back, by the river. It stretched wide, flat, and placid, to Laos, about three-quarters of a mile away: a broad, calm river the color of red mud.

The waiter, in white shirt and tie, brought us some dusty menus with an English translation, and we selected a hot seafood and rice concoction, but we didn't do as well as when Hiney was with us.

A concrete sidewalk, with a stone wall on the river side, extended north of the town for quite a distance. After dinner we walked along the Mekong, talking about this story, about Vietnam, about working for Brown, walking further than we actually had time to walk. We had to get back to the hotel for our scheduled contact.

There was alleged to be a guerrilla encampment about fifteen kilometers north of town. Colonel Boon Lert was supposed to be making arrangements for us to go into Laos with them.

Tom placed the call. He understood Boon Lert's accent

over the phone better than I did. He sat on the bed, surrounded by field gear: packs, poncho, patrol harness, his M-5 aid kit, and field chow, mostly beanie weenies.

By now maids in the hotel had undoubtedly conveyed a complete inventory of this stuff to the local gendarmes.

"They haven't been able to set anything up," Tom said. "The Thais have called some kind of moratorium on guerrilla operations. Some kind of big meeting is going on."

"Wonderful," I said. "Only they told us before we left that it already *was* set up. All we had to do was wait until they picked us up."

"Well, I guess we'll just have to wait a little longer," he said. He put a Meat Loaf tape into his cassette deck and started waiting.

I went back to my room and fretted. Then I went to sleep.

We spent the next two days prowling the town and the banks of the Mekong, hovering over the phone, listening to the same tap dance from Bangkok.

By breakfast the third day I was snarling, "Fuck this! Either they come through today or we go back to Bangkok, and I have a little chat with Chan and the Colonel."

Suddenly there was an ungodly series of internal combustions out in the parking lot. It sounded like a two-stroke firefight. Then it ceased. An Ichabod Crane–like young man, about twenty-four, sauntered self-assured into the lobby. A mop of curly red hair tumbled all over his head. He spied us, turned, and walked to our table, sat down, crossed his legs and smiled as though we were long lost fraternity brothers.

"Hi, I'm R-r-roger W-warner." He held out his hand. We shook and introduced ourselves. "Do either of you know where I might get my motorcycle repaired?"

We couldn't read Thai, but we could read the word "Honda," so we knew where that shop was. We told him, and he joined us for breakfast.

Roger told us his story over breakfast. He was a freelance journalist, here to do a story on the refugees. Roger was a Yale graduate. He had been a rewrite man for *Time* for a year after graduation, and then taken what little money he could scrape together and headed for the Orient with a camera and a portable typewriter. His objective was to sell enough stuff so he didn't have to use his return ticket. So far he had made it nine months, which impressed me. Free-lancing is a tough gig.

Roger was six-four, 170 lbs., broad at the shoulders, narrow at the hips, twenty-four years old, good-looking, a graduate of one of the three best universities in the U.S., and off on the adventure of his life. I envied him. Like Captain America in Cambodia, he could take his adventure as it came. I felt compelled to tie my adventure to something that was long gone.

He seemed to have that bland assurance taught in Ivy League schools that pretty much anything he did would be okay. I had known his type in the Army, and they had not done well. They tended to wander, oozing charm and ad hoc analyses, into situations that would either get you shot by the other side or arrested by your own.

But Roger was not in the Army and could wander anywhere he wanted. People would usually decide he was amiable enough, and give him whatever he asked for.

I have long used the down-home Okie version of the same technique, which works in the army, but not on the State Department.

"What brings you gentlemen to this unlikely place?" he inquired.

I saw no reason not to tell him.

He smiled. "I speak a little Lao," he said, and held up a Lao dictionary to prove it. "How about joining forces. I could cover it for another magazine. We can hire a tuk-tuk and cruise the villages along the river until we find one that's affiliated with the resistance."

I shrugged. "Might as well. It beats sitting here on our duffs, waiting for something to happen."

We put Roger's bike in the shop, and that afternoon he

and I took a long walk upriver, while T.R. went to see *The Jazz Singer* at the local moviehouse. Roger had great freelance stories to tell. Somehow he had managed to get the Heng Samrin government to let him into Ankhor Wat, which had been closed for years, to Khmer and foreigners alike.

Finally, Roger and I walked the paddy dikes across a rice field past a small boy prodding a water buffalo, who eyed us curiously as we passed. We walked around the village and found a sheltered spot by the river, stripped and went swimming.

By nine-thirty the next morning, thanks to Roger's dictionary, we were in a small resistance village, and my spirits soared. We were going to get in without Chan, without Boon Lert, without Dr. Seuss. The village was hidden in a grove of trees by the road, on the side away from the river. It was a small village, maybe fifty people, a collection of bamboo, rattan, and thatch shacks. There were families, but all the men were of military age.

With the aid of his dictionary, Roger was in painstaking conversation with a tall Lao in cut-offs.

"Ask them if there are any sick people I can treat?" Tom said. His M-5 kit was slung from his shoulder.

As soon as Roger had dragged this message out of his dictionary the man he spoke to led us into his hut, where his own baby lay dying.

Swiftly and efficiently Tom opened his kit and went to work. The problem, as it turned out, was that the boy's mother was also sick; her milk was killing the child. Tom also ministered to the mother, and that afternoon we brought a six-week supply of infant formula to the village. Through Roger, Tom delivered a half-hour lecture on field sanitation. That's how long it took to say, "Always boil water," with the aid of the dictionary. But for the time being, at least, he had saved the child, and possibly the mother as well. We were in with the people of the village.

They seemed a simple, happy people, just as my Montagnards had been, and I felt an open warmth and friendship coming from them, such as I had not felt in many years.

That afternoon though, when we came back with the infant formula, the headman of the village told us we would have to deal with someone higher up in the hierarchy.

I had just assumed they would take us over that night, and we would hook up with the people they fought with on the other side of the Mekong. When was anything ever so simple in Southeast Asia?

The next day we rented a truck to take us to one of the large refugee camps nearby, to pick up the man who was supposed to make it all happen, a "major" in the Lao resistance. After a long, anxious wait at the gate, closely scrutinized by Thai guards, our man showed. He was tall for a Lao, and slim, and wore neatly pressed slacks, sandals, and a white shirt. Like our guide, he was smiling; but unlike the headman, whose smile was open, friendly and ingenuous, this man's smile was the phony smirk of a used car salesman. But he did speak excellent English, and we talked some in the truck.

He had a military bearing, but not the look of someone who had seen much combat. I guessed correctly that he had been an administrative officer, a first lieutenant in the *Force Armee du Royoume* of Laos.

I didn't find this news particularly reassuring. I never fought in Laos, but I did serve for a time with the Allied Officer Liaison Office at Ft. Benning, where we ministered to the needs of foreign students at the Infantry School. I had been highly impressed by some of those officers, and appalled by others. The ones who had appalled me the most were the Laotians and the Iranians. For arrogance, ignorance, and inefficiency they were unrivaled, although later I was to find their like throughout the so-called "upper classes" of the Third World.

With a surprisingly warm and hospitable manner, he explained that it would take another day to arrange for weapons for us to take across. The Thai government tolerated the Lao resistance, but they would not allow the Lao to bring weapons into Thai territory. This seemed reasonable enough, since they didn't want to give the Vietnamese an excuse to invade. Then he asked us to a party in the village that night. All the while we were driving from the refugee camp into NKP.

By the time we reached town he had sprung the happy news that while the Lao were giving the party for us, *SOF* was paying for it. He made it seem so reasonable. As hosts with honored guests, etiquette demanded that they throw a party, but these people were poor and had nothing, so we must buy the stuff for it. Noblesse oblige! It was as slick a con as I had ever seen, and, low as the stakes were, and as much as we stood to gain, I decided to let it run on to see how far it would go. We bought a few cases of beer, a couple of bottles of Mekong Whiskey, a couple of 100 kilo bags of rice, enough actually to last the village for about six weeks, and some odd groceries. It came to about a hundred and twenty bucks.

That night Roger, T.R., and I sat cross-legged around a fire in the village with lukewarm beers in our hands, the village men seated around us. The women served a thick soup in battered tin bowls, rice in the same, corn on the cob, and later, papaya.

Until sunset, the sky was clear and blue and the forest crowded our little clearing of bamboo huts. The men wore only pants or cut-offs; the women wore sarongs, stained from being washed in muddy water, some wore tops, and some did not. Some of the women wore turbans, and some smoked green cheroots. It was a moment of peace such as I had not known since Vietnam.

As it got dark they built a huge fire. It blazed in the dark and sparks flew off into the night. The air was light and fragrant, clear and sweet. It was to city air as champagne is to sludge. For a moment I felt . . . did I actually feel it or only remember as it dopplered away? For an instant I was back in the mountains, a natural man.

The next evening T.R. and I went out to the village dressed normally, but carrying our field gear in kit bags. Once there, we suited up. Normally I don't wear socks on a combat patrol. What they do to your feet after walking across a river is not nice. But the only boots I'd been able to get on short notice were too wide and I had no choice but to wear two pair.

I had also thoughtfully put a taped hacksaw blade in one boot and a woodsaw blade in the other, in case of capture. I had no illusions about the quality of the troops we were going in with. I wore a regular Vietnam-style tiger suit, bush hat, and standard load bearing equipment, ammo pouches, two canteens, field dressing bandage, knife, compass secured to the harness by three feet of parachute suspension line—and no weapon. Weapons were on the other side of the Mekong.

Roger wore jeans and a dark shirt. He was guided by standard journalistic ethics and had no plans to carry a weapon. Besides, he'd never fired an automatic weapon before, and this was not the place or time to learn. The troops wore motley camo.

At dark we set out. The troops took up a good interval and moved silently, and very swiftly. I wasn't having any trouble keeping up, but my glasses were bifocals, and my feet were lost in a fog below. The ground was irregular, giving me a mild case of the stumbles. Nothing I couldn't handle, but I hated feeling awkward in the field. And I knew we wouldn't be out long enough to get over it. It takes about two weeks to get used to the field, and about six to get good at it.

But the air was clear, and it felt good to be out in the night. We crossed the highway and entered the dry paddy on the other side. The troops lengthened their stride and it was a bitch to keep up with them. I focused my total attention on the task, and stayed that way until we entered the jungle by the river. Then everything slowed down and the air became dank and ripe.

Slowly we groped our way down to the river's edge, where the boats were, and took up a defensive position while we waited for the light on the other side that would signal us to come over. We spread out and sat down. I found my insect repellent and gave myself another good coat. They buzzed around my face all night, but I got only two or three bites. In that situation you can't smoke, and you can't talk. You can't move around. You just sit and wait for word to move out.

I sat in the dark and felt the power of the river. This was life. No cities, no hustle, just the power of the river and the clean air, the moon, and clear bright stars. I had not expected that moment, but I would have come to Thailand for it alone.

Good thing, because the light on the other side of the river never shined.

The Laotian resistance major looked up at me with big sorrowful eyes, unable to believe that we and our traveler's cheques were actually leaving. He would have to go back to the refugee camp. Word was that the Thais were still cracking down on the resistance. There was no action on the border.

"We can go across without guns," he said desperately. "You can see the other side."

And what? Take pictures of village life; take a picture of a Russian-made truck on the highway? "Look, Major," I snapped. "You don't get it; we're a gun magazine. No guns, no story."

We finally agreed to his bringing some young leaders of the resistance over to the hotel that afternoon, to tell us their stories of derring-do from the other side.

When we got back to the hotel T.R. said, "Boy, am I glad

you decided not to go over tonight. Those guys don't have it."

"That motherfucker," I said of the major. "I'm tempted to start a fund to buy salt for the Vietnamese, so they can turn Laos into a desert."

That afternoon the major brought over three or four of the young Lao resistance leaders. They were real guys, and you only had to look at them to know they dealt with death on a daily basis. They were young and dark, not light-skinned like the upper-class Lao, and their eyes blazed. Three days before they had raided a Soviet information center in Savanaket, on motorcycles; cheap little trail bikes. Five guys had ridden into town on bikes, thrown a grenade apiece into the center, fired up a magazine apiece and zoomed back out of town.

They sat in our hotel room, quiet and stolid, telling their story when the phone rang. I picked it up and heard Brown's conspiratorial snicker. I quickly filled him in on what had happened.

"Never mind that," he snapped. "We're through here. Coyne and I got in with the Afghan rebels. We attacked a Russian A-camp. There were about twelve of them holed up with maybe four hundred Afghan troops. We laid out on the next hillside and pasted them all day with mortars and a 12.7 anti-aircraft machine gun. Killed two Russians and God knows how many Afghans."

"You rotten bastard!" I screamed. "You beat me again!"

Again the snicker. "So how about you and Kat going to Israel for a couple of weeks on your way to Beirut?"

22
ALOHA, VIETNAM

The night before Kat and I left for Israel I dreamed of my first leave-taking from Vietnam and of a jump I'd made when, as I'd told Mark Smith on the Mitrapab jump, everything was for the first time.

Four of us, Special Forces officers, squeezed under the porch of the ops shack to get out of the rain.

I had just brought my last patrol back into our camp, four klicks north of Cheo Reo, after having taken Walt Swain, a good friend and executive officer of our replacement detachment, on his orientation patrol. We had killed three VC and captured a Walther PPK pistol that I confiscated as my personal war trophy. We had sprung the ambush at two-thirty in the afternoon, less than eight klicks from a Vietnamese district headquarters. Even Captain

Charley Judge, Walt's CO, was impressed, not something that happened often. Judge turned the Walther over and over in his hands. Swain told the story of how it happened. "So you didn't put out flank guards?" the Old Man, Captain Crews McCulloch, said.

"Nope," Swain replied. "Just got on the trail and barreled on through."

The Old Man looked a little embarrassed. "We usually keep off the trails and put out flankers," he said.

I started to explain that it was a fairly safe area—our intelligence had put the VC crossing the ambush site at a certain time—and that I had wanted Swain's first patrol to be a success, so they'd stay with our concept of operations.

I'd made my decision based on the best facts available and had been right. I didn't need to apologize to anybody. "I'm going to get cleaned up," I said, moving off into the rain, toward the wash house.

I was proud of that operation. We had spent our first four months wandering around in the woods trolling for ambushes. But by then the Old Man had evolved a concept of operations that got us in solid with the tribespeople, one that didn't involve shooting buffalo or burning villages, and from that I had been able to set up a superb intel net. For the past two months we had been going on short patrols, setting up on the trails, waiting for an appointment that Victor Charlie didn't know he had.

We knew that place cold. The Old Man could stand anywhere in Phu Bon province and call out a four digit coordinate without reference to a map. We had the highest kill score in II Corps, and we had got two-thirds of it in the past sixty days. Never in my life had I been anyplace that I wanted to leave less.

My stomach cramped badly. I'd been operating with a constant bellyache for more than two months, losing a steady five pounds a month to amoebic dysentery for six months.

That night at supper the Old Man said there wasn't time

for any more patrols. "The operational fund has to be taken into finance at Nha Trang by an officer. Judge and I have to inventory weapons tomorrow, so you're elected."

I wasn't happy about it because there was still one patrol planned. But that night I packed an AWOL bag and shined up a pair of jungle boots. The following morning I caught the II Corps courier aircraft, a Caribou, at the airstrip.

It was still the dry season in Nha Trang and the sky was a hard, pale blue from the mountains to the sea. The air was lemon yellow and the sun baked my bones. I was covered with a fine film of sweat as soon as I jumped off the Caribou. It felt good. The passengers stood with their baggage beside a long row of new, whitewashed concrete hangars, the hard concrete of the runway stretching off in the distance.

I went inside one of the hangars, blinking to adjust to the light, my body turning suddenly cool as I passed into the shade. The 7th Aerial Port Squadron's passenger desk was an upright, homemade counter painted a glossy grey. It was manned by a young Airman 2nd class in fatigues and a blue baseball cap.

"How do I get to the new Special Forces Headquarters?" I asked. I hadn't been to Nha Trang since we came in country.

"It's way across on the other side of the runway, sir," he said. "Just a minute and I'll call over and get you a ride."

I took the manila folder with the ops fund in it inside the door marked FINANCE. A fat Spec 5 behind a big steel desk took it, turned and handed it to a pretty Vietnamese girl, who put it at the bottom of a pile of paper on her desk. "Where's the transient officer's quarters?" I asked the specialist.

"All the way down the street and to your left, sir," he said.

I grunted thanks and went back through the door, out into the hard yellow sunshine. I looked around, always feeling uneasy in Nha Trang. Mountains loom over the town, within easy mortar range.

I walked down the street and turned left where a row of barracks stretched off to the right. Like the rest of the buildings, they were gleaming white one-story structures with pitched roofs and lots of windows to let in the air. A walkway ran in front of the barracks, and across from the barracks was another row of bigger buildings, three of them. The sound of splashing water indicated they were latrines. In front of each barracks was a small teal and gold metal sign hanging from an inverted L-shaped bracket. The sign in front of the first barracks said, BRODT BARRACKS, and there was another over the door that said, "Transit Officers Quarters." It should have read "transient," but who was I to bitch?

Every barracks was named after a Special Forces man killed in Vietnam. Too many had been friends of mine.

The last time I saw Jim Brodt, he and I and a guy named Morgan Jones sat in the bar of the Ft. Buckner Officers Club on Okinawa. Morgan and I made up rowdy songs, and Brodt bought beer to keep us fueled.

A kid named Neil McIver was killed in the same action as Brodt. His building was down the street. He and Mike Iten, our junior commo man, had gone through basic, jump school, and training group together. Mike was in Vietnam on his first tour when they were killed. He and McIver used to talk in Morse code back and forth in the evening. Then McIver quit sending. Mike didn't find out why for a couple of weeks. His team sergeant got him drunk, told him, then sent him to Dalat for three days. Mike and McIver were both eighteen at the time.

We were free enough for that sort of kindness in those days.

It seemed almost indecent to be sleeping in Jim Brodt's memorial. I went inside and threw my gear on the first empty bunk. In back was a Dutch door with the top part open and a sign that said, "Transient Personal, Check in

Here." There was a fat, gray-haired "leg" sergeant back there, reading a true adventure magazine.

"I sign in here?"

"Yes, sir, and check your sidearm."

I signed his register and slipped my scrounged USMC shoulder holster over my head. "Anywhere around here to get a drink?"

"Prayboy Crub's down at the end of the barracks row, sir," he said.

"Is it open?"

"Noon to midnight, sir."

I went back into the sunshine. The white rows of buildings closed in around me, and for a moment my eyes started flicking from shadow to shadow. Then I realized what I was doing and walked with my eyes fixed straight ahead, to the end of the row.

It was dark inside the Playboy Club after the brightness outside. The club was in a regular barracks building, long and narrow, but there were rows of chrome and leatherette couches on the left, with round, black Formica-topped coffee tables. The bar ran almost the entire length of the right side, and the mirror behind it ran the length of the bar. It was two o'clock in the afternoon. The bar was three-quarters empty. Mostly the customers were transients like me, with bleak faces and very wide eyes. Their shoulders slumped and they seemed to cluster on the couches, with their backs to a wall. Over in one corner was a bunch of young PFCs and Spec 4s.

They were very clean and eager and talked loudly. Most likely off-duty commo men and truck drivers. Next to them was a glowing, multicolored Seeburg juke box. At the other end of the room were two pinball machines.

I went over to the bar and sat down, staring at the rows of canned cashews, Polish sausages, and my own face in the mirror. It looked ten years older than it had six months before. The barmaid came over. She was almost thirty, and had aged fast, too, become stringy and hard-faced. She wore black capri pants and a purple blouse. But she had beautiful long, straight black hair, drawn into a ponytail, flipped over her shoulder, and spilling down the front of her blouse in a shimmering cascade. "Gimme a San Miguel and a bag of Fritos, Angel," I said.

I took my beer and went over to the jukebox. There were three good songs on it, loud and rhythmic enough to preclude rational thought. I put in a dollar's worth of quarters and played them four times apiece: *Twist and Shout* by the Beatles, *Deep Purple* by Nino Tempo and April Stevens, and *Green Onions* by Booker T. and the M.G.'s.

The hard-driving rhythm drew me out of myself, and I stood, letting the beat drive me along. I killed my beer and went back for another.

Then I took the beer and the Fritos and sank into one of the deep chairs along the wall. I flipped my feet up on the low coffee table and let a long gurgle of beer slide down my throat.

I sat there until my twelve records played through, then broke a five, put in another dollar and played them again, four more times apiece. I did it fast, before anybody else could have a chance to make a selection, but somebody had slipped in a dime and Sinatra sang *All the Way*.

I got another beer and some pork skins. I ate a lot of junk food that afternoon, missed lunch, and drank through suppertime.

Some guys I knew came in. I grunted enough greeting to acknowledge their presence without inviting conversation.

My belly felt kind of crumby and my head was hot and it seemed a good idea to roll the cold beer bottle over my forehead. As soon as the beer was gone I got up, thinking I might go downtown.

But then I felt very sick and walked quickly out the door and across the space to the latrine building. It was dark and stars shone down between the buildings. Then there was the brightly lighted latrine with a row of stalls on the left and porcelain sinks on the right, each with its little square of mirror. I bolted for one of the stalls.

I got my pants down just in time. My bowels emptied in great racking spasms. I sat on the stool and rocked back and forth, trying to hold my stomach down. Then I grabbed the chain on the French-style crapper and, holding my trouser tops in my hands, whirled and watched the last of the stool swirl down the drain, as I threw my guts up in a sour green and yellow gusher, just finishing in time to sit back down again. This time it was all liquid.

I alternated like that for half an hour, until finally there was nothing left. Then I buckled up and went back to the Playboy Club, the closest place where there was help.

I barely got the door open, and stood there in the doorway, looking into the dim interior at all the green butts on barstools. *Green Onions* was still playing, and I couldn't have cared less.

Two young sergeants I had known on Okinawa came up. One of them said, "Sir, you all right?"

"No," I said.

One of them clamped a hand over my forehead. "You better believe it," he said. They half-dragged, half-carried me to a jeep, got my AWOL bag and weapon from the BOQ and drove me to the 8th Field Hospital on the other side of the airstrip. The ride was a dark blur.

A white-coated medic gave me a card to fill out and stuck a thermometer in my mouth. "Hundred and five," he said when he took it out.

For three days I lay in a bed in the hospital, between crisp, clean sheets, floating free in a bright white swirling cloud of feverish hallucinations.

It got cold, so cold I shivered for a long time, floating in the cloud. Then it turned warm again, and I became conscious and ate a clean meal off a clean tray, with salad.

"What have I got, Doc?"

"Gastroenteritis."

"What's that?"

"It's a badly upset stomach condition, characterized by diarrhea, vomiting, and a high fever."

I slept, twelve, fourteen, sixteen hours a day. Three days later I woke up. I grabbed a medic and said, "Man, I gotta get out of here. My team leaves Vietnam day after tomorrow, and I got stuff scattered all over that camp."

"You sure you feel well enough to go?"

"Sure, sure. I feel great. See!" I swung down out of the bed and walked about four steps, briskly, with my head held high. Then I stopped and grabbed a bedpost so I wouldn't fall down.

"Okay," he said. "Get your gear and check out."

As soon as I could get dressed and clear the hospital, I lurched weakly into the street, AWOL bag in hand, and thumbed a ride on a passing three-quarter.

The driver let me off at the little building beside the warehouses: the Transportation Movement Control office.

I pushed through the screen door and leaned on the counter. My stomach still had a few butterflies, but by and large, I felt okay. There was a sleek, efficient-looking Airman 1st class with a boogie haircut, ducktails on the sides and crewcut on top, and a clipboard, working behind the desk. Two pilots sat in back, drinking coffee, their feet up on desks. They wore flight suits and S&W .38s in cowboy rigs. They both had survival knives and good boots. One wore a U.S. army blocked fatigue cap and the other a camouflage duck hunting cap. They looked tired, but real solid. I didn't trust anybody in Vietnam who didn't look tired. They were Air Commandos.

"You got anything going to Cheo Reo this afternoon?" I asked.

"Yes, sir," the Airman 1st said. "Leaves at 1200 hours."

"Okay," I replied. "Book me on it. Name's Morris."

As soon as I got my name on the manifest I went back up to Special Forces headquarters and picked up our clearance for the ops fund and my pistol, got some lunch, and came back down to the TMC.

"Sorry, sir," the airman said as I came through the door. "That aircraft is a scrub. The right wheel is flat."

It was already too late to catch the courier, and even if I could, it only went to Pleiku today, then back to Cheo Reo tomorrow. By that route I'd be lucky to get back before the team left. "You got anything else going that way?"

"No, sir, not until day after tomorrow."

"Aw," I said, "I have to get there. You got anything going over it?"

"Yes, sir. There's an air drop at Plei Ta Nangle this afternoon. But it won't land at Cheo Reo."

"Have you got a weather check?" I asked. "What's the ground winds?"

"Eight to ten knots, sir," he said, checking the chart behind him.

"Okay, what time's the aircraft take off?"

"Fourteen-hundred, sir."

"Book me on it." I went to the Special Forces supply office next door. There was another clerk behind a desk there, an Army guy.

"Who do I see to draw a backpack, reserve, and kit bag? And preferably a helmet," I asked him.

"Chief McKee, sir," he said. "He's the rigger officer."

"Where's he at?"

He pointed toward the back of the office, on the other side of a partition. I went back there and found an earnest gentleman in his forties, laboriously pouring over some paperwork. He had a shaved fringe of hair around a gleaming bald head, and his face looked far older than his years.

"Chief McKee?" I said.

"Yes, sir." He stood up, and I saw he wore master parachutist wings and rigger wings. He was well-built, actually in a lot better shape than I was, a highly conscientious man.

I explained the situation to him and asked for a T-10 parachute assembly.

"Sir," he said. "I don't approve of jumping in on these

unprepared DZs. That's a very unsafe practice. I highly recommend against that."

From his standpoint, of course, the chief was absolutely right. But that didn't help solve my problem.

"Approve of it or not," I said, "will you give me the rig?"

"No, sir," he said. "I won't."

"The hell with it. You must work for somebody around here that can authorize it. Where's he at?"

"Major Kollat is the S-4, sir. His office is in the front."

I walked back up to the front of the supply office and through the door marked "Supply Officer."

He was seated behind his desk. The desk had a nameplate on it that said Zoltan F. Kollat, Major, United States Army. He was a very muscular man with brown curly hair. He had been physical training instructor for my class at the Special Forces Officers' Course at Ft. Bragg, and with his shirt off, from behind, if he wiggled a finger, his entire back looked like a flag waving. He sat at his desk, staring off into space. Perhaps he was practicing his glower.

"Major Kollat," I said.

He reached up and scratched his nose, almost splitting his sleeve up around his bicep. "What?" he replied.

"You mind if I borrow a T-10 assembly? I want to jump into my camp this afternoon."

"Naw, I don't care."

"Thanks." I got out of his office fast, before he could change his mind. Avoiding Chief McKee, I went to the warehouse and drew the rig and a helmet. Then I went back to the TMC.

There was still an hour to wait, so I got a cup of coffee and sat down with it. They had some old magazines for the flight crews to read. I picked up a dog-eared *Argosy*.

At one forty-five the Airman 1st class came back and said, "About time to load up, sir."

"Thanks." I slipped my shoulder holster over my head and picked up the heavy kit bag with the two parachutes in it, and my AWOL bag with the other hand.

"You want some help with that, sir?"

"Nope."

The crew squatted over their map under the wing of their C-47. Over by the door a fork lift put cargo pallets up on the conveyer inside the aircraft. Up inside, two door-bundle kickers tied on G-13 cargo chutes. Directing the whole operation was Chief McKee.

"Major Kollat loaned me a rig," I said.

"All right," he replied, but he didn't look very happy about it. An old jumper, he must have seen a lot of guys bent out of shape on better drop zones than the Cheo Reo airstrip. I sat down my kit bag and went over under the wing to talk to the crew. "Going to Cheo Reo?" I asked.

The pilot looked up. "Can't land there," he said. "Not on the flight plan."

"Just go over the airstrip at about twelve hundred," I said. "I'm going to jump."

"Okay, fine."

I squatted down over the map and showed him the approach I wanted. He suggested a better one and I agreed to it. "Look," I said, "if you got one of these little message-dropping jazzers, why don't you come down over Buon Beng and I'll lob it in and have somebody meet me at the airstrip. I don't relish walking all the way out to camp."

"Sure," he said. He reached into his flight suit and came out with an iridescent red streamer, about fifteen feet long, with a small weighted pocket for messages in one end.

The pilot got up and looked questioningly at his aircraft. "All right," he said. "Let's see if this sucker'll fly."

He went back to climb up the ladder. Chief McKee's men had already stowed my chute in the back.

The flight took about two hours, which gave me plenty of time to write out, "Have somebody meet me with the ambulance at the airstrip. Will jump about a half hour from now. —Morris."

Then I went up to the door and looked out. This pilot was flying a lot lower than the one who'd taken my team in.

That was because the weather had been better then. No clouds. We followed the flat, looping river, Song Ba, all the way up from the coast. The country was as beautiful as ever. The green seemed to shimmer in the rainy season, and the flat square paddies were filled with water that gave off a sheen, like a thousand mirrors laid out on the ground, stubbled by uniform sprigs of rice. I watched the shadow of the airplane flying off to the left and the reflection of it just below. The three of them: the real one in the sky, the shadow on the ground, and the reflection in the stagnant water, flew in perfect formation until we came to the mountains. The reflection disappeared and the shadow broke apart on irregular country.

Down below was the district headquarters on Highway 14, and I could see the big trail that ran a hundred feet from where we had ambushed the VC company commander and his two buddies four days before. A little to the west was the spot where Bill Foody, our junior medic, got hit in the leg. It was saddening to look down and see the ground we had made our own with so much effort, only to have our tour end just as we had achieved a real mastery of the area.

Our past was written all over the land below. And the future was written in the past, if you could see it.

I could see some of it. We knew the Montagnard revolt of September 1964 was coming, had reported that intelligence to higher headquarters, and not been believed.

The first bundle blocked the door and I couldn't lean out, so I ducked back inside and went up to talk to the crew chief.

"Drop down over Buon Beng," I howled over the engines, "and I'll lob out the message. Then I'll jump on the way back from Plei Ta Nangle."

"Rodge," he said. He turned and spoke into his microphone, nodding to the pilot. Then he turned back to me.

"We're ten minutes out from Cheo Reo now," he bellowed. "We'll be dropping down in about five."

I nodded and went back to the door, working my way

around the door bundles and the conveyer belt all the way back. The wind caught my face again as I got to the door. It seemed only a moment later that the aircraft started dropping. I knelt and took the message streamer from the front of my shirt, peering around the bundle. The ground below rose swiftly, and we started passing over the road complex around Cheo Reo. I could have reached out and touched the treetops underneath.

I leaned out as far as I could and made out the great oval of dozed trees around the camp, thatched-roofed buildings, and the shiny tin roofs of the supply building, commo shack, and dispensary up ahead and closing fast. Then the dozed trees were underneath, scattered helter-skelter with great dried clumps of dirt clinging to their snarled roots. We passed over the trenches, like parallel brown mole burrows, and a water buffalo ran over a pig to get out from under the shadow of the wing. We couldn't have been over forty feet off the ground.

I thought, I better get rid of this, and threw the message streamer out the door as hard as I could. It immediately disappeared from sight. I wondered where it landed. The aircraft ascended.

Fifteen minutes later we were circling Plei Ta Nangle, the great triangle of the camp laid out on a plateau. We circled once. Then the first bundle got jammed in the door and we took it around again. The aircraft flew about a hundred and fifty feet over the DZ, high enough to give the cargo chutes time to open, low enough that they wouldn't drift far. We had plenty of time, plenty of fuel, and a small DZ, so the pilot made one pass per bundle. Mr. McKee and his two riggers hooked up the static lines and manhandled the bundles into the door. As the aircraft made its approach, the two kickers tipped the bundle out so it was just balanced on the edge of the door. They had to lean back hard to hold it in. Mr. McKee leaned around and stuck his head out the door to judge the exact moment they passed over the panel. Then he looked back and yelled, "GO!" and the door was suddenly empty, the static line dragging back and down, taut and hard. Then the two kickers dragged the static line back in and dumped it in the back.

Figuring the time to get back to Cheo Reo, I decided to chute up. I went aft and opened my kit bag, reached down and pulled out the rig.

I ran the leg straps through the handle of my AWOL bag so I wouldn't have to carry that. By the time the last bundle was out, I was ready for some help with the reserve. Chief McKee cinched it up for me and made a thorough rigger check. The helmet was a little loose, but it was too late to worry about that. I wrapped my glasses in my beret and shoved them down the front of my shirt. Mr. McKee went around and behind me to check the backpack and then he handed the static line over my left shoulder.

My adrenaline was up and I was ready to go. I started waddling back to the door. When I got about six feet away I stopped and hooked up the static line, inserting the safety wire through the snap link.

Then I moved into the door. Below were the trails and jungles we had run over for this too-short time. We passed over the village where Ksor Ay, our oldest platoon leader, who had fought for the French before us, whose front teeth were filed and whose earlobes were pierced and stretched into big loops in the old Jarai manner, would be assassinated when he went home on leave wearing a uniform. We passed over the spot where Nay Re, our psychotic company commander, was to be executed for mortaring a Vietnamese district headquarters during the revolt. But of course, I didn't know about those things yet. Knowing Nay Re, though, it was predictable that something similar would happen. It was also predictable that a convoy of government troops would be ambushed on the same road where I used to drive a jeep alone and unmolested, because they didn't understand the principle of not setting a pattern. Six Americans were killed on that ambush, and it wouldn't have happened if even one member of our team had been there.

We were being withdrawn because of a peculiarity of the Department of Defense joint travel regulations which only permitted us to stay for six months. Don't ask why; that would only lead to thirty-two pages of bureaucratic gobble-dygook that would still make no sense. The Old Man had volunteered to extend us, which we all wanted, and been turned down.

I had to come back, not just this time to get my stuff, but because we had led the Montagnards way out on a limb and shouldn't have quit until they were safe. When you fight with people there is an implied obligation to stand with them until the fight is over. It was something we all felt keenly, personally, but our government felt not at all.

The U.S. didn't do that, but we stuck with them another nine years, and without that, their culture wouldn't have survived *either* Vietnamese regime.

I'd keep coming back as long as it was there to come back to.

I moved close to the door and took the wind blast full in my face. Down below was the canopy of trees to the left of Highway 14, and back on the other side of the highway were the Chudleya Mountains. And below the tree canopy, on the small trails, were little skinny guys in black shortie pajamas and tire sandals, with wicker helmets and cap-tured American weapons, or the new family of Chinese weapons which were just beginning to appear.

I became conscious of Chief McKee there beside me, a worried frown on his face. He kept his balance by hanging onto the cable. We passed over some more green moun-tains, the camp, and the town of Cheo Reo on the left. We came up on the Cheo Reo airstrip, more than three-quarters completed now, but still with a great clutter of ill-main-tained construction equipment at the unfinished end. I grinned, fired up and ready to go, and the AWOL bag flapped against my legs as the pilot turned to make his downwind leg.

When we got past the construction equipment at the other end, he turned again and started his approach run.

I leaned way out the door and caught the wind blast full in the face. I squinted and my eyes watered, but I could make out the red cross on top of the ambulance. We were about four hundred and fifty yards from the desired exit point.

"Sir," said Chief McKee, beside me. "I don't see any smoke on that DZ."

"I didn't ask for smoke, Chief," I yelled. They'd only put out red smoke for no drop.

"You can't hardly judge the wind without smoke, sir. I don't think you better jump." In his mind's eye he probably saw me slamming into the runway at about thirty knots and being dragged to death before I could get the chute collapsed. All this time we were steadily eating up DZ. I leaned way back in the door, with my fingers hooked around the outside.

"You got a point there, Chief," I said, jumping up and out. The blast whirled me away as I shouted, "One thousand, two thousand, three thousand, four thousand." I was away and free.

23
PEACE
FOR
GALILEE

The Israeli tank, a Centurion, lay about forty feet off the winding mountain road, its right track blown off by an anti-tank mine. That should have told me something.

There is a particular mindset you need for combat, but we were a day behind the point of Operation Peace for Galilee and I felt quite safe.

"Peace for Galilee" was the official name for the 1982 Israeli invasion of Lebanon. Kat and I had flown into Tel Aviv ten days before, to do a couple of small stories on the Israeli Defense Force before going on to Beirut for the Lebanese Forces Commando Course. We had spent about a week getting our press credentials, touring Jerusalem, Jericho, and the site of the Dead Sea Scrolls while we waited for approval. The preceding Friday, Major Irit Atsmoun, the very attractive press liasion officer in the IDF spokesman's office, had told us to come back Monday. "I think we may have something for you." That Sunday they invaded Lebanon.

Now we were part of a convoy of journalists in rented cars, each car accompanied by an Israeli officer from the spokesman's office. Our little convoy of civilian cars was stopped in the middle of a dun-colored column of tanks and armored personnel carriers. The mountains were beautiful, the air crisp and clean. What's to worry?

For a close-up of what this particular mine had done to this particular tank, I stepped over a piece of engineer's tape, and walked toward it.

"Jim, *STOP!*" Bill Gross yelled before I had gone two steps. He ran down the road, Uzi slapping against his side, an Incredible Hulk in flak jacket and billowing afro. "There are anti-personnel mines out there. We had to send another vehicle out to retrieve the crew."

Bill had moved from Minneapolis to Tel Aviv a few years before, to go into the diamond business. He was a lieutenant in the Israeli reserve, called up for the Galilee operations.

After I left the minefield, we were still stalled in the road, waiting for a Caterpillar tractor to smooth off a bend that two days of tank columns had made impassable.

I climbed up a dirt bank and scrambled onto an armored personnel carrier. The infantry squad, who rode into combat inside, now lounged on top, with the insolent idleness of young soldiers who had nothing to do but bitch and make bum jokes while they waited for the order to move out.

Thoroughly bored, they made me immediately welcome, and showed me their vehicular-mounted machine guns and personal weapons.

"Are you getting a good story?" one collegiate-looking blond kid asked.

I laughed and told him I had come to do a story on Israeli airborne training. "This is a bonus."

From their fearsome reputation, I had expected the Israelis to be an army of smartly turned out, gung-ho troops. I soon learned that military courtesy and spit and polish were far down on a list of priorities headed by tactics and training.

I was told that the more elite the unit, the sloppier it is. Boots are bloused or not, at the whim of the individual. Berets are worn folded, shoved through an epaulet. They wouldn't fit on the hair anyway; the Israelis see no inverse correlation between hair-length and combat effectiveness.

On my way to Metulla, on the northeast border, on the first day of Operation Galilee, I gave a ride to a young paratrooper on his way to his unit. His boots were unshined, but his SAR was spotless.

Israeli soldiers carry their personal weapons everywhere, and I never saw an obvious demerit on one. They were lightly oiled and perfectly cleaned, with all the creases, cracks, and crevices immaculate. "It's like a second wife," one Israeli lieutenant said.

The Israeli Defense Force consists of every man with four limbs and two eyes between the ages of 18 and 55. For women, the ages are 19 to 35. Most battalion commanders are under thirty. But beyond that, the entire nation is part of the defense effort.

Israel, in the best of times, is a nation on alert. The Israeli Army, as far as I know, is the only one that hitchhikes to combat. All reservists keep personal weapons and web gear at home, and upon mobilization, troops hitchhike to designated points, ready to fight. Any Israeli travelers, military or civilian, will give them a ride.

Their basic fighting unit is the tank-infantry team. In 1973, during the Yom Kippur War, the Israelis became temporarily infatuated with the notion they could fight with tanks alone—and lost a bunch of them. Now they fight with each tank paired with an infantry squad in an APC—except for their own Merkava, which has room for a squad in it, and is, therefore, both a tank and an APC.

The infantry carried Galil assault rifles. The Galil SARs are for paratroops and commandos, the M-16s for artillery and support troops. Rumor has it the Israelis captured so many AKs in Lebanon that they planned to start making ammo for them and issue them to troops.

The Israeli Defense Force is informal, but because of their training and discipline, they don't take many casualties. They can't afford to; there aren't that many of them. They were taken by surprise in 1973 and had two thousand casualties, their worst to date. It seems as though everybody in Israel lost a member of his immediate family in that war.

One of the kids we gave a ride told me, "If one of us kills twenty PLO and gets killed himself, he has failed, because he was more valuable to us than those twenty were to them."

After heavy losses in 1973, the Israelis set out to revamp their military force. They built a bigger and better military, with more sophisticated weapons, more troops, better equipment, and new tactics.

In 1973 the IDF had only 2,000 tanks; in 1982 it had 3,500. APCs had increased from 3,000 to 8,000. The few dated anti-tank missiles it had in 1973 were replaced with thousands of state-of-the-art weapons. Similar improvements were made in the air force.

More than 600 combat aircraft were available in 1982, including many American-built F-16 Fighting Falcons and F-15 Eagle fighters. "Smart" weapons, television-guided for pinpoint accuracy, and electronic anti-radar devices had greatly improved the Israeli Air Force. The Israelis had amassed an awesome military force, one in which they were very confident.

"Motivation," one soldier explained to me, "is the key to the Israeli Army."

I thought I knew what he meant, but later I saw a perfect example.

One morning in Metulla, on the fourth day of the operation, kids were going to school. Metulla is Israel's northern-most city, and looks like a suburb of Phoenix, except that every house has immediate access to a bomb shelter. Metulla and Kiryat Shemona, the first city south, had taken plenty of Katyusha rockets from the PLO in Lebanon. They had lost a few people, and were in constant jeopardy. That was part of the original rationale for the invasion.

The kids looked like American school children. Mothers escorted young children along streets clogged with olive drab APCs, half-tracks, and trucks.

At one corner, a young mother and her daughter, about seven, stood waiting to cross while a three-quarter-ton truck drove by. The two soldiers in front were tired, bearded and dirty, maybe four hours out of the fighting, and maybe the same before going back in.

The little girl squealed and jumped on the running board of the truck to give the driver a big hug. Dust from southern Lebanon smeared her school dress; his dirty, bearded face scraped the soft skin of her neck. He was a reservist from Metulla; she was his daughter.

Nabatiye, about thirty miles into Lebanon, a beautiful hillside town of maybe a hundred thousand, had been a major southern base for the PFLP (Popular Force for the Liberation of Palestine), a radical PLO faction. For seven years the PFLP had occupied Nabatiye. People spoke of them with fear, recalling forced evictions, looting, rapes, and senseless killings.

The Israelis hadn't shelled in Nabatiye; they didn't have to. The PFLP pulled out rather than defend. The Israelis were greeted by open shops, fresh fruit and vegetable vendors, and joyous people; some of them said they were smiling for the first time in years.

In Nabatiye the Israelis captured three times as much PFLP ammo as their own intelligence estimates had indicated, all Soviet. I saw cache after cache of it, in houses and garages. As in Tyre and Sidon, the entire town was an ammo dump. It made me wonder how much of the damage to these cities, for which the Israelis were being consistently denounced in the press, was caused by secondary explosions of PLO ammo.

Bookshelves in PFLP-occupied houses were full of Marxist propaganda, on the walls were hammer and sickle posters of Lenin, Marx, and Ho. It reminded me of the stuff Coyne and I had seen at Surat Thani in Thailand, also all Soviet. When you see the same stuff in lots of different places, it tells you something.

I was reminded of the doctrine proclaimed at a party congress in 1976, to support "Wars of National Liberation" wherever they might arise, worldwide. I was beginning to see that these small wars, funded, armed, and trained by the same source, were coordinated; therefore, they must have a common objective.

If a "War of National Liberation," backed by the Soviet Union, were successfully waged in every vulnerable Third World country—and at present there was very little to prevent that—the result would be a chain of wretched Marxist-Leninist Soviet client states controlling enough of the world's vital resources to lock the United States out of twenty-first century technology, and control enough sea lanes to prevent our deployment of military forces to strategic areas.

This strategy alone, successfully pursued, could relegate the United States to the status of a second-rank power, leaving one and only one superpower, the Union of Soviet Socialist Republics. That would leave only one thing between the Soviet Union and world domination, the U.S. nuclear deterrent; and I did not think we would destroy the world to prevent them from taking it.

If the Katyn Massacre in Poland after WWII, in which all non-Communist Polish officers were simply slaughtered by the Soviets, the genocide in Cambodia, the "re-education" camps in Indochina, and the executions in Cuba after the Castro takeover were any indication, it was also their objective to line me, these Israeli troops, and everybody like us up against a wall and silence us forever.

The taking of the ruins of Beaufort, the old Crusader castle high on a mountain, was the first objective of the operation. For years Beaufort had been the symbol of PLO domination of southern Lebanon. From the square, jagged peaks of Beaufort, on a clear day, you can see the Litani River, Nabatiye and Marjayoun in Lebanon, and the Israeli cities of Metulla and Kiryat Shemona. It was such a clear shot with a Katyusha rocket that all forward observation and fire-direction functions had been handled by the gunner.

The mountain on which the castle sat was extremely steep, almost straight up, with a clear field of fire down the slopes.

With enough food, ammo, and water, a well-trained and motivated squad could defend it forever against anybody.

In Beaufort's 800 year history, with the exception of a couple of starve-outs, and a negotiated peace, it had never been taken. The Israelis took it on the second day, at the price of six killed in action.

Staring down the slopes from its summit, overlooking the broad, green agricultural valley, I asked Bill Gross, "Who did this?"

"A two-hundred-man commando unit of the Golani brigade, one of our best units," he answered. "Heliborne to the mountain's base, then a night assault straight up the hill. It took from one in the morning until seven to do it. Night operations are a specialty of ours. The Palestinians don't like them, and they aren't very good at them."

Only a highly trained and disciplined force could have done it at night. If the slope had been ten degrees steeper, it would have been a cliff.

24
HIGH
ADVENTURE

The lobby of the Arazim Hotel in Metulla, Israel, was filled with Israeli soldiers and an international smorgasbord of correspondents. Most of the Israelis wore fatigues or the olive drab, zippered jumpsuits favored by some of the tankers. A variety of pistols hung from their hips; from their shoulders hung Galils, Uzis, and M-16s. Most of the Israelis were covered by a fine khaki dust, except for the pink raccoon mask where their goggles had been, with dark-rimmed, bloodshot eyes peering out from those ghost goggles.

The Israeli way of playing the role is to underplay it, and these guys were really tired, anyway. The only people acting heavily macho were the correspondents. They swaggered around in their camera vests and safari jackets, affecting a bored and knowledgeable air, chain-smoking their cigarettes overhand, demonstrating that, even though they were noncombatants, they were *real guys.*

The most macho of them all were the female correspondents, many of whom appeared to be working up a Chesty Puller imitation for the Marine Corps birthday ball.

The major exception to this rule was Kat, quietly amused in her safari suit, with red, heart-shaped sunglasses on her forehead.

The glasses were a gift from me, and a lucky one, for while the Israeli G.I.s had little use for macho noncombatants, they were all suckers for a cute girl in Lolita glasses and a Cambodian bush hat. That day, on the road to Beaufort Castle, which two days before had been the PLO stronghold in southern Lebanon, and today was an Israeli tourist attraction, an Israeli armored personnel carrier had clanked past thirty clamoring photographers to stop in front of Kat, who dangled from the back of a three-quarter-ton truck. But she couldn't get them to look grim and war-like. All they wanted to do was grin and give her the thumbs up.

Into the lobby of the Arazim strode a grinning trucker from any truck stop in America. He wore blue jeans, cowboy boots, a blue Kentucky Wildcats Windbreaker and matching baseball cap. Blond hair curled out from under the cap, which was pushed back on his head. Stocky and muscular, he appeared to be in his late-thirties/early-forties, but his face was so unlined, the concept of "worry" seemed entirely alien to him. He looked as though he had just won the Publisher's Clearinghouse Sweepstakes.

"We took the tail fin off one of them Syrian MIGs you guys shot down in the field today," he announced to the Israelis at large. "I had a farmer drag it back to the station. That thang was brand-spankin' new, built in 1981," he drawled. I caught his eye and waved him over.

"Where you from?" I grinned.

"Lexington, Kentucky," he replied as we shook hands. "Why?"

"I'm Jim Morris, and this's my wife, Kathy. I'm from Oklahoma, and she's from Arkansas. We've been chasing the wars for almost six months now. You're the first person in a long time we've heard talk right."

He laughed and sat down. "I'm Harold Cox," he said.

"What are you doing in the middle of this war?" I asked.

He laughed again. "I'm with High Adventure," he said, and pointed toward a flag-sized banner on the wall over the serving counter that led back into the kitchen. It was a navy-blue banner, with a white dove very like Picasso's, except it seemed to be flying faster and wasn't carrying an olive branch. The lettering read, *High Adventure Broadcasting—the Voice of Hope.*

When Kat and I first arrived at the Arazim three days before, Bill Gross had told us that there were some American Christian broadcasters who maintained an office in this hotel, living in Israel and operating a radio and TV station three klicks over the border in Lebanon. "They're just super people," he said.

The idea had seemed so bizarre that I had erased it from my mind. But here was Harold Cox, smiling and immensely likeable.

"Don't write nothin' bad about these Jews," he said. "God loves 'em."

I laughed. "I haven't seen them do anything bad," I said. "They're good folks, and I'm no fan of the PLO.

"You're easy enough to spot as a Pentecostal Christian," I went on, "but you don't look like a broadcaster."

"I'm a truck driver," he said.

I was about to ask him what a Jesus-freak truck driver was doing in Metulla when the cook opened the doors to the dining room. Dinner was served.

Kat and I shared a glance of agreement, and I said, "Join us for dinner?"

"Sure." He grinned.

"Meat or dairy?" the young lady in jeans and black blouse asked as we walked through the door. You can find any kind of restaurant in Israel, but by law the hotel restaurants are kosher; no cheeseburgers, no BLT's. There were no menus, because the Arazim served only one entree in each category. Half the time we didn't know what we were eating, but it was always wonderful.

We took our seats and Kat and I ordered a bottle of Carmel Avdat, a local red wine, and Harold asked for water. Around us the crowd was seating itself in revealing groups. The correspondents all sat with correspondents, and the Israeli soldiers always sat with each other.

Kathy and I were the only correspondents who sat with the soldiers, which we preferred to do most of the time.

Sometimes we sat with the correspondents. Except for Terry Anderson, who was a veteran, they were mostly quiet around me, but they were more open with Kat when I wasn't there. She got to watch a process I never saw. She got to watch them all get together and decide what was news and what was not. The facts were never in dispute, but even in so-called objective reporting, the order in which those facts are presented, the weight given them, and the connotations of the words used to describe them, can slant the story. The invisible subhead on every story these guys were writing was, "Get the Yids."

"So what brings you here?" I asked Harold, when we were comfortably seated.

"Well," he said, "I was livin' in California, drivin' my truck. One day I was on my way home when a voice said, 'Harold, you can't go on livin' the way you have been.'

"Nothin' like that had ever happened to me before, but I knew Who it was, and what He was talkin' about. 'What you want me to do, Lord?' I asked.

" 'Turn left at the next block. About two blocks down, on the left-hand side, there's a little church. Go in there and talk to the pastor.'

"Which I did. We talked for quite a while, and I made an appointment to talk to him again. He gave me his card.

"When I got home, my wife was all packed up, and she was going to leave me. I told her what happened.

" 'You've told so many lies,' she said. 'Why should I believe this one?'

"So I whipped out the preacher's card and gave it to her. 'Call him,' I said.

"He told her to wait a few days and she'd know by then. She saw I was serious and she stayed.

"Then the Lord told me to quit my job and put the house up for sale. She figured I'd gone nuts and started to leave again. I told her she could go where she wanted, and she could have everything. When she saw I was serious, she decided to stick it out.

"I quit my job and put the house up for sale. We had to wait eighteen months and that was a strange time. My neighbor next door played for the '49ers, and I built him a hot tub. We became friends and I spent some time with the team, went on a couple of road trips. I was just waitin'."

Something about his shoulders and the way he walked made me ask, "Were you ever an athlete?"

He nodded. "Boxed middleweight. I was good enough that for a year nobody would fight me but light-heavies. Then they discovered I had a soft head. A good blow to the center of the forehead and I was out like a light."

"Ever been in the service?"

"Air Force communications. Korea."

"So you were awaiting instructions?"

"Yeah. Long before the house sold I knew I was going to come to the Holy Land and be in television. My neighbors and my in-laws figured I was crazy." He laughed. "Anyway, for about a year and a half we didn't get a single call on the house. Then one day this Jewish couple from New York came and offered me $165,000 for it. That wasn't what I was asking, so I said, 'I'll have to pray on it.' The Lord said, 'Don't be greedy, Harold. I doubled your investment.' So I took it.

"Everybody thought I was nuts."

This statement kept cropping up in Harold's conversation. They said it again when Harold told them he was going to Israel to work in television, pointing out that all he knew about television was how to wiggle the rabbit ears.

It was not until he got to Israel that he even heard of George Otis.

George Otis was a former vice-president of the LearJet Corporation who had produced and hosted a television show about the romance of aviation called *High Adventure*. When he became a Pentecostal Christian, divine inspiration led him to raise the money to found a radio station in the seemingly inhospitable religious climate of southern Lebanon. Everybody within range of his broadcasts was already either a Jew, Muslim, or Maronite Christian. There were no Protestants, and certainly no Pentecostals. But everybody liked the music, and at least the news wasn't slanted in favor of any one of their rivals. The station was an instant success.

In fact it was such a success that Otis decided to expand into television, and to that end, a remote studio fitted into a motor home had been purchased.

"It was still on the docks when I arrived," Harold said, "sitting on the floor of the crate it was shipped in. They'd tried to back it off, and did eleven thousand dollars' worth of damage to the transmission."

Nobody in Israel could drive the mobile studio. It had six forward gears and four reverse gears. It was the same transmission as had been in Harold's semi.

On his first day in Israel he met George Otis in a hotel lobby and moved the mobile studio that afternoon. He ploughed most of his profits from the house into High Adventure, sent for his wife, and learned to engineer the TV remote system. "I'm doing fill-in shifts for the other engineers now," he said.

"That's a pretty miraculous chain of events," I interjected. "But why does God want a TV station in southern Lebanon?"

Harold nodded. "Well," he said, "the Israelis have just built the most modern air base in the world in the Valley of Megiddo. All the hangars are underground, and the planes are brought up on elevators, like an aircraft carrier. Anyhow, the Israelis are going to win this war here. The Syrians aren't going to come into it. Then, for the first time, the Israelis are going to be at peace for years. Then the Russians are going to attack, with some of the Arab countries as allies. It's all in the 38th Chapter of Ezekiel. Where it says Gog and Magog, that's Russia.

"Anyway the Russians are gonna sweep down right through Lebanon, in just too great a number for the Israelis to handle them. That's when they're gonna turn to God and get in the synagogues and start praying.

"The Russians are going to stop to consolidate right there in the valley of Megiddo, and God's gonna destroy 'em there."

"How?" I asked.

"Bible says fire, earthquake, pestilence, the whole nine yards."

I made a mental note to look up Ezekial 38 when I got back to the room. "Okay," I said, "that's all very interesting, but what's it got to do with you?"

Harold nodded. "Up in the mountains overlooking the valley there's a flat concrete slab with a road leading to it. I've never seen it, but I know it's there. There's a millionaire oilman from Denver who's a Christian and owns the land. He called and told me God told him to build the slab. Anyhow, when God destroys the Russians in the valley of Megiddo, I'm gonna have a TV camera on it and you'll see it live in your living room via satellite."

"Okay."

"The networks will be ringing their hands and not knowing what to make of it, but the Christian stations will know, and that will be our witness."

That was kind of hard to take at one sitting, but when we got back to our room that night I looked up the passage in the beat up old copy of the *Living Bible* that Crews McCulloch, my first CO in Vietnam, gave me just before I went to Cambodia in 1973.

In that version, Ezekial 38 says, *"The Lord God says to Gog: When my people are living in peace in their land then you will rouse yourself. You will come from all over the north with your vast host of cavalry and cover the land like a cloud. This will happen in the distant future in the latter days of history. I will bring you against my land, and my holiness will be vindicated in your terrible destruction before their eyes, so that all the nations will know that I am God.*

"The Lord God says: You are the one I spoke of long ago through the prophets of Israel, saying that after many years had passed I would bring you against my people. But when you come to destroy the land of Israel my fury will rise. For in my jealously and blazing wrath I promise a mighty shaking of the land of Israel on that day. All living things will quake in terror at my presence; mountains shall be thrown down, cliffs shall tumble; walls shall crumble to the earth. I shall summon every kind of terror against you, says the Lord God, and you will fight against yourselves in mortal combat. I will fight you with sword, disease, torrential floods, great hailstones, fire and brimstone! Thus I will show my greatness and bring honor upon my name, and all the nations of the world will hear what I have done and know that I am God!"

Harold came in again the following evening at supper. He suggested that we get permission from the IDF to go in with him the next day. They didn't like journalists running around with no escort all over southern Lebanon, especially not since Mosi's Italian TV crew had stumbled into the PLO and been held prisoner for a day.

Harold reckoned that if he asked them they'd give us a pass to go in with him.

The next day, while we were at his radio station, Harold got a call that the generator on their transmitter, on a mountaintop thirty miles east, had quit, and his expert hand was called for. We headed back to the TV remote van to await the station's Lebanese engineer.

The motor home remote unit was parked just on the Lebanese side of the Good Fence, as it was called, that marked the border, opposite an Israeli observation platform. They had set up a couple of machine gun positions there, but primarily it was a place for tourists to look over into Lebanon. There was a restaurant and a gift shop back behind the platform, both closed now. There was a sandbagged M-60 machine gun emplacement atop the restaurant.

Waiting for the engineer, we witnessed the arrival of the first load of tourists since the war started. Just days before, artillery had boomed across the valley all night; now there were tourists, sunburned and giggling, taking each other's pictures in shorts, fat thighs, and funny white hats with "I (little red heart) Israel" inscribed on them.

When the engineer arrived, he gave us a handy-talkie to put on the dashboard of our rented Autobianchi. We followed Harold for almost an hour over the twisting mountain roads of southern Lebanon. It was beautiful country, fairly big hills, rocky, sandy-brown, with little vegetation, sparsely populated. The towns were old, and there were stooped and stolid elderly people in the streets and on the roadside. It was easy to get a feel of what Galilee must have been like in Biblical times. That feeling was frequently interrupted by a dusty new Mercedes booming over the hill with ten or fifteen Lebanese inside.

Under the PLO, southern Lebanon had been a collection point for stolen autos from all over Europe. It was possible to buy a car there that would have cost $25,000 in the States for $600, but there was no way to get it out after you bought it.

Finally we reached the transmitter. Harold grabbed his tools and went into the shed to work on the generator. He worked swiftly and efficiently. Harold was not an average guy, but one thing he was not was nuts. I didn't really know what to make of his story about the Russian Army in the Valley of Megiddo, but I would not have bet anything *against* its happening.

A young man in boots and a fatigue uniform wandered over while Harold worked. He was introduced to us as Fares, a fighter in Major Saad Haddad's Army of Southern Lebanon, a predominantly Christian militia, although it contained many Moslems, Fares among them. Fares was assigned to guard the transmitter. The surprising thing about Fares was that, although he had an olive complexion, he was blond and had European features. Then I remembered that the crusaders had been in this area for centuries.

Fares had news. Not an hour before, a Syrian jet had roared in low, dropped a 500-pound bomb on a house in the nearby town, and killed every member of the family, a mother, father, and two children. He asked whether we wanted to go to take pictures of the damage, which, of course, we did. We went in our car, leaving Harold to work on the transmitter.

The funeral was already underway when we reached the town. Not having any embalmers there, these people didn't mess around before they buried their dead. We drove in on a rocky road. The funeral was taking place further on down the hill to our right. A fairly large crowd that must have been half the town was gathered around the grave site. They were just lowering a tiny coffin into the ground as we drove by.

I started to take a picture, but Kathy put her hand on my arm. She had covered plenty of car wrecks for the Arkansas *Gazette*, and a fat woman from Illinois, with her hair in curlers, called her a "ghoul" at Elvis Presley's funeral, but something about these simple people's tragedy was just too personal to film.

The town was built of ancient Moorish buildings, terraced into hillsides. We drove through, twisting and turning on the narrow streets as we wound up the hillside to the house where the bomb had fallen.

Soon we came to it, a flat-topped, two-story concrete house smashed, with the roof collapsed at an angle, debris scattered for a hundred feet around. A smaller crowd was gathered around the house, mostly young men in slacks and shirts that fit tight around the waist. They were mostly poor, and wore cheap, shoddy clothing, but the look they aspired to was Vegas dealer.

Kathy went to work with her camera. I decided to wander on up the hill and see whether I could get a good shot from above. There were other houses on up the hillside, but they were surrounded by shrubbery, and it was hard to get a clear shot. I wandered out into a yard, but to get a clear view I had to step into the garden.

I walked very carefully between rows and tried not to step on any plants, but that didn't seem to make any difference to the two angry women, probably mother and daughter, heads covered with kerchiefs, who stormed out of the house.

I pointed to my camera and smiled. They poured forth a torrent of verbal abuse. I don't think they really objected to the camera. I was just a representative of the outside world who had come into their village and done this terrible thing. Almost everybody in Lebanon speaks French. *"Merci, merci, pardonez moi,"* I said and started edging out of the garden. I had already taken a couple of shots anyway, and I could tell they would be lousy. *"Merci, merci,"* I muttered.

Then a strange thing happened. When they saw I was genuinely contrite, they smiled and invited me back. I took two more photos, just to be polite.

When I got back down the hill the crowd had grown. Two of the young men angrily demanded of Fares to know who in the hell we were and what in the hell we were doing there. He patiently explained that we were good people who were here to help.

Some of them looked like they were buying it, and others did not. The nonbuyers were the most vocal. I had faced down a couple of Vietnamese mini-mutinies, but I couldn't read these people. I looked at Kat, just checking to see that nobody threatening was near her, and prepared to start smiling and jiving. I wondered just how far this might go.

Harold arrived at that moment, parked on the road, and walked up to the crowd. Apparently they knew him, because they immediately led him to where fragments of the bomb had landed.

"They say a Syrian jet came over heading south, chased by two Israeli jets," he said. "Nobody knows which side dropped the bomb." He dusted off the fragments to see whether they were of Russian or American manufacture, but he couldn't tell.

Two of the boys brought me a black-and-white photo of the man who had been killed. In the photo he was a nice-looking, smiling, smallish man, about thirty-five, in a dark suit and tie, walking on one of the roads of the village.

Harold still had some work to do on the generator, so we went back to the transmitter site.

Fares and the Lebanese engineer were concerned lest we be bored, standing around on the barren hilltop while Harold fiddled with the machinery, so he led us over to the little shack that housed the transmitter and gave us a tour. Floor to ceiling banks of grey-metal cabinets, covered with lights and dials. There was one tiny monitor that showed what the station was broadcasting.

A tiny lady in leotards was going through a series of leg raises, showing the ladies of northern Israel and southern Lebanon how to reduce the size of their thighs.

25
CHEESEBURGERS
IN
NAZARETH

It was not until the Israelis surrounded West Beirut on June 8 that reporters were allowed to catch up to the actual combat. Even so, IDF policy required that we be back in Israel by nightfall.

The practical effect of this rule was to send us each morning hell-bent, in convoys of uninsured rental cars, over rutted and shell-pocked highways, through the blasted, shattered cities of Sidon, Tyre, and Damour, a Christian city which had been destroyed and its populace massacred by the PLO in 1976, past a blasted and shattered seaside amusement park, to Beirut, a bigger blasted and shattered city. In the evenings we returned separately, at the last minute, racing the sunset down sniper alley.

When we crossed the Israeli border in the evening it was like entering the U.S. from revolutionary Mexico. We

kicked back, Kathy and I, and teased each other in our re-
spective hick accents, maintaining our roots.

Since Thailand, we had maintained a running argument
about women in combat. I have no reservations about
women's courage or intelligence. But I maintain that much
of an infantryman's job is to be a beast of burden, and
women are not suited to that.

"God!" she said once, as we slowed to pass a column of
tanks, parked beside the Metulla–Tel Aviv highway. "It kills
me to look at these kids, wondering which ones aren't going
to live out the week."

"You get used to it."

She shook her head. "I don't think women are supposed
to get used to it. Maybe you're right about women and combat. I'm beginning to feel that women's true role is to nur-
ture. Without that there'd be no society to defend."

We passed a pole posted with road signs, one to Megiddo.
A bit later we passed the Sea of Galilee to our left. Far out
on calm blue water a guy skied behind a boat. Beyond were
the hills of Jordan. We stopped for a cheeseburger, fries,
and a shake at an Arab restaurant in Nazareth, and checked
back into the Plaza in Tel Aviv that night.

In Lebanon, CBS alone lost five Peugeot 504s on the
roads. One was run over by a tank, another hit by a PLO
rocket; the others, I don't know.

Lebanon was the first story Kathy and I covered as a
team. She became a partner, as cool as Coyne and more
diligent. This was not her idea of a good time; she was there
to work. She seemed to lapse only once, as we roared past a
bombed-out shopping center in East Beirut. Her head
whipped around to read a sign. "Oh, Charles Jourdan sandals!" she cried. Then she smiled wryly.

As we drove into the city of Tyre the first day, rubble and
shattered buildings lay everywhere. The only thing untouched on that stretch of road was a mosque. Obviously
Israeli gunners had been ordered not to hit it, for public

relations purposes if nothing else. But with the entire city blanketed by artillery, it had taken tremendous skill to miss it.

The smell was horrific. Kathy was thinking, *Did they leave every refrigerator door in this town open?* when Roy Uaval, the ginger-bearded, English-born Israeli photographer who was driving, asked, "Anybody want to see the mass grave?"

"God, no!" I blurted.

In Sidon, the next town up the road, a PLO terrorist academy was found in the underground floor of a United Nations–administered vocational school, complete with cutaway models of rockets and machine guns, and a dormitory set up like a barracks, with uniforms in wall lockers and double-decker bunks. The U.N. had taken sides, voluntarily or through coercion, in this conflict.

There was disagreement over civilian casualty figures in southern Lebanon. The International Red Cross's initial estimate was 1,541 deaths—no differentiation between civilians and terrorists—in Tyre alone, and 300,000 homeless. In contrast, Israeli estimates were 450 civilian fatalities in the two cities, and no more than 20,000 homeless in southern Lebanon.

Nearing Beirut we encountered a long line of refugee traffic moving south. People were leaving West Beirut before the Israelis moved in on the PLO. They came down that dusty alley of destruction, a single column of Okies going to California in Mercedes. We slowed now to a crawl, past a huge tractor hauling a demolished tank, moving around APCs parked outside a store. Dusty G.I.s leaned against them, smoking and drinking warm Coke.

Finally we pulled up behind a three-quarter-ton truck and stopped. We'd be moving in a minute.

I looked to the left. Israeli G.I.s had established a roadblock and were thoroughly searching a black Mercedes with a very large family in it. I felt a blast of the sheerest hate, and did a take into a pair of blazing almond eyes. In the backseat were four people. The two in the middle, one staring lasers through me, were well-built young men of military age, in civilian clothes, but with military haircuts.

We moved on again. Now I carefully watched the backseats of oncoming cars. Every second or third one had what I was sure was a PLO fighter in it. They were so obvious that I wondered why the Israelis were letting them through. Later I learned they had collected about 700 of them further south.

There was a bad run after we left the main road, before we got to the Israeli headquarters at Ba'abda. It was in the winding hills south of Beirut, surrounded by stone fences and olive groves.

On this road we were in range of PLO gunners. A barrage of high explosive 82-millimeter mortar rounds crashed into the grove to our left. Arnold Sherman, our IDF escort, a red-haired transplanted New York author and Israeli reservist, took off his steel helmet and made Kat wear it. It looked great with her Lolita shades.

Our first day in Beirut we had a gourmet lunch at Emil's atop a high hill overlooking the city, and watched artillery and rockets exchanged between East and West Beirut, while a waiter in black pants and a red mess jacket poured the wine. During the dessert course a flight of F-15s smoked down out of the sky directly over our heads and poured rockets into West Beirut.

After lunch I found a pay phone and called Fouad to tell him we were in town and would be by to see him.

The Lebanese Forces command was in a new headquarters, set up in a row of buildings in a military compound. As we pulled into the parking lot I saw a familiar walk, yelled, "Sam!" and bailed out of the car before it came to a stop.

We grabbed each other and hugged. "Jim!" he exclaimed. "We were expecting you to come in from Jounieh."

I quickly explained what had happened, and introduced Kathy, Arnold, and Roy.

"Come inside," he said. "Rick will want to see you." In a small room Rick sat at a desk, talking to correspondents, very official-looking in pressed, tailored fatigues, with a cammo T-shirt underneath, clean-shaven, hair neatly combed. The picture of a young staff officer.

"Jesus!" I said, barging through the door at the head of my troops. "I never thought they'd get you into uniform."

"Jim!" He grinned, and came from behind the desk. His fatigue pants were jean cut, and under them he wore his old roughout cowboy boots. They hadn't quite got him into uniform yet.

Sam quickly explained that we were here with the Israelis. "Why don't you just blow them off and stay here?" Rick asked.

I looked at Arnold.

His brow furrowed. "I can't stop you," he said. "But if you do, I'll be in terrible trouble."

This was the man who had put his own helmet on Kathy as we drove through a mortar barrage. I looked at Rick and shrugged. "No can do," I said.

Sam gave me one of his more mournful looks. "We have a house for you two," he said.

I shook my head.

We watched, with about two dozen other correspondents, as Fouad explained why the Lebanese Forces weren't going to attack West Beirut, as the Israelis wanted. The Israeli notion was that they had fought their way up the highway and given the "Phalangists" their chance to settle all scores. Now it was up to them.

"This is our city," Fouad said, standing in uniform beside a map, pointer in hand. "We have relatives over there. Our boys are not going in to kill their relatives." Either his English had improved in the past year or he had rehearsed this briefing.

In fact the Israeli battle to surround the city had been a cakewalk compared to the nightmare of casualties they would incur going into West Beirut. The PLO had fought only to delay as they fell back, assuming that the Israelis would stop when they came to their announced objective, 25 kilometers into Lebanon.

I'm still not convinced that the original objective was to go further than that. I think maybe it was just too easy not to drive on north.

But now the Israelis were confronted by the chilling prospect of having to root out thousands of PLO fighters, who would be fighting for their lives with their backs to the sea, from superb defensive positions.

Nobody wanted to do it. It would be block to block, house to house, room to room, hunting cornered fighters who were armed with AKs and RPGs, with artillery and tanks at their backs, determined that if they had to go, they were going to take as many with them as they could.

The Lebanese Forces' volunteers hadn't signed on for anything like that. They volunteered on a mission by mission basis, mostly to defend their own neighborhoods. Only a few commandos and elite units fought offensive actions, and most of those were raids. No one was up for a frontal assault into what looked like, and probably was, almost certain death.

After you, my dear Alphonse.

So for three days we toured a static front, kidding around with the militia kids, going into gutted apartments to peer through holes Katyushas had left in the walls—PLO fighters sunbathing on a balcony a hundred meters away—photographing Israeli artillerists, and dining splendidly.

On the third day the incoming held your attention, and there was machine-gun fire about two blocks away. Driving out was the worst, with the incoming very close, right at the same place we had taken mortar fire two days before. This time we screamed and slewed down the dirt road like Grand Prix racers, mortar rounds and artillery coming in all around us, although nothing hit the car.

On the last hill overlooking the city, the air was shattered by the crack of outgoing 155s; then there was a noise as though the sky were made of silk and had suddenly been ripped from horizon to horizon. We stopped and got out.

In the distance, we heard a muffled WHOOM, WHOOM, and two grey puffs billowed out of the dark haze that over-lay the Burj Al Barajneh Palestinian camp, just north of the airport.

The press habitually called it a refugee camp, but it could just as accurately have been called Fort Burj Al Barajneh. By then I had come to think of my press colleagues as so many Eskimos at the Super Bowl.

We got out of the car and walked to a shelled apartment house on the point of the hill. A couple of guys with a big battery commander scope sat on a third-floor balcony, ad-justing fire. I gradually became aware of a cracking roar overhead that swept from the south up the Mediterranean coast and then turned in to a high, keening shriek over the airport.

The sound of anti-aircraft fire came drifting up from the valley . . . pom-pom-pom . . . pom-pom-pom.

A series of loud crumps followed as the bombs hit and the shriek ascended and disappeared. For all we could see of the airplanes, we might as well have been listening to the radio, but bright flashes came from the center of the smoky haze over Burj Al Barajneh. Twice there were ballooning orange and black secondary explosions—ammunition caches.

The minutes of dead silence followed. Way below, the smoke drifted. Then the whole sequence of aerial attack repeated itself, and after that, once more. The papers the next day did not mention the secondary explosions, just a helpless refugee camp, vandalized by naughty Jews.

I decided it was getting too hot to take Kathy in. I broke the news at dinner that night, after a day of dodging mor-tars and snipers, as we ate in the dining room of a luxury hotel on the Mediterranean.

"I have to go in," she said in almost desperate exasperation. "It's my job. You're the one that's always going on about 'professionalism.'"

"Yeah," I insisted. "But that's not what's going on here. What's happening here is that my baby's gettin' shot at. You're doing your job, but I'm not doing mine. All I'm doing is watching to see if you're okay. That's the final argument against women in combat. The men won't be worrying about the enemy. They'll be worrying about the women."

"But . . ."

"You're not going in," I said calmly.

The next morning at the kibbutz on the border where the correspondents gathered, I found the IDF spokesman's office had reached the same conclusion. No female correspondents allowed in the forseeable future.

Nonetheless, it was a light day. I saw nothing that was newsworthy.

That night Kat and I talked it over. We had everything we needed for the *SOF* invasion special, and were both bone-deep tired from a month on the road, eight to twelve hours every day. I decided on one more run to say good-bye to Sam, Rick, and Fouad. Who knew when, or if, we'd ever see them again?

But when I got to the kibbutz the IDF was permitting runs only to the Bekaa Valley. I could not convince the major in charge to let me go to Beirut, so I wrote Sam a letter, which the major promised to deliver, and the next day we flew out of Tel Aviv.

That day, June 27, was our first anniversary. The stewardess brought Kathy a rose and served champagne with our meal.

When we collapsed into the bed at our London hotel, I called our friend, Graeme, to see whether he and Caroline were free for dinner the following evening.

"Oh, Jim," he said, "pity you didn't arrive yesterday. We had two extra tickets for the Stones concert."

I managed a weak smile into the receiver. "That's okay, Graeme. We weren't looking for excitement yesterday."

26
EL SALVADOR

A week back from Israel, sick and soul-weary of death and the smell of death, I walked into Brown's office. He sat with his beat-up shitkickers on his desk, howling into one phone while he held the other a foot from his face.

In thirty-second intervals between frantic overseas phone calls, people bursting in and out of his office, we talked.

"Brown, I've been in three wars in the last six months . . ."

"I know. I sent you."

"Everywhere I go the bad guys went to the same schools, use the same gear, exchange personnel, and read the same books. When we dumped Vietnam, they decided they had a winning strategy, and now Vietnam is measles. It's everywhere, and it's all the same war."

"Everybody knows that." He spat a glob of Skol into a clear glass.

"No, they don't, Bob. Nobody knows it but people who've seen it firsthand, because it ain't in the papers, and it ain't on TV.

"I want to do a book about it. To make it convincing, I need to go to one more area. Africa, Central America—it doesn't matter."

I had seen ample evidence of Soviet involvement in Lebanon—no surprise, since they do not conceal their backing for Syria—but it really came home when I saw those posters with Lenin and Ho on them, hammer and sickle, and the writing in Arabic.

The Soviets backed the Vietnamese in Laos and Cambodia; the Soviets also backed Libya, which was backing Muslim separatists in Thailand and Malaysia and the Philippines, for that matter. At Surat Thani, Coyne and I had seen an entire arsenal of Communist Party of Malaysia weapons, and they were all Soviet, as was their communications equipment and their mines and booby traps. They backed Syria, which armed international terrorists, threatened Israel, and had occupied most of Lebanon.

I wanted to see it with my own eyes in one other theater of operations. That wouldn't constitute proof, but the proof was well-known to foreign policy and military professionals; it was just not widely publicized. I wanted to tell the story in a popular format, one that would be widely read and, I hoped, believed.

I intended to hang around Boulder for a couple of months, get some of my Lebanon and Thailand stuff written, rest up, run, lift weights, eat some American food for a change. I was still jetlagged; my ears still rang from self-propelled 105mm howitzers. But I wanted to get my bid for another expedition in early. Sometimes it takes a while to set these things up.

"Fine," he said, "you can go to El Salvador Friday."

He was sending a reporter with a congressional delegation led by congressman Bob Dornan of California, and including Major General Jack Singlaub and Andy Messing of the National Defense Council. No way could I pass that up.

"As long as you're down there you might as well stick around for a couple of weeks, try to get in some combat, then go to Honduras and Guatemala."

That night Kat and I had one of our few really bad fights. She knew I was in no shape to go. Her face showed real anguish. "Look," she said, "we're just moving into a new apartment. I need you here now."

"Ah, bullshit!" I said. "If you were going, you'd be champing at the bit."

"Maybe so," she admitted. "But I'll be scared to death with you down there."

I shrugged. "Can't help it," I said. "If I don't do this one, the book won't get written, and Thailand and Lebanon will be wasted. Stories in *SOF* won't accomplish anything; that's preaching to the choir."

My first week in El Salvador, August 1982, we traveled to briefings and cocktail parties in air-conditioned vans. I went from one air-conditioned environment to another, half the time with a drink in my hand. It was only toward the end of the week that I noticed the van was bullet-proofed. A year before I would have picked that up immediately. I had become so jaded, and tired, that now I did not see the obvious.

We were wined and dined by people who desperately wanted our help. The Salvadorean Right wanted U.S. Support; the U.S. Special Forces trainers wanted to know that the people they were risking their lives for cared.

The trainers felt betrayed by the recent ruling that they could not carry rifles, only pistols. A New York *Times* reporter, Ray Bonner, had run a story that he had seen a U.S. lieutenant colonel, an engineer advisor, carrying an M-16 while working with a bridge crew in guerrilla territory. Bonner cited the M-16 as proof that the trainers were leading combat ops, something they were forbidden by law to do.

Against assault rifles, the pistol is nothing. Not without reason, the trainers felt ill-used by their country, that nobody in the States cared about them. Not the army, not the government, and certainly not the people.

What kept them going was professionalism and a belief they would be vindicated in the end.

I mentioned to General Singlaub my thesis that we were *in* a *Third World* war, WWIII in two meanings, a worldwide conflict being waged in the underdeveloped nations. General Singlaub is a kind of cross between Mickey Rooney and Buster Keaton, a grown up all-American kid with a deadpan manner. He seldom makes a joke, and when he does it's usually so dry it's easy to miss. He's about 5'7", maybe 150 pounds. I once told him that I had this image of him as the smallest guy on his college basketball team, who lettered by outhustling everybody. "UCLA football," he said. "Third string guard and center."

To my assertion that we were in a worldwide guerrilla war, he replied, "Yes, of course. That's quite correct."

General Singlaub became famous when he was fired for publicizing his displeasure at the Carter Administration's plan to withdraw two divisions of troops from South Korea, but his real field of expertise is guerrilla warfare. He fought with the Maquis, the anti-Nazi underground in France, and was in training to go in as an advisor to Ho Chi Minh's guerrillas, whom the allies backed in WWII, when the war ended. He ran guerrillas into North Korea during the war there, and ran the Special Operations Group in Vietnam—where Hiney Aderholt had been his deputy for air—where he had run cross-border ops and other secret missions.

He also has a significant intelligence background. Since his retirement he had toured the world, visiting anti-Communist guerrillas and visiting countries threatened by "Wars of National Liberation."

General Singlaub, Andy Messing, and I spent an evening with officials of the ARENA Party, the ultra-conservative group blamed for the Death Squads. The meeting was held at the stately, three-story home of Billy Sol, a Salvadorean businessman, graduate of Texas A&M. He had been a huge landowner before the land reform program went into effect. After his land was confiscated he went into the insurance business. He wasn't living on the scale he had, but he was doing all right. He had his home and servants to staff it.

On the other hand, our dinner was carry-out chicken and beer. Good chicken and great beer, but not in the style of old.

"I flew over my rancho week before last," said Sr. Sol, a chubby man with heavily framed glasses, gesturing with a drumstick. He walked with a slight limp, recovering from an assassination attempt by the insurgents. Almost every official of the ARENA Party carried scars or fragments. The Death Squads in El Salvador weren't all right-wing.

He went on, "The jungle had grown up around all our modern, concrete loading pens.

"When the peasants took over our land, the first thing they did was kill and eat the breeding stock. Now they are barely making a subsistence.

"They are good people, very hard-working, but they do not have the knowledge to run a modern cattle ranch. They are much worse off economically than they were before."

This seemed to distress him as much as the loss of his own holdings.

A short time after dinner the doorbell rang.

Major Roberto d'Aubuisson, president of the ARENA Party, later a candidate for president of El Salvador, and his entourage swept through the front door. D'Aubuisson had been a major in the National Guard prior to a preceding change of regimes, then he had been a fugitive, and a prisoner condemned to death.

He was a small man; physically he reminded me of Joel Grey, the actor, but with a cocky air and military bearing. He was dressed in a Swiss Army shirt and slacks, very self-possessed, but did not speak English. His translation was handled by Ricardo Valdivieso, a Salvadorean who had grown up in the U.S. and been a U.S. paratrooper in Germany during Vietnam.

Later I got to know Valdivieso. He was a very likeable man, a burly, handsome Latin, full of good will and charm. A leftist journalist described him to me as a "fascist with a heart of gold," but he was no fascist; he was just a guy fighting for his life and the lives of his family, and his property. He had only come back from the States to settle his grandfather's estate. He figured he'd be there at the most six weeks. That had been sixteen years before. He fell in love with the country, but more than that he fell in love with his wife, Patricia. Together they had fought and farmed and been fugitives with d'Aubuisson.

"We lived in Guatemala and made runs in and out of the country. Sometimes we changed cars three times a day; we wore disguises. We could never spend more than three hours in any one place."

Finally they gained legitimacy and set up as a political party, only to become targets of leftist guerrillas.

"We were in jail with Roberto—Billy and I and the rest," he said. He leaned forward earnestly. "We were put against the wall in front of a firing squad. Roberto said, 'These men are guilty of nothing. They are only my friends. If you must kill somebody, kill me, and let them go.' The officer in charge was so impressed he dismissed the firing squad and had them put us back in our cells.

"Then one of the guards offered to open the doors and provide us with weapons. It sounded like a setup to us, so we stayed put." Finally, they were released.

I was entranced with d'Aubuisson's bodyguards. There seemed to be a dozen of them. They wore mustaches and carried pistols, submachine guns, and shotguns. They brandished their weapons. They were . . . perfect.

Also with d'Aubuisson and Ricardo were a couple of men in suits, one a lean, scholarly type, the other a stocky, Zapata-mustachioed goon, in a suit made of a fabric that looked like burnished aluminum.

D'Aubisson sat at the coffee table and spread out a map of Central America. General Singlaub and I leaned over the map as d'Aubuisson explained how guerrilla supplies were delivered. Roads in central America are few and bad, so there is a lot of civil aviation. Guerrilla supplies were flown in from Nicaragua in light aircraft at night and landed on roads in guerrilla territory. Some stuff also came across the Gulf of Fonseca in boats.

The goon in the suit lolled, legs crossed, in a Louis XIV chair, jiving with the other goons. He let out a burst of laughter and gestured, working his trigger finger.

We chatted about Salvadorean politics and guerrilla warfare. Ricardo translated one of d'Aubuisson's questions as, "What's the big deal about the nuns?" He referred to four American women, three nuns and a lay worker, who had recently been killed by four drunks guarding a roadblock near the airport.

"Respect for women, respect for the Church," I said.

His look held no comprehension. They were Maryknoll sisters. *Subversivos* had been seen going in and out of the Maryknoll Chapter House. As far as he was concerned that made them Communist spies, fair game.

Congressman Dornan didn't arrive until three days after we did. Dornan was another believer in the *Third World* War theory. As a congressman he had traveled the world on fact-finding missions, and the War was what he had seen. He came directly to El Salvador from Beirut.

A Catholic, he said, "There is nothing the Communists would like more than to take over a country named for Jesus Christ." Dornan, a redheaded, former TV newsman from California, was ebullient; I think the Salvos found his personality a little overwhelming.

He was very proud of having been an Air Force fighter jock and having flown every jet aircraft in the U.S. inventory. "Nothing I like better than to get an F-16 up to about forty thousand feet, find a rock 'n' roll station on the radio, and just . . . rock 'n' roll," he said.

Our delegation was given a tour of Salvadorean military installations. Since the trainers couldn't carry anything heavier than pistols, Andy and I were pressed into service as Dornan's and Singlaub's bodyguards.

The second-in-command of the U.S. army trainers, Lieutenant Colonel John Boykin, a big, dark-haired man who wears a mustache and is built like a weightlifter, gave us a couple of old Danish Madsen submachine guns to carry, and showed us how to work the safeties. Andy and I slung the SMGs over our shoulders.

Since he worked out of the embassy, John wore civilian clothes, polo shirt stretched tight over bodybuilder's muscles, designer jeans and Dingo boots, .45 tucked into the small of his back. We were all dressed pretty much the same, except that Andy and I were better armed.

Standing there chatting, I explained my *Third World* War theory to him. He gave me a look as though I had just grown two heads, and said, "Where the fuck have you been?" He had gone in the army after I had, but had been in during the years since I had got out, most of that time in Special Forces. Having spent his life in the *Third World* War, and among others who lived the same life, it was incomprehensible to him that most civilians don't realize what is going on.

Starting from such a world view, our foreign policy, to the extent we have one, must have seemed insane to him.

To me it seemed strange that there was common acceptance by everyone I met in the field that war was being waged against the United States, while the American public was *totally unaware* of it.

* * *

One evening, after we had been there a week, I called
Kathy. She had been badly scared and was angry that I
wasn't home. A man in the next block had gone crazy and
was shooting people from an upstairs window. Police advised everyone in that block, and ours, to stay indoors,
while they lay siege to his house.

Great! I'd been in El Salvador a week, hadn't heard a shot
fired, and Kathy was pinned down by a sniper in Denver.

We met the archbishop, and we met the acting president,
and the Congressional delegation went home, leaving me to
try for a combat story with the best set of introductions I
could have asked for.

By the end of a week there, I was sure El Salvador would
be the next domino to fall. The hapless government, the
oligarchy entrenched and vulnerable, had so obviously
been a straight-out fascist dictatorship until recently that I
was convinced only a miracle could save them.

But now, six years later the situation in El Salvador has
improved wonderfully. The army is more professional and
the government more compassionate. The Death Squads
have all but disappeared. I credit that to the patience and
professionalism of our army trainers, and to the fact that
the Salvadoreans, both sides, are among the gutsiest people
on Earth. They don't do things very well by our standards,
but they keep going.

27
TWO DAYS WITH THE PARACAIDISTAS

One of the advisors, Tony, a compact, almost criminally handsome Puerto Rican sergeant, worked in the military training group's headquarters at the embassy. He had also volunteered to train the Salvadorean paratroops, on the side—a job that would normally be full time for a six- or twelve-man detachment.

With only fifty-five men in-country, the trainers met themselves coming and going. They voluntarily worked nights and weekends to make up for the congressionally imposed lack of personnel.

Tony arranged a jump with the *paracaidistas* for me. The night before the jump he called.

"No go," he said. "Over seven hundred insurgents have been reported near Tenango. We got one company that just completed training going in as a blocking force. The jump's off."

"I'd rather go on an operation anyway. Is it possible?"

"Probable," he said. "I'll pick you up at 0600. We'll go out to the airbase and see."

Since U.S. advisors aren't allowed in combat, Tony wanted an evaluation of the paras from me.

At the airbase, Major Turcios, the paras' commander, told Tony it was fine with him if I went along, but he would rather I got out of civvies and into a suit of fatigues. He didn't want his men to have to sneak through the jungle with a huge, redheaded gringo in civilian clothes.

I had met Turcios before, with General Singlaub. He was a compactly built young officer, and, although starched and spit-shined, a relaxed and friendly man. His troops both liked and respected him.

"Good," I said. "How about a weapon?"

"You want to carry a weapon?"

Oh, yes I did. By putting on a green suit I was dealing myself into the game, and the game in El Salvador was played under a very rough set of rules.

The custom was to keep your last round for yourself.

They gave me the largest suit of fatigues they had—a bit snug, but I could move—and a Heckler and Koch G-3 assault rifle, with four loaded magazines and 300 loose rounds in a pack. I could see myself burrowing into the dirt while trying to reclip those mags in a firefight.

Having carried an M-16 for years, my G-3 seemed as heavy as an artillery piece. And this one, although immaculate and well-oiled, was old enough to have most of the bluing knocked off. How accurate could it be? How prone to malfunction? I asked one of the paras to show me how the selector switch worked before we climbed aboard the chopper.

We lifted off the main runway at Ilopango and soon were where it's high and cold and your pant legs flutter frantically in the blast from the door. I looked at the Salvadorean paratrooper beside me. Ripples from the wind ran through his cheeks.

Flying over Vietnam, I had believed it was the most beautiful place on earth. Now, fifteen years later, I felt the same about El Salvador. The fields were smaller, without rice paddies. There were huge lakes and volcanoes. Everywhere the land was flat, there were houses: farmhouses, ranch houses, haciendas. But the tropical vegetation and the feel of danger were like Vietnam.

Our choppers flew in two V's in trail. By craning my neck, I could see another Huey rising and falling through the windshield over the co-pilot's shoulder. It had been a long time, fourteen years, since I sat in the open door of a helicopter at 3,000 feet. I gripped the edge of the door and hoped the kid with his knee in my back wouldn't decide to shift his weight.

We flew for about fifteen minutes. The door gunner pulled the pin that held his M-60 down and brought it up, ready to fire. There were no gunships.

We circled and landed without contact.

The paras deployed around the grassy clearing to provide security for the next two lifts, but they tended to bunch up at the perimeter.

The Salvadorean army was a young army, and only since the insurgency had it tried to develop into a modern force. Until recently, everything technical, complicated, or difficult had to be supervised by an officer.

John Hoagland, an ex-G.I. *Newsweek* photographer, told me he had been astonished to see a .57mm recoilless rifle set up by two grunts, then a lieutenant come up to fire it.

Julian Harrison, a British television reporter, told me of having seen a Salvadorean accidentally kill two of his own men with a rifle grenade. He was called over by his commander, who made him bend over and grab his ankles, then proceeded to beat his ass with a swagger stick.

Hoagland said that until the last couple of years, an NCO

in El Salvador was somebody who got too old and fat to
hack it in the field; so they gave him three stripes and a
clipboard and set him out front of the headquarters to write
down names.

They still lacked an infrastructure of experienced leaders.

It was the first week of August, noon, and very close to
the equator. Going from the chopper to the perimeter of the
LZ, my head buzzed from the suffocating heat. Sundazzle
spots drifted before my eyes, and I broke out in a sick,
feverish sweat. I was in trouble, even before we got off the
LZ. Maybe I'll be okay once we get moving, I thought.

I melted into the minimal shade on the edge of the LZ.
The men were bunching up, and once satisfied they weren't
taking fire, most of them sat down and lit up. There was a
low buzz of Spanish conversation.

Perdomo, the commander, stood with his radio headset
pressed into one ear, hand over the other, calling in the
next lift.

He looked up. "They put us too far from the objective," he
said. "We must walk five kilometers, not two."

I nodded. Five klicks. How bad can it be? In Denver I ran
further than that every day.

When all the troops had landed, we walked single-file
across the open jungle, going almost straight down toward
a rushing creek below.

It was the worst five klicks of my life. In the Rockies it
would have been a workout, but not much of a challenge,
yet here in this heat, it was murder. All of it was either
straight up or straight down. Stretched out it would have
been about twelve klicks. Years before, I had scrambled
over worse terrain in heat as bad all day every day, for
weeks at a time, but even then it took a few days to get used
to it.

We slid down slick mountain trails and slipped up them.
All the wait-a-minute vines that the Salvos passed through
caught me square in the face.

We went slowly; the point was moving cautiously, and

when we stopped the paras sat quietly. I flopped on my back in the trail and panted like an old dog.

I wondered, very seriously, whether they knew the treatment for heatstroke.

Crawling over a stone fence, I tripped, fell six feet straight down, smashing my jaw on a rock. I didn't feel it, just dragged myself back to my feet and lurched ahead to catch up.

The next to last hill, one para had my rifle and another had my pack, and I crawled up it, using both hands.

Perdomo took a break at the top. "I'm slowing you down," I said.

He shrugged. "It's no problem."

"Well, I made it this far."

He stubbed his cigarette and grinned. "Come on," he said. "We are going to the *chingada*," the whorehouse.

I grinned too, but it was a bluff. We moved out.

At the top of the hill I found Perdomo sitting, totally alert.

"That's it," he said softly, pointing to a small stone house with a red tile roof on top of the next hill. He scanned it for signs of occupation. We sat there for a long time. The shadows lengthened; the land cooled. I found my strength returning.

When Perdomo was satisfied, we moved out again. This time he was pretty sure there were guerrillas in the area. The stone house had been an observation post/way station. He figured they had vacated it when his column appeared, but he also assumed they had kept it under observation.

We cut down a little draw and up another long, steep hill, single file on the narrow trail. Shadows were starting to lengthen. The temperature had dropped a few degrees; I had no trouble at all.

When I reached the top of the hill Perdomo held out something like an adhesive-wrapped tennis ball. *"Bomba contact,"* he said. It was guerrilla ordnance; they had been here, recently. It looked like an overgrown cherry bomb, and I didn't take it too seriously.

Perdomo set up his CP at the stone house. It occurred to me that if I were a guerrilla I'd already have a mortar concentration on it. But Perdomo wasn't worried about that, and we didn't get mortared.

Perdomo told Elga, his radio operator, to set the radio on a low stone fence about six feet from the house. He picked up the handset and gave instructions to his troops. "I am putting ambushes at the four cardinal compass points," he told me. One squad moved by us heading into the bush to the north, carrying an M-60. Another moved back down the hill to the west, taking up a position in a smaller stone house at the base of the hill.

Since we seemed to be settling in for the night, I laid down my G-3 and started to take off my shirt. Around the corner of the house a couple of Perdomo's soldiers started building a small fire.

Elga, a tall, likeable kid, eyed my camera with an admiring glint in his eye. He had been a tour guide in civilian life, and after Perdomo, he spoke the best English in the company. "If you get killed, can I have your camera?" he asked.

I grinned. One of his buddies lurked nearby, eyeing me. "You can't both have it," I said.

"He wants your watch."

I laughed out loud. That stuff would never get back with me if I bought it, and these kids might as well have it as anybody. "Sure," I said. But I didn't like being on combat patrol with people who would profit if I got killed. I stripped off my shirt. I was soaked through with sweat: T-shirt, shirt, lapels, epaulets, pockets, everything. Pants the same way.

A six-round burst from an M-16 snapped over my head and I found myself flat on the ground by the stone house. *You may just earn your money this time, my boy,* I thought.

G-3s returned fire from the north and east, none from the other two directions, as far as I could tell. Everybody in the CP was cool and collected. Perdomo was on the radio, too fast to follow, but I heard the word *"putas"* several times. A few rounds still snapped overhead, and there was a lot of outgoing. I slithered over to my weapon and took up a position facing down the hill to the west. It was the only field of fire available where I wouldn't hit one of his men. "The north ambush killed one insurgent," he said, looking up from his radio.

The firing died and there was a series of insults shouted in Spanish. The paras answered in kind.

When that died down Perdomo said, "I want a cup of coffee. Would you like some?" A few rounds were still passing back and forth. One ricocheted over our heads.

"Yes," I replied. "That would be nice."

"Eh, Guatemala," he called to one of his troopers, under the lean-to at the side of the house. *"Cafe."*

"Capitan!" Elga said. *"Una columna de putas."* He pointed across the valley to the west. *Putas,* whores, was what they called the guerrillas.

Perdomo and I faced to the west. The shadows were very long and I couldn't pick out any movement in the jungle across the valley. In rapid-fire Spanish, Elga gave Perdomo directions as to where he had seen the guerrillas.

Perdomo placed six single shots from his G-3 into where he thought they were, and since we were already facing that way, we paused to enjoy the sunset. The sky turned a vivid mauve behind the mountains across the jungle below. The breeze grew cool and night sounds started.

Guatemala brought Perdomo a blackened canteen cup of coffee. He took a sip and handed it to me. It was hot, sweet, and killer strong. I took a long sip. Perdomo handed me a paper sack and said, "Eat!"

Oatmeal cookies. We sat as the last of the sun went down, drinking coffee and eating oatmeal cookies.

Something flew by. Perdomo snagged it out of the air and popped it into his mouth.

"This captain eats insects," Elga said, choosing his words carefully. Perdomo had picked up insect-eating at the Columbian "Lancero" school, their version of our Ranger school.

"We will get you a nice fat butterfly for breakfast," said Perdomo.

"My Montagnards used to scrape locusts off window screens and eat 'em like cocktail peanuts," I said.

They wearied of the search for foreign words and the conversation drifted into Spanish. I dropped out and tried to listen. The young troopers talked and chuckled, talked and chuckled. They were at an age where everything is a joke.

I wanted very badly to wander off in the bushes and urinate, but every time I tried to move, my leg cramped. I devoted almost an hour and a half to taking a piss.

By then it was pitch black. When I got back to my seat on the wet ground, one of the troopies asked another, "Who was that?" in Spanish.

"El Gringo," was the response, followed by the sound of panting like an old dog, the sound I had made on the trail that day. *Fuck you, kid,* I thought. *If you went where I live, all the clothes you own wouldn't keep you warm.*

I had hoped my clothes would dry by the time it got cold, but they didn't. I had no poncho, and I started to shake. What a letdown, sleeping in a muddy ditch in wet clothes without even a poncho.

It started to rain. Nice fat drops fell on my face. Perfect, I thought. I wondered whether I would die.

"Go in the house," I heard Perdomo say. Even in a semi-sleep that seemed like a good idea. I staggered into the house, carrying my rifle and dragging my pack. Inside the house I lay with my head on the pack, head cradled on 300 loose 7.62 rounds. I shook for another hour and a half. Finally I shook my clothes dry and went to sleep.

I awoke the next morning feeling looser and better than I had for weeks, a little tired from lack of sleep, but good.

I shuffled and limped around until I found Perdomo just

waking up under a poncho liner, using a folded, grey issue blanket for a pillow.

"Where's the body of the guerrilla?" I asked. "I want to get a picture of it."

"They drag it away," he said, sitting up.

I nodded. Everybody wants their dead back. He handed me a cup of his killer coffee.

Just before we left that morning he hollered down the hill to make sure his outpost in the little stone house below had pulled in, then hurled the contact bomb we had captured down the hill. The throw was about twenty-five meters out and at least fifty down; it couldn't have dropped into the wet jungle with much impact. But it exploded violently and smoke rolled out of the valley for two minutes, finally building to a grey column about thirty-five feet high.

At the bottom of the hill we connected with a level dirt road leading due north. Perdomo put a squad out on both flanks and we headed right up the road. *Easy day*, I thought.

The roadside was a museum of guerrilla life. As we advanced north I collected several samples of propaganda leaflets from both sides. Perdomo handed me a homemade ammo pouch he found, a small blue denim pouch with a half-dozen .223 rounds in it.

The road was a pleasant, tree-shaded lane, lined on either side by stone houses with red tile roofs. Behind them lay fields of corn and pasture land. There was plenty of evidence that the houses had been occupied by guerrillas. We found a one-room schoolhouse, set up to teach drill and squad tactics to the tiniest children, with little wooden rifles. But no people.

The troops attempted to destroy everything, but it was largely a futile effort. Stone and tile don't burn. They booted a few tiles out of roofs and kicked down a few corrugated tin walls.

The paras brought whatever they found novel or interesting out of the houses. They pushed a wooden-wheeled cart until it fell apart on the rocks in the road. One of them found an ornately framed print of the Virgin Mary, and carried it from then on, probably to take home to his mother.

There was a festive air; we moved up the road, eating fruit from the trees, telling jokes, kicking down walls.

Until the firing started.

Perdomo was immediately on the radio. I unslung my G-3 and dropped three feet off the road into the yard of the house his troops were attempting to kick apart. The left flank security must have made contact. I put my selector on semi-auto and peered around the corner of the house to see where the firing came from.

When I first started running combat patrols in 1964, I experienced an elation which surpassed anything I had felt before. Then I got badly hit.

After that, combat caused a sour feeling in the pit of my stomach. I did my work, but I didn't like it. Only pride and determination not to let my friends down kept me going. Then I got hit again, worse than before.

I've been shot at a few times since, mostly while working for *SOF*, but this patrol was my first as a participant. I felt no elation and no fear; I was just doing a job. I might have been taking out the garbage.

"They are killing cows," Perdomo called.

"What?"

"They found guerrilla cows. They are killing them."

"Son of a bitch!" I put the G-3 on safe, slung it and went back to the road.

Gutierrez, Perdomo's second-in-command, screamed into the radio in Spanish. "Your guns are for men, not for animals," followed by a long burst I couldn't translate, but it got quiet quickly.

The paras and the Third Brigade were closing in on each other's positions; sporadic gunfire on all sides, but too far out to be coming at us. Perdomo was busy on the radio.

Finally we came to a large, open, barbed-wire-fenced field to the right of the road. Paras fanned out inside it, taking up defensive positions. They weren't bunching up as much as they had; they were taking this pretty seriously. Perdomo stayed on the radio. Both Gutierrez and Ordonez hustled around, trying to be everywhere at once.

Suddenly a Huey appeared over the horizon and circled the LZ.

Ordonez popped yellow smoke out on the LZ, and from across the road eight paras dragged three bodies, hastily slung in ponchos. The soldiers had handkerchiefs over their noses. The corpses were in their underwear, but from their haircuts they seemed to be government troops. One wore macho maroon bikini briefs, and one black sock. They were dead limp and bloated in the ponchos. But they couldn't have been paras, because if we had lost anybody, it would have been in the past ten minutes, and these bodies had been dead for a while.

I went over to Perdomo and asked, "Who are those guys?"

"Soldiers of the Third Brigade," he said. "They were killed by mortars." No wonder our guys had quit bunching up.

The chopper crew was quick to get handkerchiefs over their noses. The soldiers dumped the bodies in a random pile on the floor of the chopper and got out as quickly as possible. The rotors whirled and the chopper lifted off.

There was intermittent helicopter activity for the rest of the morning. The next flight brought in huge gunny sacks of rations. I took mine over to the shade by the road. Swilling down a small can of pineapple juice at a gulp, I opened up a can of tamales. Not as bad as you might think, under the circumstances.

I was almost through when an explosion shattered the calm. It came from about a hundred meters away, in the woodline to the northeast. A half-dozen guys ran toward the sound.

I hung back until the medics had gone into the treeline and then followed them in.

Down a slight depression in the woods a soldier lay. He

looked dead. A cluster of maybe eight men stood around him. One of them threw a jungle boot, with the canvas top completely ripped down to the leather, into the bush. They quickly got an IV into him—he wasn't dead after all—and dragged him across the clearing back into the shade where I had been sitting. One soldier held a plasma bottle over the kid as they moved him.

He became conscious then, moaning. The medic drew a clear liquid into a hypodermic and knelt to give him a shot. He got quiet very quickly.

They didn't bother to throw smoke this time. The chopper knew where to go. He just came in and landed, and they ran the wounded man out. I wasn't sure but I think he was one of the new kids on his first patrol.

"He stepped on a mine?" I asked Perdomo.

He nodded. "Contact bomb, under a rock."

"He'll live, but he'll lose the leg, right?"

He nodded. "He will lose the foot."

We waited around the LZ for another hour. Some troops led five or six apprehensively mooing cattle onto the field. Perdomo had told me earlier that they had captured 22 cattle and were taking them back to the mess hall.

They led a fat Guernsey into the center of the field. She and Perdomo circled each other for a few minutes.

The two soldiers holding her rope scurried around to get out of Perdomo's way while he tried to line up a clear shot. The cow had become frisky, and Perdomo had to be more nimble as a result. Finally he dropped her with one shot.

She jerked and flopped over on her side.

The sun was high again.

Three choppers came in. Troops loaded onto two of them, and eight or ten guys managed to load the cow onto the deck of the chopper. Three paras hopped on with her.

Perdomo turned and yelled to me, "Time to go home."

I grabbed my pack and rifle and jogged to the ship, ducking under the rotor blades, hitching my butt up onto the floor of the Huey. The dead cow's eyes looked at me blankly. She was still warm to the touch. I leaned back against the warm, dead cow and the chopper lifted off.

28
DIVING INTO BROOKLYN

My physical incapacity on that patrol hit me hard. I went to Honduras sick. In my hotel room I lay near delirium, time after time watching Bo Derek's *Tarzan* without sound, waiting for phone calls that never came, rising occasionally to throw my guts up. I had never before been so depressed.

I was sure that with thirty days of training, I could out-walk most of the *paracaidistas*. Later, Brown sent more reporters and also financed a couple of training teams. In those mountains they all had a rough go at first, no matter what their age or how good their physical condition.

But in my feverish depression I wondered why I should kill myself to be mediocre at something I had been good at twenty years before. Especially when there were young guys coming up who were in great shape and still possessed of a sense of wonder.

Pride, of course. Pride only.

Perhaps my proper mission was to use my writing and editorial skills to explain the *Third World* War, rather than roam the jungle, looking for a firefight with people younger and quicker than I was. It was time for subjective journalism.

I fought in the Tet Offensive, so I don't even want to hear the term "objective journalism." It's one of those joke oxymorons, like "military intelligence" or "business ethics."

Not only had the press not covered the war in Lebanon objectively, but no one had done the story of how or why the war was not covered objectively. "Objective" reporters don't fink on each other, not even in the interest of objective journalism.

Consider this. Almost all the foreign news in this country goes through about fifteen editors—New York *Times*, Washington *Post*, the three networks, *Time*, *Newsweek*, *U.S. News*, AP, UPI. There's not much more than that. And for that matter, the networks follow the *Times*.

Network producers read the *Times* on the way to work in the morning, and whatever the lead story is, that's what they want film on. Cover a war and you'll find TV guys sucking up to the *Times* correspondent to find out what he's going to write so they can cover it. Whatever the foreign editor of the *Times* says is news *is* what's foreign news in the U.S., and if the KGB finds some way to get to that guy, then they control what you learn about what goes on in the world.

I don't know whether they have such a way or not, but I do know that one Vietnam vet who worked for the *Times* finally quit because he could no longer stomach seeing stories which supported a "progressive" view played out of proportion, and important stories that supported a "reactionary" view spiked. At one point I tried to shame him into doing a book about it. "It's your duty," I insisted.

"Yeah, well, I've got four kids, and if I do that book I'll never work as a journalist again," he replied. "What about my duty to them?"

As a journalist, and as a former Special Forces officer who has had his nose rubbed in the *Third World* War, I felt it was my duty to do as much as one person could to correct that imbalance.

Shortly after returning from Central America, I left *SOF* for New York, to become editor of their main competition, *Eagle*. I sat behind a desk in a swivel chair, half the day at a typewriter or with a blue pencil in my hand, half a day with a telephone mashed to my ear.

I had reporters on five continents, and everything they found served to reinforce my belief that most of the wars in the Third World were part of a global conflict directed by Moscow; their ultimate target being the U.S., and their principle weapon—disinformation.

One of my reporters went through I.R.A. Provo roadblocks in *West Beirut*. Another discovered a Sandinista recruiting booth at a street fair in *Mexico*. Recruits were sent to Nicaragua for thirty days of guerrilla warfare training. After that they simply returned to Mexico, to their regular jobs.

But, of course, their names were on a computer in Managua, ready to be activated when the time came to start the revolution in Mexico.

About a year after I came to *Eagle*, the regular newspapers began to acknowledge that guerrilla weapons in El Salvador came from U.S. stocks in *Vietnam*. Even then they didn't draw the obvious conclusion, that they came by way of the Soviet Union, Cuba, and Nicaragua.

A statement one hears often: "We don't want another Vietnam." From a strategic standpoint it's not "another" Vietnam. It's the *same* one. We've just got in the habit of naming wars after the patient rather than the disease. The war is not "Vietnam." It's us against the strategy of the "War of National Liberation." Once the U.S. abandoned Vietnam, the other guys decided they had found the winning formula and extended it to the *entire Third World*.

Almost every nation in the world has had its Vietnam now. France, the U.S., and China have had their Vietnams in Vietnam. Vietnam has her Vietnam in Cambodia. England has her Vietnam in Northern Ireland. Israel has her Vietnam in Lebanon. The Soviet Union has her Vietnam in Afghanistan. The U.S. has a new Vietnam in Central America. Want it or not, that's the deal.

The press used to talk about the Domino Theory, and how it failed. But the Domino Effect rolled up three countries immediately; Vietnam, Laos, and Cambodia. It stopped at Thailand, because the Thais: a) have never been colonized by anybody, and aren't about to start now; b) have in the King a unifying national symbol who is universally loved; and c) really practice the counterinsurgency principles that we taught them.

But if the Domino Effect failed in Thailand, it still jumped to three other theaters of operations: Africa, Central America, and the Middle East.

Whether capitalist or socialist, the factor which makes a country subject to such a war is a rigid class structure. Anywhere a society is rigidly stratified, whether by race, religion, or class, it becomes vulnerable to subversion.

This is obvious in South Africa. It was also obvious in El Salvador. A poor kid there was destined to spend his life chopping cane or picking coffee beans, watching his wife grow old quickly and his kids die of easily curable diseases.

Then the Communists came along and provided another option. In the guerrillas, a man could rise as fast as his talent could carry him. And if they succeeded in taking over the country, he could really be somebody.

If your kids were dying of some easily curable disease, you'd kill anybody who stood between you and the medicine that would cure them. In the Third World there's always disease, and the medicine is always controlled by a monopoly. You can't afford it . . . unless you become a Communist guerrilla, or unless the Americans come along and make the government change the rules.

Those of our allies who have successfully resisted the War of National Liberation have been those who have succeeded in opening their societies so that capable people from the ranks of the *Outs* have been allowed *In*. Two examples that come immediately to mind are Thailand and Malaysia.

It does not particularly concern me that Congress has kept our aid to El Salvador and the Contras down to a thin trickle, although it would concern me deeply if it stopped altogether. Our experience in Indochina indicates that aid given too lavishly leads to an indigenous leadership diverted from fighting the war to slicing the pie. Careful control of the thin trickle of aid gives us the leverage we need to require the oligarchy to reform its own society.

The Thais and the Guatemalans, for two, have done better without or with little aid than the Vietnamese and the Laotians did with lavish backing.

It's time for the *Right* in this country to accept that our problems in the Third World are in many ways of our own making, because we have supported governments that were antithetical to our own principles. It's time for the *Left* to acknowledge that while the roots of these insurgencies come from within, the rain, the sunshine, and the fertilizer come from the Soviet Union. Their ultimate objective is to wipe democracy, personal freedom, and human dignity from the planet.

It takes a generation of counterinsurgency work to teach the ruling classes in these countries that they will have to share the wealth to survive. In Vietnam, we were halfway through with that task when we quit, and we lost. You have to start with second lieutenants, and low-level bureaucrats, and hold on until these people become generals and presidents. We could have won in Vietnam with one-tenth, or even one one-hundredth the people we sent, but with professional people: experts, committed for a twenty- to thirty-year period.

War is being waged primarily in the Third World now, but it would require only a policy decision on the part of the Soviets to expand it. They now encourage limited terrorism in western Europe, but withhold funding for any terrorist group that wants to operate in the United States, because they don't want to raise public awareness here. They want America asleep until they have a lock on the Third World's raw materials, without which a technological society cannot survive.

People talk about how they don't want another Vietnam, as though the choice were between that and some sort of wonderful Eisenhower America. The choice may be that we have to fight Vietnam over and over again in every little ceiling fan, rat-and-fly infested Third World country, until we get it right—or face the prospect of seeing the U.S. turned into an oversized version of Lebanon.

If this narrative has not convinced the reader that we are at war, I recommend the following experiment. Every day for three months read in the New York *Times* every article about guerrilla warfare anywhere in the world. You have to read all of it, particularly the last three paragraphs where the really significant information is buried. It would help to underline every time the word "Soviet," or any synonym appears.

For myself, I found New York jungle enough, and a challenge of a different kind. Kat found us a great apartment in Brooklyn, top two floors in an old brownstone, huge living room with a cathedral ceiling. In Manhattan the rent would have been three times what we paid. But it was in a neighborhood which strongly resembles Calcutta. We have a storefront Shiite Mosque backing our place, on the next street over.

These Shiites are black guys who hate Whitey so much they joined the Ayatollah's religion.

To the front we are across from the Patrice Lumumba School for Wayward Girls. Working the nearest corner one can usually find the second, fourth, fifth, and seventh ugliest hookers I have ever seen.

Six blocks over is a Haitian neighborhood that looks like Hiroshima.

But we've never been bothered in our own neighborhood. I once had a guy pull a knife on me on the fashionable Upper West Side; Kat pulled me off him before either of us did the other any damage. Once a guy hassled her on the subway; she clipped him in the nuts with her attache case.

I wasn't in very good shape psychologically when we first came to New York. Several times on the subway I hallucinated that the passengers were all dead. I saw their skin go waxy and they didn't seem to move. This sometimes happened when the light changed as we came out of the tunnel to cross the Manhattan Bridge.

I usually looked out the window and watched the illusion of the Statue of Liberty moving across the Brooklyn Bridge in the distance. It looked as though the statue, actually way off in the distance, was mounted on the bridge and crossing as we did. Then we hit the top of the arc of the bridge and started gathering speed as we approached the tunnel, diving into Brooklyn.

Rick, my friend from Lebanon, has come to visit several times. Things deteriorated in Lebanon, and his brother had been killed shortly before his first visit. Outwardly he projected his old suave manner, but at lunch, when a waiter dropped a tray of dishes behind him, he winced, and almost went under the table.

He and Christine had split up. She wanted marriage and a family; he couldn't see bringing a kid into the world he knew.

He stayed in the States several months, dividing his time between New York and Washington. Christine came to visit.

She and Kathy had not met, but they became close friends almost immediately. But she seemed drawn and sad. Shortly after she left, Rick returned to Europe. They have since married and Christine became pregnant.

Between my writing the second and third drafts of this book, Rick called. He and Christine have a "three kilo, two hundred" baby girl.

Fouad, the Lebanese Forces press officer, came to New York on official business about a year after I started with *Eagle*. He brought a new girlfriend, a sweet young lady named Nadia, who had been French-language anchor on the Beirut evening news.

At dinner I asked Fouad how his brother Teddy was. His face fell. Teddy had finally decided on an operation to restore partial use of his leg and had died under anesthetic on an operating table in Dallas six months before.

Later Fouad got caught on the wrong side of a Christian intramural squabble and left Lebanon. He and Nadia have married and he practices law in Indianapolis.

Sam, our other Lebanese friend, who looked like either a mad monk or a tong killer, had been scheduled to lead a detachment of troops into the Sabra Refugee Camp the night of the massacre. He and his men got off to a late start, and when they reached the main gate the firing didn't sound right. It wasn't like a firefight, too sporadic, too one-sided. He took his detachment and left. Since then he has left the militia altogether. I understand he has taken up with a beautiful Italian lady with children and lives in Byblos, where he is cultivating a magnificent tan.

The Lebanese Christians who did enter those camps were all volunteers from towns that had been massacred by Palestinians.

Of the 460 people killed in that "massacre," more than four hundred were men of military age, and more than half of them were not Palestinians at all, but free-lance terrorists from countries other than Lebanon. This information comes from the official Lebanese investigation of the massacre, which has never been seriously challenged.

But you could search the headlines and lead paragraphs of every story on that issue in every newspaper in the U.S. without learning that fact.

Larry Dring went back to Lebanon twice. Once, in a car with a couple of Lebanese Forces press bureau guys, a French woman photographer, and a Druze driver, their car was attacked and shot full of holes by Druze militiamen. The French lady screamed, and Larry hurt his arm when the car turned over.

The driver crawled out, shrieking curses at their attackers, who then realized they had hit the wrong car, apologized, and asked everybody in for coffee.

When he got back from that trip, Larry reported in to the *SOF* office with a duffelbag full of bombs, rockets, and grenades he had collected. They weren't just souvenirs. Larry was fully conversant with the Army technical manuals on Soviet weapons, and this was new stuff that wasn't in them. He had strolled blithely through customs with it, and his duffel had never been touched. *SOF* did a piece about it, and Brown turned the stuff over to the DIA.

Larry was preparing for his fourth trip to Lebanon for *SOF*. One Sunday afternoon at a cookout in his backyard in Summerville, SC, he complained of not feeling well. He lay down on the couch in his living room and died of a massive heart failure. He was forty-three. I believe his heart had been weakened by fifteen years of painkillers. I know several guys like that, who finally succumbed to wounds incurred in Vietnam.

Haney Howell went back to CBS in New York as a producer, and then to produce an overseas news feed for CONUS Communications in Minneapolis. He now teaches communications at Winthrop College in South Carolina and has written a novel set during the war in Cambodia. Al Rockoff gained a measure of fame when John Malkovich played him in *The Killing Fields* and is still one of the best combat photographers in the world. Captain America is a multimillionaire commodities broker who buys and sells with the same killer instinct that made him so happy in Cambodia.

I recently received word that my friend, Kpa Doh, was not, as we all thought, killed right after the Khmer Rouge took over Cambodia. Probably because he was not a Cambodian national, they offered him a job fighting the Vietnamese on the border. It has been reported that he fought on for another two years before finally being killed in combat. He had finally found another backer for his war with the Vietnamese.

I was shocked when I heard that he had collaborated with the KR. Then I realized that this was his only means to keep his family alive. To whom did he owe not to do that? The Americans who deserted him twice; the Cambodians who sold him out over and over again? Of his family there is no news.

In Bangkok, Dawson, my correspondent friend from the Bangkok *Post*, and his girlfriend, Tuk, have married and have a son, Patrick Michael; I call him Sluggo. Dawson has left the *Post* and is free-lancing and working as technical advisor on Vietnam movies being made in Thailand.

Roger Warner has also returned to the States, married, fathered a child, and written two excellent books.

Brigadier General Hiney Aderholt is back in Florida, developing an autogyro as a cheap alternative to helicopters for Third World countries with a counterinsurgency problem.

Coyne has also married. His wife, Thuy, is an intelligence analyst for the U.S. government. They live in Washington with their daughter, Tricia. Coyne is writing a novel.

Mme. Suon, the KPNLF press liaison officer, is no longer with the resistance. She is raising her children in Paris.

Neil Davis, the CBS correspondent who went into Cambodia with Kat and T.R., was killed in '85, in a little Mickey

Mouse coup attempt in Bangkok. He filmed his own death, and it was shown on the NBC Nightly News.

Bill Gross, our first escort officer, is still in Tel Aviv, off active duty and back in the diamond business. Arnold Sherman was forced to retire from the IDF reserves when he reached fifty-five. He has moved to Athens and is writing a thriller.

Terry Anderson, the best friend we made among the American correspondents in Lebanon, a Marine combat vet from Vietnam, has been hostage in Lebanon for several years now. Oliver North and company were a week away from getting him out when Terry's colleague, Jack Anderson, printed the Iranscam story.

Ironic indeed. I have been angry at the press for continually printing stories that jeopardize the lives and slander the accomplishments of American servicemen. But what are we to think of an institution that eats its own?

Roberto d'Aubuisson was narrowly elected president of El Salvador; they like macho men there. But the vote count was rigged by the CIA to give the election to Duarte. D'Aubuisson's right-wing views are so unpalatable to Congress that it would rather let the Communists win than support him.

The day after I left El Salvador, Julian Harrison, my British friend, was shot in the chest. A very able Salvadorean army doctor saved his life, but he'll never fully recover. About a year later John Hoagland, the American who filled me in on background in El Salvador, was killed in an ambush.

29
THE MONTAGNARDS

Cambodia, 1984, Colonel Y Guk Hlom lay almost naked, his face pressed into the dark jungle earth. The one piece of clothing he wore was an old pair of tiger suit cutoffs, bleached white with repeated washings, then recamouflaged by months in the jungle. Slowly he raised his shaggy head and looked in hatred at the six PAVN *bo doi*, Vietnamese Communist soldiers, ahead of them on the trail.

He had meticulously planned a route that circumvented all enemy troop concentrations, but nothing could prevent the occasional encounter with a recon team. Y Guk was not much impressed with their quality. As a young man, he had run recons with B-50, a U.S. Special Forces reconnaissance project.

They were so sure of being alone out here that they had

no security out. He looked with contempt at the *bo doi* as they sat cooking rice beside the trail. The unrestrained singsong lilt of their conversation made him shudder. He had hated these people all his life, and for the first half of it he had feared them. Then the Americans had taught him he was as good as any man, and they had treated him and his Rhade brothers, all his Montagnard brothers, as though they were equals.

On his first leave to Ban Me Thuot after his Mike Force training, he and two of his friends went into town in their new slacks and jeans, in polo shirts and flip-flops, feeling very good. They had just earned American parachute wings; they were somebody.

Coming down the street a South Vietnamese Ranger, a sniveling, limpwristed pfc, his beret ironed into a coxcomb, a cigarette dangling from his lip, broke off holding hands with one of his buddies long enough to shoulder Y Guk off the sidewalk and into the street.

Y Guk had heard stories from his Jarai friends about ARVN Rangers coming into the Mike Force villages near Pleiku, raping women, stealing chickens and goats, killing some of them for no reason, not even for food. Since the Montagnard Revolt in 1964, the Mike Force had been forbidden to take their weapons home, but Vietnamese Rangers carried theirs wherever they willed. If Montagnard men were in those villages, they were held at gunpoint while the Rangers did what they wanted. The Americans stopped it by staying in the villages with their own weapons.

"You die now," Y Guk muttered in his guttural tribal language to the ARVN who had pushed him, but his buddies held him back.

"You never leave ARVN jail," Y Blik muttered.

"Wait!" Ksor Drong had whispered in his ear.

Y Guk had fought with the Americans for four years, but then they left. His unit was itself made an ARVN Ranger outfit, and Y Guk wouldn't be an ARVN Ranger, so he joined FULRO in the jungle. He had fought in the defense of

Ban Me Thuot when South Vietnam fell—word had gone out that the Americans had sent for the Montagnards to fight there—and then he had run raids and ambushes until their ammo ran out and their weapons all broke.

They took fewer casualties than the PAVN, but the PAVN had replacements. They lost fewer weapons, but the PAVN had more.

For five years they had lived on the myth that the Americans would come back. He had believed that; he had preached it to his men.

But he could not preach it when he did not believe it anymore. In 1980, FULRO had sent a delegation that got as far as Bangkok, to talk to two Americans who would say only that they "worked for the government." The delegation was not permitted to see the Ambassador. They were sent to the Khmer Rouge for help—to the Khmer Rouge, who had slaughtered a third to half of their own countrymen.

They realized then that there was no way they could win, and so sent everybody who could go safely back to the village. But for four thousand of them that was not an option. They were marked for death by name. In four groups they set out for Thailand, to find their friends, their only hope, the Americans.

So Y Guk was still fighting now, eleven years later, though he had nothing left to fight with.

Strung out on the trail behind him, lying quiet next to the jungle floor, were eight hundred people, mostly men of military age; there were only about fifty women. Almost everyone was sick—malaria, scurvy, tuberculosis, yaws—and all of them were slowly starving to death. In his entire column Y Guk had only seventy-three men who were fit to fight, and they were weak. They had foraged their way halfway across Cambodia, and the pickings had been slim. He had last eaten meat two weeks before, an iguanid lizard called a tokay. He ate grass and roots and the bark off trees. You could live on it, barely, but you lacked an energy reserve.

Intense hunger pangs came and went, as did cramps, fever, dysentery.

On top of that there were only six working weapons in the column. Without ordnance support, their delicate M-16s had fallen apart within two years after the Americans left. What they had were three ancient M-1 carbines, an M-1 rifle, which he carried himself, and two captured AKs. They had five or six rounds for each weapon.

He remembered being on patrol with the Green Berets, flying in, sitting in the cool wind at the door of a helicopter, the adrenal thrill building in the cold air above small arms' range, then slamming into the LZ and running through the prop blast to the perimeter, ammo thudding against his pelvis, so much ammo that he complained of the weight of it. He wished he had some of it now. Some choppers to get the hell out of here wouldn't be bad either.

He looked briefly at the Khmer Rouge guide beside him in the dirt. As it had turned out they would help, to the degree it suited their purposes. This one was strange, not bright, but with moody fanatic eyes. His solution to almost every problem was to kill somebody. This time he was right, however. No way could Y Guk sneak this entire column of people past these *bo doi*.

He signaled for four more men with weapons. He wanted this quick and final. One by one the men came down the trail. They moved silently. When they were in close behind him he gave a sudden gesture with his arm that meant to move on line through the jungle, and fire only on his command. These guys had been at this a long time.

It took more than two hours for each man to pick and crawl his way through the jungle without making a sound, vines pulled aside, branches parted and replaced carefully.

When he was sure everybody was in position, he slowly brought the ancient M-1 to his shoulder. He got a good sight picture on the leader of the *bo doi* and squeezed off a round. The man jerked backwards and went down as more shots rang out.

Y Guk waited a while and then went forward.

Six good weapons for his impoverished command. And some food. His decision was to give half of the *bo doi* rations to the armed men, and half to the sickest in the column. For himself he took nothing. He was a good leader.

About six months after I left *Eagle* to do this book, my phone rang. It was a guy named Peter Geismar, from *West 57th*, the CBS magazine program. He wanted to know about the 220 Montagnards who had fought their way across Cambodia and were now in a refugee camp in Thailand.

These people were the remnants of FULRO, the Montagnard revolutionary organization. After the Americans left they had fought on alone until 1980, when they recognized that without outside support their cause was hopeless.

A force of four thousand of them set out for Thailand in six groups. Many of them had to leave their wives and children behind; they had no illusions about their chances of crossing Cambodia successfully. They were betting on an almost certain death against an absolutely certain one.

It took them two years to cross Cambodia. When they arrived at the Thai-Cambodian border, instead of turning them loose, the Khmer Rouge interned them in a camp in the jungle, eight klicks from Thailand.

Finally, they escaped in February 1985, when the Vietnamese hit the Khmer Rouge in that year's dry season offensive and destroyed all the Cambodian resistance's bases on the border.

Only two hundred and twenty made it to Thailand. Some were interviewed by Barbara Crossette of the New York *Times*. After all they had been through, they said they wanted to emigrate to the U.S., but they were determined to stay together. They wanted to immigrate as a tribe, and the Immigration and Naturalization Service had no provisions for that.

Having spent two of three tours working with Montagnards, I wanted to help them. But how?

Then the call from CBS. *West 57th* wanted to do a story on them, and that story could only work in their favor. Regardless of any personal bias I might feel toward General Westmoreland and his lawsuit against the network, CBS was the only handle I had. I gave them every name I knew, every telephone number of people who had worked with the Montagnards, who had a deep affection for them. Among them was that of Don Scott.

Don Scott had been the in-country chief of Project Concern, a civilian nondenominational charitable foundation that ran a hospital in Tuyen Duc province, about an hour and a half from Dalat, and also ran schools, well-digging projects, and much more.

Once Scott, alone in a jeep, stormed into a village that had been occupied by an NVA battalion and confronted its commander. God knows what this guy thought when an enraged American civilian appeared and screamed in his face, "You can't stay in this village. The Americans will come out and bomb it flat. Get these people out of here!"

But he took his battalion and left.

Their headquarters was in an abandoned Special Forces camp, but they flew no flag, and their hospital took all comers. It was not unusual to find a wounded NVA trooper in bed next to a wounded South Vietnamese G.I. from the same battle. At one point, Scott got an invitation from an NVA general to visit Hanoi, because the hospital had saved his son's life.

Scott also formed a personal friendship with General Westmoreland, and once took him, alone and in civilian clothes, into a village that was "VC controlled." It was a Montagnard village, and the general had such a good time that he didn't get back until very late. He and Scott paused and leaned against a fence and looked at the stars for a long time on their way back to the Project Concern compound.

"You know, I don't get many moments like this," the general said wistfully.

The general's aide gave them both hell when they returned. "Sir, you can't do this. You can't just disappear like that."

"They pay me to take this," the general muttered to Don.

In December 1968, Don Scott found out about the group at Site II in Thailand. He also found out that one of them had been his friend and interpreter, Ha Doi.

Don had been informed by a reliable source that Ha Doi had been assassinated. He had to go to see for himself. Accompanied by his fourteen-year-old adopted son, Bryn, who is Vietnamese; by Ha Kin Lienghot, a Koho Montagnard who has lived in the States since he was thirteen; and by Hugh Brown, a *Time-Life* photographer and Vietnam combat veteran, Scott set out for Thailand to find Ha Doi.

He found more than Ha Doi. Several of the Montagnards in the camp were people who had worked for him. Fourteen of them were in jail in Bangkok, charged with illegal entry. Our embassy had done nothing for them.

Don hit the ceiling. He paid all their fines. Then he called the U.S. Embassy. Normally he would have had a hard time getting through to a high-level official, but, as it happened, he called at lunchtime, so the Deputy Chief of Mission's secretary was out. This official, one Charles Freeman, answered the phone himself. He told Don, "The Vietnam War was a long time ago. There is no reason these Montagnards should have any higher priority than anybody else. If they're on the agenda at all, they're at the bottom, and personally, I don't think they're on the agenda at all."

Scott slammed the phone down and muttered an expletive that he has asked me not to quote, as he is trying to teach his kids not to talk like that.

Having done all he could, he returned home to Brunswick, Maine, to get in direct contact with his Senator, Bill

Cohen. He intended to devote himself, full time if necessary, to getting the Montagnards to this country.

Don had kept contact with almost all the Montagnards in
the U.S. It was not hard to do; there were only twenty-four
of them. After he got back he called Pierre-Marie K'briuh,
in Bakersfield, California. K'briuh claimed to be in possession of the minutes of a meeting that took place at the U.S.
Embassy in Saigon in 1975, during the waning days of the
Thieu regime, at which the Montagnards were specifically
empowered to form a resistance movement, in the name of
the United States.

A week later, Rob Hershman, the producer of this *West
57th* segment, had struck a deal with Scott. "If you return to
Thailand to see the Montagnards, we'll bring a crew and
film the reunion, as well as all the byplay with the State
Department and the Montagnards in the refugee camp."

When he told me that, I immediately called Brown, who
gave me an assignment to cover the trip for *Soldier of Fortune*. On the plane over I read all the paperwork Don had
brought. There were no "minutes" of the meeting, only a
memorandum of record that the meeting had taken place.
It was extremely vague as to what was said. Certainly there
was nothing we could use to prove the U.S. had reneged on
an agreement.

But one thing that was there was a list of who was present, and one of those was Ed Sprague, my friend from the
1973 trip to Vietnam and Cambodia. If I could find Ed, and
the U.S. had made such a commitment, I had no doubt he
would testify to it.

The first thing I did in Bangkok was to go down Patpong
Road, looking for a journalist friend of mine. He was at his
usual spot at the bar when I arrived.

He laughed when I explained to him what I wanted and
why. An old Indochina hand, he is a member in good standing of the Montagnard Mafia. "There were two guys from

the embassy here last night," he said. "I told them they better do what they could to get those Yards out of here as a group, and right away, or they'd have veterans' groups and congressional inquiries out the ass, and I'd personally see to it."

I grinned at that. "Do they know the Special Operations Association is having their annual reunion in Bangkok in December?" I asked.

He laughed. "No shit! That's great. If they don't have those guys out of there by then it's going to be like the last scene in *Rambo* with two hundred Rambos."

He told me, though, that it would take at least a week to get a pass to enter the camp. I didn't have a week to get the pass. I had to be back in the States within ten days.

He had been in the camps the week before and had a pass with his name on it that had two days to run. "The Thais won't ask to see your passport," he said. "Just give them my name and go on in."

I put his phony pass in my pocket and rented a car.

That night I told Don about my friend's conversation with the guys from the embassy. He laughed. "They received a letter from Senator Cohen. That probably happened the day after he threatened them. Then today I called and got an appointment with the Ambassador. They know this CBS crew is here. Couldn't be more cooperative."

We talked for a long time that evening. I told him about the daughter of my Montagnard friend, Philippe, a.k.a. "the Cowboy," whom I had worried about for years.

Phil had been my patrol buddy. On more than one occasion he had risked his life for me. And the best operation I ever ran was one where I gave him the mission and went along for the ride. We ambushed a VC battalion headquarters, killed the commander and most of his staff, captured all their gear and a load of valuable documents.

I got a Bronze Star with "V," and he got a $25.00 bonus and a three-day pass.

We put him in for a U.S. medal, but, as a civilian, he was

ineligible, and he wouldn't take a medal from the Vietnamese.

His daughter, Marina, had been only two when I last saw her. She was a kind of rusty blonde; some Montagnards are. There had been a rumor that she had not been Phil's daughter at all, but the daughter of one of the CIA guys who set up the Special Forces program in the Central Highlands. Easy to believe, because Philippe's woman was absolutely stunning, with rusty, reddish-black hair. Allegedly the Agency man had persuaded Phil to take over the woman and the baby when he left.

To be a good-looking half-American, half-Montagnard girl in Vietnam is just about the least enviable situation I can think of. What's more, her Montagnard father had been the most famous Cong-killer in the Highlands.

Don said that there was indeed such a girl in the camp. A rusty blond, not classically beautiful, but very striking; she was the best weaver they had.

Don and I agreed that he would stay in Bangkok for a couple of days and come down with the CBS crew. I would go ahead, spend a couple of days with the Yards, and try to negotiate a fraudulent extension on my phony pass.

The next morning at four o'clock I was on the road from Bangkok to Aranyapathet. It had been four years since I'd driven on the left side of the road, and even longer since I'd been someplace where the cops don't particularly care how fast you go. I managed to cut about two hours off the average time for the trip, Pink Floyd blasting from my cassette recorder, driving like a kamikaze, as I winged in and out of maniacal Thai traffic.

I stopped in Aran and picked up seven cartons of cigarettes and four big jars of instant coffee. Then I headed for Site II, five kilometers from the Vietnamese army in Cambodia, well within range of their artillery.

It was another 45 minute drive to the camps, through six or seven Royal Thai Army checkpoints, the road progressively more full of potholes, until finally it became a nightmare. I crawled along at five miles an hour behind convoys of tanker trucks carrying water to the refugees.

The camps were well back from the road; you could only dimly perceive them through the dust and the trees, huge cities of small thatch and rattan buildings.

Site II is the second largest city of Cambodians, after Phnom Penh, in the world. These regularly spaced buildings stretched for more than a mile before I came to the road leading to the camp entrance.

I missed the entrance to the small checkpoint I'd been directed to, and turned in at the main checkpoint, where the headquarters for the guard detachment was located. The barrier pole came down, and I stopped. A guard in black jungle fatigues came out and his eyes quickly locked on my jacket, which I had thrown over the coffee and cigarettes.

I had dealt with the Thai Rangers at Khoa Kor, and found them to be good people. But I'd been warned in Bangkok that this was a special unit, slapped together quickly by a raid on the Bangkok jail.

The guard whisked the jacket aside and smiled, then gestured for me to turn in at the headquarters.

"They're chicken thieves," I'd been told. "You have to make friends with them. Then, instead of stealing your chickens, they'll steal chickens for you."

But I didn't have time for that. Very nervously I got out of the car, confronted by the commander of the checkpoint, a Southeast Asian Burt Reynolds look-alike in black fatigues, with a very large service .45 on his hip. Smiling, he led me to his interpreter.

The interpreter, a smarmy wisp, was all smiles too. He held out his hand for my pass. "You cannot take anything into the camp," he said. "You will have to leave this material here with us." He examined my pass curiously. He looked at the name. "I will have to see your passport!" he demanded.

I patted the pocket where it was. "I, uh, seem to have forgotten it," I muttered. No way was I going to let him see that the name on the passport was not the same as the one on the pass. "Er, you must give me receipt for coffee and cigarettes."

He carefully wrote the amount of stuff he had taken on the back of my pass, but it was just a list. It didn't say he had taken it, and he didn't sign it.

We were at an impasse. If they didn't let me go in they had no excuse for not giving me my stuff back. If I demanded he sign a receipt, he would throw me out of the camp.

I smiled. He smiled. I got back in the car and drove in.

After a half hour of driving around, trying to find somebody who spoke English or French to ask whether anybody knew where the Montagnards were, I found a dispensary staffed by European medics with an organization called *Physicians Sans Frontieres.* I stopped a good-looking blond German nurse in the parking lot of their bamboo headquarters. "Do you know where the Montagnard camp is?" I asked.

She said I had to go back out the gate and to the one across the road, the one I'd missed the first time.

Surprise! When I went back through the gate my coffee and cigarettes had disappeared, and nobody seemed to know what I was talking about when I asked for them.

The kids at the other gate accepted my pass without a second look. I could have breezed through with a couple of RPGs and an AK with no problem.

Now the Montagnards were easy to find. I drove straight down the road until I found a building with a sign on it that said, "ILOT DEGA." Mountain people. I parked the car and got out, feeling not a few belly flutters. Some kids came out to see who it was. Then a few elders. They weren't wearing traditional Montagnard dress, of course. They wore western pants and shirts. But I recognized them at once. There is something distinctive about them, something straight, that you don't see in other cultures in the Far East. These were my people.

A short man with stiff hair came out, surrounded by others, small brown men in pants, shirts, and flip-flops. When he recognized me as an American, he smiled. We shook hands. He shook in the diffident Montagnard manner, pressing my hand softly. It amuses me that these people have developed a reputation for ferocity. They were always brave, but we taught them ferocity.

"Is Y Tlur Eban here?" I asked. Y Tlur's was the name I had been given as the man who had worked longest with Special Forces. He went all the way back to the first camp at Buon Enao. He had also worked for Chuck Darnell, now president of the Special Operations Association, and for the B-50 (Project Omega) Mike Force.

"No, he is at Ban Thai Samat. They are interviewing us. He is the interpreter."

I smiled. The embassy had started the interview process already. The presence of that CBS crew had certainly jerked their chain. This was no cause for complacence though. This process could take months, and stop dead at any point. It would not be smart to let up until the Montagnards arrived in the States.

My informant introduced himself as R'mah Doc. We went inside the Ilot Dega headquarters and sat down. I was served a glass of hot water, which I received gratefully. They had no tea or coffee. Doc and I talked, and other Montagnards gathered. This group was made up of members of four tribes, although most of them were Rhade. But they called themselves "The Dega People." Montagnard, after all, is a French word. These folks had claimed the right to name and define themselves. From this and other clues I began to recognize that these were not the simple primitives who had first slipped their bracelet on my wrist on December of 1963. They had taken the grand tour of hell, and learned.

R'mah Doc was a Jarai from Pleiku. My people had been

from Cheo Reo. I asked him whether he knew what had happened to them. He did; they were all dead, except maybe Nay Phin.

I asked him about Philippe's daughter. Marina. I knew Phil was dead, and I supposed his wife as well. But their daughter would be 24 now. R'mah Doc told me that he had heard she had married and had a child, but she had not come on this trek.

There was one person there from my old camp, a girl. She was in her twenties now, married, and with a baby of her own. She had been one of two sisters whose parents had been killed in the war. She had been "adopted" by an American SF captain. This was a couple of years after I left the camp, and I wasn't able to figure out who that captain was. She couldn't remember his name; she had only been two or so at the time. They told me how it had been in the Highlands when the North Vietnamese took over.

H'bia's small brown feet padded on the packed cool earth of the trail back to Plei M'nang. She paused and adjusted the weight of the wicker rice basket on her back. She had walked two hours to a small stand of corn that grew by the river. She put fifteen or twenty ears of corn and a couple of hands of stubby green bananas into the basket. They were for her wedding tomorrow, to Ksor Blem, the warrior who had come home.

Her heart beat a little faster at the thought. They couldn't afford to sacrifice a water buffalo as they had in the old days, but there would be rice wine—the men would sip it from crocks through reeds and grow morose or jolly, depending on their natures—and corn and bananas. All the old wives would tell stories of their own wedding days, in the guise of advise, and the younger girls would look at H'bia in awe.

She swung the basket off her shoulders and felt the breeze in the shady spot she had chosen to cool the perspiration on her budding fourteen-year-old breasts. She could remember when the American missionaries had made her mother wear a cotton blouse, and was glad she didn't have to. She filled a crooked pipe with harsh, homegrown tobacco and took a pull through the brass mouthpiece. Checking the tuck on her black sarong and another on the loose turban that kept her long hair off her neck and back, she repressed a giggle at the thought of undoing them for Ksor Blem. Then she set off down the trail, singing a song from the days before the Americans left. "Oh helicopters, you came and took my man away. Helicopters, please bring my man back to me."

Something didn't feel right as she approached the village. The birds weren't singing; they were twittering excitedly, and as she got closer to home they were dead quiet. Then she heard two gunshots and an excited jabber of Vietnamese.

A big American truck was parked at the gate, half-full of unhappy Montagnard men. Two excited *bo doi* in khakis and pith helmets were angrily shoving more men toward the truck. A ring of *bo doi* with AKs stood around all the men in the village, who stood dejectedly, submissively, in their loincloths.

She gasped. Ksor Blem was one of them.

The leader of the *bo doi* called out names from a clipboard, and he called out Ksor Blem's.

One of the soldiers started to shove him toward the truck, but the leader demurred. "Not that one. Kill him with the others." It was only then that she saw the corpses across the road from the truck. Roughly they led Ksor Blem to the edge of the field. A downy-cheeked *bo doi*, too young to have been in the fighting, fired directly into Ksor Blem's stomach, and, as Ksor Blem lay screaming on the ground, looked at his buddies to see whether they were impressed with his toughness.

"Quit screwing around with that *moi*," the one with the clipboard called. "We got work to do!"

One of the older ones sighed and blew Ksor Blem's brains out. They went back to their work.

Her hand flew to her mouth. Eyes wide, she fled back into the jungle. She'd heard of a village deep in the forest where the men still wore tiger suits and carried M-16s. They went out at night and attacked small Vietnamese outposts and ambushed truck columns. With Ksor Blem gone, she needed a man like that.

R'mah Doc told me how it had been. How they went into the villages with lists, and put some people in re-education camps, but many were just shot on the spot. He had been in a re-education camp for three years, then escaped by simply wandering off one day when the guard wasn't paying much attention.

He joined the resistance in the jungle; he had never been a fighter before, but he became one, because he had no choice.

Next he introduced me to Y Bhuat Eban, who was acting as civilian leader of this group. He was an intensely sincere and decent person, but his most marked feature was the suffering that showed in his eyes.

We went to Y Bhuat's hooch. The striking, rusty blond weaver was there, working at her loom. She was his wife; she wasn't Marina.

I stayed for a couple of hours, photographing, touring the area, then headed back to Aran for a shower and to buy some more coffee and cigarettes.

Next day I went back out and had no trouble smuggling my stuff in. Coffee and cigarettes for all. It was Sunday, no interviews. Y Tlur was there.

Not what I expected, a thin, middle-aged man with a receding hairline and a thin mustache. He introduced himself as Thoraban, a name many of the Americans had called him. We had a couple of laughs talking about Special Forces, jump stories and all that, and I asked him how it had been after the Americans left.

His face became grave. It had been bad. The North Vietnamese had been so bad in the mountains that even lowland Vietnamese had joined in the fight. "They were brave," he said. "But they could not live on grass and bark from the trees as we did."

Finally they had nothing. Not enough weapons, no ammo for what they had. The minuscule amount of help they got from Beijing disappeared in a policy change. They were left alone out there with nothing but the grass and the bark.

"We never lost a battle," he said, "but we never gained a thing. Everybody that was wounded died, and we came out of every victory with less than we had before."

The miracle was that they weren't bitter at the Americans.

The next day Don Scott and the TV crew arrived. Rob Hershman, the producer, was a no-nonsense get-the-story type of journalist. Meredith Vieira, the reporter, was warm and friendly from the start. But it's fair to say that they began with a cool, professional approach.

Thirty minutes after they arrived the Yards were singing hymns in Rhade in their church, and Hershman was all over the camp in his khaki shorts, sunglasses pushed up on top of his head, rubbing his hands, saying, "This is great! This is great!" Not only because it was a great story but because he had fallen in love with the people.

Later we went to Ban Thai Samat to cover the interviews. Young American refugee workers doing the screening were 100% behind the Dega people. One young lady led me aside and said, "Make all the noise you can when you get home. That's the only way to get them there."

I laughed. "Don't worry," I said. "That's the plan."

Don had an appointment with the ambassador in Bangkok for the following day, so we left before the crew. As we pulled away they were all wreathed in smiles, Meredith standing there with a baby on each hip.

That night, after a hellish ride around Bangkok trying to find our hotel in a city where we couldn't read the signs and nobody spoke English, Lacy Wright, who handles refugee problems at the embassy, came over for a drink. It was a cordial talk. There was no question that Don's congressional inquiry and the CBS crew had changed things. But I got the impression that what we had done was give the old Asia hands in the embassy ammunition to make the case for us. They had wanted to help the Yards all along. So far the only serious opposition had come from the dyspeptic Mr. Freeman.

Lacy visibly paled, however, when I told him about the SOA Reunion being in Bangkok. "I think we'll have them out of here by then," he said nervously.

The embassy insisted that there be no press present for Don's interview with the Ambassador, especially not CBS, but not me, either. I could go as an interested party, but if I went I had to agree not to write about it. He went alone.

The interview couldn't have been more cordial. The Ambassador turned out to be an old paratrooper. When he found out that more than thirty of the Dega people were qualified to wear U.S. wings, and that some of them had earned the 101st Airborne Division combat patch during Tet, he said, "I've got to get up there and meet those people."

Back in the States, Peter Geismar of CBS found Ed Sprague, my friend who had been at the meeting at the embassy in Saigon, the one where the Yards were allegedly promised support for their revolution. As soon as we returned I called him. He confirmed that the meeting had been held. "Did the embassy promise to get the resistance out?" I asked.

"Look, they dazzled them with footwork. The Yards left with the impression that certain promises had been made. But they weren't really. They were flimflammed."

After that conversation I went back to the original memorandum and looked at it more closely. K'briuh, who was at the meeting as Secretary General of the Ministry of Ethnic Minorities, states unequivocally that a Montagnard resistance was established at that meeting. The memo quotes

Nay Luette, the minister, as having proposed such a resistance movement, or to have Montagnard forces start moving toward Saigon for the last-ditch defense of the city. There are no quotes for G. D. Jacobson, the American who chaired the meeting, a curious omission in view of the gravity of the situation, but this sentence does appear: "Mr. Jacobson said that all our information indicated that the GVN intended to defend Saigon and he was confident they would consolidate their forces to do so."

In the Montagnard culture there are no weasel-words, no diplomatic language. If you ask a man a straight yes or no question, and he nods and smiles and says something that sounds positive, that means yes. It was obvious to me that whether the U.S. had authorized a Montagnard uprising or not, the Montagnards thought it had. They had fought on for five more years in the full belief that they were acting as our agents.

I called Sprague back. "I know that's what they thought," he said. "That's why I was so pissed off. That's why they threw me out of the country. I told them what the Montagnards thought, but they didn't care about Montagnards. They were getting ready to get out."

Our two hundred and twenty Montagnards are in the United States now. It took Don and me and several others eight months of hard work to get them here. Eight months of jet travel, meetings, and telephone calls. The only real action we saw during that time was running down a jetway with suit bags over our shoulders.

I have a new Montagnard bracelet to replace the one I gave Sam in Lebanon. It was made in North Carolina by a Montagnard I helped get there. It is the VIP model, like John Wayne had, and like him, I intend to wear it to my grave.

INDEX